Palliative Care

Palliative Care

A Guide for Health Social Workers

EDITED BY BRIDGET SUMSER,

MEAGAN LYON LEIMENA,

AND

TERRY ALTILIO

OXFORD
UNIVERSITY PRESS

Oxford University Press is a department of the University of Oxford. It furthers
the University's objective of excellence in research, scholarship, and education
by publishing worldwide. Oxford is a registered trade mark of Oxford University
Press in the UK and certain other countries.

Published in the United States of America by Oxford University Press
198 Madison Avenue, New York, NY 10016, United States of America.

© Oxford University Press 2019

Library of Congress Cataloging-in-Publication Data
Names: Sumser, Bridget, 1983– editor. |
Leimena, Meagan Lyon, 1981– editor. | Altilio, Terry, editor.
Title: Palliative care : a guide for health social workers / Bridget Sumser,
Meagan Lyon Leimena, and Terry Altilio.
Description: New York, NY : Oxford University Press, [2019] |
Includes bibliographical references and index.
Identifiers: LCCN 2018028279 (print) | LCCN 2018043426 (ebook) |
ISBN 9780190669614 (updf) | ISBN 9780190669621 (epub) |
ISBN 9780190669607 (pbk. : alk. paper)
Subjects: LCSH: Social work with the terminally ill. |
Palliative treatment. | Terminal care.
Classification: LCC HV3001.A4 (ebook) |
LCC HV3001.A4 P35 2019 (print) | DDC 362.17/5—dc23
LC record available at https://lccn.loc.gov/2018028279

9 8 7 6 5 4 3 2

Printed by Webcom, Inc., Canada

It is the vulnerability we all share, that of being human, mortal, and interconnected, that makes this work central to all of our lives. May this shared vulnerability invite discovery and wonder.

CONTENTS

List of Illustrations ix
Foreword xi
 Shirley Otis-Green, Mercedes Bern-Klug, Barbara Jones, and Stacy Remke
Acknowledgments xvii
Contributors xix

Introduction: In Plain Sight 1
 Terry Altilio, Meagan Lyon Leimena, and Bridget Sumser

1. The Convergence of Social Work Practice: Integrating Health Social Work
 and Specialized Palliative Care 17
 Colleen M. Mulkerin

2. Structure and Processes of Care 31
 Anne Kelemen and Regina Tosca

3. Physical Aspects of Care 52
 Terry Altilio and Meagan Lyon Leimena

4. Psychological Aspects of Care 71
 Christopher Onderdonk and Kathryn Thornberry

5. Social Aspects of Care 97
 Karra Bikson

6. Spiritual, Religious, and Existential Dimensions of Care 122
 Dana Ribeiro Miller, Melissa Stewart, and Bridget Sumser

7. Cultural Aspects of Care 148
 Yvette Colón

8. Care of Patients and Families at the End of Life 165
 Susan Conceicao and Ginny Swenson

9. Legal and Ethical Aspects of Care 192
    Kathryn M. Smolinski

10. Special Issues in Children and Older Adults 226
    Terry Altilio, Meagan Lyon Leimena, Bridget Sumser, Allie Shukraft,
    Martha Schermer, Mercedes Bern-Klug, and Amy L. Lemke

Epilogue 253
    Terry Altilio

Appendix 255
    Patient Narratives 255
    General Resources 259
    Technical Reports and Issue Briefs 259
    Timeline of Seminal Publications, Decisions, and Events 261
    Training Opportunities 262
    Domestic Resources and Organizations 263
    International Resources and Organizations 263
    Hospice Eligibility and Benefits Information 264
    Multimedia 264
    Additional Reading 264
Index 267

This work invites us to consider our own mortality. We (and those we love) will one day be cared for by the health care system we are called to co-create. Whether as clinicians, educators, or researchers, we must find the courage to embrace the disruption inherent in societal change and ensure that quality *caring* is prioritized throughout the transformation of health care. This is the work of health social work—both affirmed and buoyed by the principles and practice of palliative care.

Shirley Otis-Green

The Institute of Medicine's report, *Retooling for an Aging America*, anticipates a severe shortage of professionals in all areas of health care, including social workers educationally prepared to meet the needs of a growing older adult population. It will soon be necessary for all social workers to have basic competencies in working with older adults, and this book, with its emphasis on intersectionality, is a good match for the needs of these contemporary health social workers. In fact, the World Health Organization, in its "Active Ageing" paradigm, underscores the need to factor in gender and aspects of culture when designing policies and programs to meet the needs of older adults. The following chapters have been designed to underscore aspects of intersectionality and to create opportunities to identify and build on a person's strengths, regardless of age.

Serious illness can rupture a person's sense of wholeness. A palliative approach seeks to support persons and families toward healing and a renewed sense of wholeness—a vision consistent with Carl Jung's ideas about the core psychosocial challenge in older adulthood—to maintain a sense of wholeness in the face of multiple losses and to experience a sense of completeness. Use the information and insights in this book to improve the lives of current older adults, and recognize that the 5-year-old, the 15-year-old, and the 35-year-old you are working with today are future older adults, as are you. Their experiences of today can set a precedent for willingness to seek, influence, and accept health care services in the future. What you do and how you do it matters. Good social work requires integrity, hope, courage, knowledge, skill, tenacity, and creativity. Creativity is putting together ideas that have not been put together before. So soak up the information in the following pages, creatively apply it to your social work practice, and build upon it. The world is waiting!

Mercedes Bern-Klug

Children both live with illness in their own bodies and live with illness in their families, watching, observing, or participating in the experience as siblings, parents, grandparents, and friends of all ages negotiate diagnosis, disease, dying, and death. There are many invitations for social workers, both in pediatric and adult settings, to join with children and families living with the dynamic uncertainty serious illness presents. Invitations lead to inquiry and ongoing exploration of the impact of acute or chronic illness and disability on a child and family system. Curiosity and cultural humility lay the groundwork for therapeutic relationships that create space to address the intersections of identity, power, and privilege while attending to the developmental needs of children and their families. Health disparities can be particularly serious in the context of serious, life-threatening illness creating lifelong impacts. Engaging with children and families living with serious illness creates the possibility of affecting the present and future functioning of a family. Interventions can influence family functioning as well as legacy, supporting the potential restructuring of family systems to integrate an illness experience and to organize in such a way that the child's needs can be addressed. We continually see the resilience and commitment in families as they care for each other, whether the patient is child, parent, sibling, or grandparent.

Social workers are often first responders to the psychosocial and emotional needs of families. Knowing the basics of how to talk to children, in developmentally appropriate ways, about their illness or that of another requires knowledge, skill, and heart. This is family systems work; often the door opens to the children through their parents, and at other times, the opposite is true. Exploring the responses of the children, their needs, questions, or wonderings, may lead to the feelings, fears, and worries of the adults, creating a context for shared communication and a focus for therapeutic work. The process is one of building relationships that serve the evolving and dynamic needs of the family system over time. The unit of care is the child and family.

Pediatric palliative care is best defined as whole-child care in the context of their family and community. Children have access to palliative care regardless of prognosis. Care is provided by inter-professional clinicians of varied skills who work as a team. In many respects, pediatric palliative care is exemplary social work practice: whole person, person-in-environment focused, and multidimensional in approach. The guiding principles are available to all health social workers. This care emphasizes quality of life, symptom management, and familial support, with a thoughtfulness for the big picture. If the outcome is expected to be cure, hopefully the road through therapy is less burdensome. For children who will go on to live with serious illness, the focus of care includes symptom management, care continuity, defining goals of care, guidance, and psychosocial support over time. Empowering the family is key. This same attention informs the care of a dying child with legacy, support, and interventions focused on sustaining the family through the unimaginable experience of making complex decisions through the death and beyond through bereavement.

Social workers are key to providing child- and family-centered care, addressing the myriad and complex issues that emerge for both families of children with life-threatening conditions and for those families where children are impacted by siblings, parents, or grandparents with serious illness. As such, there are opportunities for leadership, research, and innovation. It is a chance to do our best work, working "at the top of our licenses," creating therapeutic alliances with, advocating for, and keeping families and children central in their experience of health care. Social workers bring a depth of expertise in interprofessional collaboration, cross-cultural communication, integrated behavioral health, group process, ethics, and family-centered care that can help ensure the children and families are receiving the best possible care. Leadership from social work practitioners will be critical in the next phases of pediatric palliative care development to ensure the field continues to grow with the needs of children and families at the center of our work. This same leadership and attention are essential to meet the needs of children who live in families with serious illness—a population that will come to the attention of health social workers across settings. Meeting the needs of children, whether as patients or family members, is within the scope of social workers who are sensitized to the developmental needs of children and who integrate the rich array of interventions and resources available.

Barbara Jones and Stacy Remke

ACKNOWLEDGMENTS

This book is born out of the work of countless social work clinicians, educators, mentors, and advocates. The charge and process of this book has humbled and inspired us, ever deepening our gratitude to all who have contributed to our shared learning, curiosity and collective wisdom. It is the thoughtfulness, skill and dedication of our contributors that have made this book possible and deeply rewarding. The challenge of integrating the work of many individuals into a whole required patience and accommodation by contributors-a graciousness we do not take for granted.

We are grateful to Shayna McElveny, MSW for her attentiveness, commitment and energy in helping us organize this book. And, to Ray Sumser, for creating an image of fluidity and grace, representing In Plain Sight throughout the text.

Bringing this book to life has been an intergenerational process. The Cynthia Zirinsky Fund sowed the seeds for this project by funding the Social Work Fellowship in Palliative Care at Mt. Sinai Beth Israel and thereby, creating the space for our relationships to begin and flourish over time.

Lastly, and most importantly, this work is dedicated to the many patients and families, in the past and future, who teach all of us what it really is to do this work.

CONTRIBUTORS

Terry Altilio, MSW, LCSW
Mt Sinai Beth Israel Medical Center,
New York, NY

Mercedes Bern-Klug, PhD,
MSW, MA
University of Iowa, Iowa City, IA

Karra Bikson, PhD, MSW, MA
University of Southern California,
Los Angeles, CA

Yvette Colón, PhD, ACSW, BCD
Eastern Michigan University,
Ypsilanti, MI

Susan Conceicao, MSW
The Denver Hospice,
Westminster, CO

Barbara Jones, PhD, MSW
University of Texas, Austin School of
Social Work, Austin, TX

Anne Kelemen, LICSW, ACHP-SW
Washington Hospital Center,
Crofton, MD

Meagan Lyon Leimena, MSW, MPH
Social Work Consultant, Ashville, NC

Amy L. Lemke, MSW, LISW, LCSW
University of Iowa, Albany, IL

Dana Ribeiro Miller, M Div, LMSW,
ACHP-SW
New York University Winthrop
Hospital, Mineola, NY

Colleen M. Mulkerin, MSW, LCSW
Hartford Hospital, Hartford, CT

Christopher Onderdonk, LCSW
University of California,
San Diego, CA

Shirley Otis-Green, MSW, MA,
ACSW, LCSW, OSW-C
Collaborative Caring, Toluca Lake, CA

Stacy Remke, MSW, LICSW,
ACHP-SW
University of Minnesota,
Minneapolis, MN

Martha Schermer, LICSW
Children's Hospitals and Clinics of
Minnesota, Minneapolis, MN

Allie Shukraft, MSW, MAT
Levine Children's Hospital,
Charlotte, NC

Kathryn M. Smolinski, MSW, JD
Wayne State University Law School,
  Detroit, MI

Melissa Stewart, LCSW-R
Memorial Sloan Kettering Cancer
  Center, New York, NY

Bridget Sumser, MSW
University of California,
  San Francisco, CA

Ginny Swenson, MA, MSW, LSW
The Denver Hospice, Denver, CO

Kathryn Thornberry, LCSW
Kaiser Permanente, Monument, CO

Regina Tosca, LICSW
MedStart Washington Hospital
  Center, Washington, DC

You will see the image that follows through out the text. It was selected for its grace and fluidity, bringing with it a message of the universality and humanity that infuses this work. You will find the graphic in places where we have identified opportunities "in plain sight"—objects, interactions, language, and more that invite immediate and accessible inquiry, curiosity and connection. These are starting places that become available and alive through our attention.

In Plain Sight

TERRY ALTILIO, MEAGAN LYON LEIMENA,
AND BRIDGET SUMSER ■

Kerry James Marshall, African-American artist, describes the intent of his work: "the museum occupies a particularly privileged place . . . not being a part of that means you surrender your place in the world as equal amongst other beings . . . if you feel it then you have to take responsibility for it . . . then you have control over your own visibility and invisibility . . . the answer is to put yourself into that space in such a way that you have to be taken into account" (Marshall, 2017). While Marshall's "place" is the museum, his words can be applied to the privileged world of health care. Social workers who choose health care as their "space" bring their humanity, skills, and a willingness to share in the universal experiences spanning birth to death. The critical intent of the authors of this book is to reaffirm the courage, mind, and heart at the core of health social work and to highlight the ways in which social work contributes to the care of seriously ill persons and their families. At a time of attention and interest in palliative care, we have a clear opportunity to assert our place in the work among equals, to reflect on the visibility of our discipline, to notice what is "in plain sight," and to choose how we will show up to care for patients and families.

Palliative care, a nascent specialty, developed and expanded over the past two decades across disciplines and settings. International and domestic organizations have offered definitions to capture its purpose and scope. Palliative care, as described by the World Health Organization (WHO), is an approach that improves the quality of life of patients and their families facing the problems associated with life-threatening illness, through the prevention and relief of suffering by means of early identification and impeccable assessment and treatment of pain and other problems, physical, psychosocial, and spiritual (World Health Organization, 2017). The Center to Advance Palliative Care (CAPC) defines *palliative care* and the medical subspecialty of palliative medicine as specialized medical care for people living with serious illness. It focuses on providing relief from the symptoms and stress of a serious illness. Appropriate for persons of any age and in any stage of illness, palliative care can be provided along with curative treatments. The goal is to improve quality of life for both the patient and family (CAPC, n.d.).

Palliative care's humanistic approach and an evolving evidence base supporting quality and cost effectiveness have fueled, and have been fueled by, national and international calls for competent, compassionate health care for seriously ill and dying patients (Gomes, Calanzani, Curiale, McCrone, & Higginson, 2013; Rabow et al., 2013). Globally, the WHO estimates that 40 million people are in need of palliative care, with 78% living in low- and middle-income countries. As populations age, the need will only increase. In addition to the lack of trained clinicians, the WHO identifies restrictive policies related to morphine and controlled medications essential to managing pain and other symptoms as barriers to quality palliative care (World Health Organization, 2014). It is estimated that 21 million children worldwide have conditions that would benefit by a palliative approach, with 8 million requiring specialized palliative care. Thus, primary clinicians will provide the majority of this care if we are to embrace a mandate to provide humanistic care of children and their families (Connor, Downing, & Marston, 2017). It also becomes clear from this international data that the Western models of medicalized palliative care will need to adapt and develop to meet the needs of resource-poor nations (Payne, 2009).

In the United States, a recent Institute of Medicine (IOM) report affirms hospice and palliative care as an established medical specialty with a strong presence in clinical education, organizations, and research communities. Their recommendations integrate micro and macro aspects of the health care experience and set expectations for high-quality health care. They include establishing palliative care as a standard of care; requiring universal clinician training and certification in palliative care, communication, and advance care planning; and policies and payment to support medical and social needs and public education and engagement (Institute of Medicine, 2015). The National Palliative Care Registry™ reports that in hospitals with palliative care teams, an average of 3.4% of admissions receive palliative care services, while estimates place the *need* for palliative care at nearly double that, between 7.5% and 8.0% of hospital admissions. Hence between 1 million and 1.8 million patients admitted to US hospitals each year could benefit from palliative care, but are not receiving it (Rogers & Dumanovsky, 2017).

These calls to action have buttressed demand, have highlighted workforce issues, and have forced analysis by all disciplines of the skills and values essential for both specialists and primary care clinicians. The disparity between the identified needs of patients and families across countries and settings and the available clinical resources has focused energy on understanding and revitalizing the potential in each discipline to affirm and infuse palliative care principles. At the micro level, there has been increased attention to competencies for both specialist- and primary-level practice. Social work competencies, national and international, have been developed to guide clinicians, educators, institutions, and care teams (see Table I.1).

Social workers have opportunities for participation and leadership at the micro, meso, and macro levels, ranging from skilled clinical interventions to community organization and policy work and advocacy, both nationally and internationally. In some parts of the world, community is the singular resource for care; in other areas, community will represent one resource in care plans

Table I.1 SOCIAL WORK COMPETENCIES IN PALLIATIVE CARE

Standards & Competencies	Author(s)	Year	Website
Standards for Social Work Practice in Palliative & End of Life established	NASW	2004	www.socialworkers. org/practice/standards/ Palliative.asp
Social Work Competencies in Palliative & End-of-Life Care published	Gwyther, L., et al.	2005	www.ncbi.nlm.nih.gov/ pubmed/17387058
NASW Certifications: Advanced Certified Hospice & Palliative Social Worker (HPSW) & Certified HPSW	(ACHP-SW) CHP-SW	2008, 2009	www.socialworkers.org/ credentials/list.asp
Creating Social Work Competencies for Practice in Hospice Palliative Care published (Canada)	Bosma, H., et al.	2009	www.chpca.net/media/ 7868/Social_Work_ Competencies_July_2009
European Association for Palliative Care Task Force on Social Work in Palliative Care established	Firth, P., & Bitschneu, K. W.	2009	www.eapcnet.eu/Themes/ Education/Socialwork. aspx
Core Competencies for Palliative Social Work in Europe: An EAPC White Paper; Parts 1 & 2 published	Hughes, S., Firth, P., & Oliviere, D.	2014, 2015	www.eapcnet.eu/Themes/ Education/Socialwork. aspx

as finance, preferences, and philosophy shift care from hospitals to long-term facilities, to home or outpatient practice settings.

Early, in the dawn of this specialty, many in the social work world quickly recognized the congruence of palliative care principles and values with core social work practice. Eliciting values and exploring the influence of culture, socioeconomic and spiritual factors, communication, self-determination and autonomy, strength-based assessment, and the importance of relationship— all key components of palliative care—have been foundational to social work practice. At our best, we attune to what we receive, verbally and nonverbally, sometimes discovered and sometimes by putting assumptions aside, and we perceive what is "in plain sight." Bringing a spirit of openness and curiosity to this work creates space for us to be present, to notice, and to begin to join with patients and families. We give back through our words, hypotheses, actions, perceptions, and documentation, giving form and visibility to shared understandings. At our best, our communication supports exploration and elicits meaning, revealing new dimensions of patient and family experience. While sometimes threatening, this depth of communication serves to bridge rather than to separate, capturing the impact on person and family when illness disrupts the order and predictability we wish for and often take for granted. When working at the top of our license, we acknowledge and honor the inextricable link of body, self, and environment and advocate for the value of ethical and therapeutic process, taking place in the moment or over time. This is as equally vital as the outcome of our shared efforts.

At the same time that congruity may be evident, social work surveys indicate self-assessed competence in many palliative care domains of practice are not learned in the course of social work education, and some of these competencies are not considered relevant to practice (Christ & Sormanti, 1999; Sumser, Remke, Leimena, Altilio, & Otis-Green, 2015). While the alignment of values and philosophy might have placed social work in the forefront, reasserting commitment to humanistic, competent, and comprehensive care for the seriously ill and their families, the focus on the "specialist" designation may have inadvertently created distance and hierarchy, rather than highlighting the commonality which bridges primary and specialist practice. This book is designed to bridge—using theory and practice, evidence and narrative—to integrate palliative care principles, and to encourage social workers across health settings to see themselves in this work, to discover "in plain sight" the additional opportunities to weave palliative care principles into the service they provide. The intent is to provide a resource for clinicians, students, and educators to identify theories and concepts that frame social work practice, strengthening the link of palliative care to health social work, the providers who are most often the first line of mental health practitioners to join with persons who are ill and their families. The current energy generated by the demand for palliative care in primary practice can provide an impetus for health social work to assert and, when needed, to reaffirm core social work values, linking to ideas, action, and institutional change. This reasserts shared humanity as the heart of providing compassionate and comprehensive services to those who are most vulnerable.

The guide is framed by the National Consensus Project's (NCP) Eight Domains of Palliative Care, listed in Table I.2 revised in 2013 (National Consensus Project, 2013) with a further revision expected in 2018.

While decidedly a document framed in Western values, the domains described by the NCP capture aspects of care and understanding that move personhood to the center of health care. In theory, these domains may appear as silos. In practice, this frame looks more like concentric circles—patient, family, and provider experience is integrated in the biopsychosocialspiritual

Table I.2 DOMAINS OF PALLIATIVE CARE

Domain	Aspect of Care	Components
1	Structure & process of care	Comprehensive assessment, interdisciplinary collaboration, team work/structure, care planning, continuity through transitions
2	Physical	Diagnosis, symptom management, medications, multidimensional interventions
3	Psychological	Mental health (anxiety, depression, delirium), adjustment & adaptation, demoralization, coping, comorbid psychiatric illness
4	Social	Family system & structures, changes in social role, concrete needs, financial concerns
5	Spiritual	Connection to spiritual/religious meaning, ritual & community, coping mechanisms, hopes & fears, being with the unknown, provider resilience & awareness
6	Cultural	Language, ritual, dietary, relationship to the health care system, illness & symptom-related beliefs & values, decision-making variation
7	Care at the end of life	Prognostication, illness trajectory, loss, grief & bereavement, active dying, funeral planning, family/caregiving needs
8	Ethical & legal	Advance directives, proxy & surrogacy decision-making, ethics committees/ consultation, physician aid in dying

and cultural model. There are opportunities for social work assessment and intervention within each domain. While advocacy and social justice issues may take different paths, they remain core driving principles. Our purpose is to guide you through so that you may locate yourself in this work regardless of setting, geographic location, and local resources.

Organizing this guide by placing patient family narratives within different settings and diagnoses, highlighting evidence and documentation, is intended to assist readers to validate and challenge current practice and to encourage a shared vision linking health social work and palliative principles. It is our intent to take the mystery out of palliative practice by integrating familiar values, theories, and concepts while honoring the uncertainty and mystery that infuse the experience of patients, families, and clinicians who share in the process of evolving illness.

THEORETICAL FRAMEWORKS

The charge of this book was significant and became more so as the work of authors was integrated into a whole. This process of reading, writing, and rewriting forced introspection and a shift in perspective, from a binary focus of primary and specialist, to a realization that the work is not binary. In parallel process to what patients and families face, adaptation and growth often demands fluidity. Social work as a discipline has the opportunity to model fluidity and grace to honor and build on the work of others, collaborating to meet the needs of those living with serious illness, while advocating to humanize the systems in which care is provided, and to recognize when one needs the assistance of specialists. To that end, we are attempting to map the universe of perspectives, needs, and opportunities in health care to be informed by the principles of palliative care. We chose theoretical tools to navigate the topography.

ECOLOGICAL SYSTEMS THEORY

Applying Bronfenbrenner's Ecological Systems Theory is one framework in considering the landscape of the US health care system and how persons living in different settings and stages of the illness continuum might interface with social workers (Bronfenbrenner, 1979). It is one way to systematize our thinking about the different levels of influence and opportunity for assessment and intervention. Originally proposed to contextualize child development and understand the influence of interacting subsystems on the child, this model has been adapted and modified over time to illustrate the ways in which complex and

---

Box I.1

MICRO TO MACRO

Micro: Individual & personal level
Support network of friends, biological & chosen family

Meso: Community & institutional level
Neighborhoods, providers, health care settings

Macro: Social & structural level
Cultural systems including capitalism, racism, patriarchy, Judeo-Christian values, cisgendered, heteronormativity, insurance, policy

---

overlapping systems act upon a single person. For our purposes, we use the lens of the micro, the meso and the macro, each of which are delineated in Box I.1, holding the realities that individuals, including providers, exist simultaneously in multiple personal and social locations and are being acted upon by larger social forces, which might contribute to their vulnerability, is not an easy undertaking. Acknowledging and developing an appreciation for the many ways individual people interact with and are acted upon by these forces is essentially aligned with the principles of social work. Viewing an experience of serious illness through these lenses might afford social workers new perspectives and insights into the complexity brought to health care settings, as these individual people become patients. At the same time, this lens invites practitioners to assist each other to recognize and negotiate the many forces in the health care world influencing individual and structural values and behaviors.

SOCIAL DETERMINANTS OF HEALTH

In a complementary framework, the Social Determinants of Health offers a perspective on illness that contextualizes health status beyond genetics and behavior (Heiman, 2015). Economic stability, neighborhood and physical environment, education, food, community and social context, and health care system are the domains considered most influential on health status and outcomes (Heiman, 2015). An individual's health and illness are embedded in the realities of her lived experience and the structural advantages she enjoys or the disadvantages she endures. The impact on health, wellness, and illness for children is especially pronounced, as children lack agency over their circumstances and are at the mercy of adults. The negative consequences of poverty and discrimination are exacerbated, as they influence not only the present but the future, imprinting as children grow and affecting development. Disparities in access to prescription medications at community pharmacies for poorer neighborhoods is one example of how geography and socioeconomic conditions interface to directly impact illness outcomes and experience (Amstislavski, 2012). Considering structural aspects of the health care system, such as access to health information in a culturally and linguistically congruent manner, it becomes clear how individuals with opportunities for education, literacy, and English language proficiency are privileged over those who have not shared these experiences. The consequences of this privileging for outcomes and experience for individuals and families who orbit around them are significant. At the same time, social work's focus on strengths counters assumptions that blind clinicians to the discovery of resilience and resources, perspectives, and values brought to illness experience by those who may be "disadvantaged," yet are privileged in ways one only discovers through humble inquiry.

The model of Social Determinants of Health includes positive influences on wellness and health, considering the impact of assets, strengths, and resources. Applying this model reminds us that wellness is an achievable and important goal beyond managing disease (see Figure I.1). There are opportunities for growth, connection, and well-being during the course of illness. In pursuit of health equity, or the right to the highest standard of health enjoyed

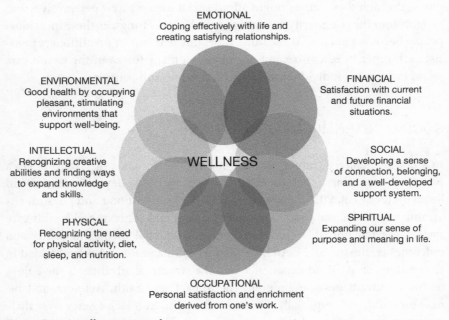

Figure I.1. A wellness approach.

by those most socially advantaged (Braveman & Guskin, 2003), a comparable idea of illness experience equity can be imagined. This means, in part, that the values, preferences, and goals of all patients are heard, and that providers work relentlessly to integrate these priorities into their care. Locating and valuing spiritual-cultural-psychosocial preferences and expressions are then considered essential to ensuring that care is responsive and centered on person and family. This is the shared mandate of health social work across specialties and settings.

INTERSECTIONALITY

As conceived by Black Womanism/Feminism, the concept and social frame of intersectionality explores social location and experience in relationship to power and oppression (Crenshaw, 1993). Working with the assumption that there are historical, systemic systems of power and privilege within US culture, intersectionality suggests that individual experience is shaped through the intersecting identities of race, class, gender, sexuality, language, nation, and ability, among others. Identity is complex—a deeply personal journey through a political socioeconomic landscape, informed through multigenerational history. Increasingly, fluidity colors these identifiers that historically have been categorized in a binary fashion. Developing and nurturing curiosity for unique experiences, while understanding the macro systems that shape and inform, restrict and promote, center and marginalize, normalize and define as "other" certain types of people and ways of being, are central to social work's commitment to social justice. This is about power, privilege, and oppression. How does social location influence what is possible, how one experiences the health care system, access to resources, health literacy, the unique configuration of stressors in an individual life, family system, and community? As a field fundamentally committed to social justice, it is social work's responsibility to show up in the space where power can be unpacked, named, and systems changed to benefit and support all people equally.

Self-awareness and reflexivity are crucial elements when considering intersectionality. We all experience intersecting identities. Social location informs world view, a lens naturally brought into clinical care and therapeutic relationships. Relational caring asks that we take stock of what we bring into the room and how this interacts with team members, colleagues, and most important, patients and families. Table I.3 explores systems of oppression as they relate to targeted and privileged groups. A border group has been added to attempt to show the fluidity which increasingly permeates identity and fosters associated shifts in social perspectives.

Table I.3 SYSTEMS OF POWER AND OPPRESSION

Type of Oppression	Target Group	Border Group	Privileged Group
Race	People of color	Biracial people	White people
Class	Poor, working class	Middle class	Wealthy, upper class
Gender	Genderqueer, transgender	Non-binary	Gender conforming
Sex	Biological females	Intersex	Biological males
Sexual orientation	Lesbian, gay	Bisexual	Heterosexual
Ability/Disability	People with disability	People with temporary disability	Able-bodied people
Religious	Non-Christians	Roman Catholics	Protestant Christians
Age	Older adults, children	Young adults	Adults
Rank/Status	People without a college degree	People with some college education	People with a college degree
Military service	Vietnam veterans	Veterans of other wars	Non-veterans
Immigrant status	Undocumented immigrants	Documented immigrants	US-born individuals
Language	Non-English	Bilingual	English

Adapted by Theodore Scheel from Adams, M., Bell, L. E., & Griffin, P. (Eds.). (2007). *Teaching for diversity and social justice* (2nd ed.). New York: Routledge.

HIGH- AND LOW-CONTEXT CULTURES

Borrowing from the anthropological field of intercultural communication, James Hallenbeck applies the concept of high- and low-context cultures to the practice of palliative care and the experience of illness and dying (Hallenbeck, 2006). In high-context cultures, communication stems from the context in which it is happening, relying on meaning, and is more implicit. In low-context cultures, communication is more direct, and less situational or related to context. High-context communication is relational, valuing the interpersonal, while low-context culture is well expressed through written and verbal communication. Cultures vary in the use of both high- and low-context communication strategies. Considered broadly, you can begin to imagine how this might apply to the different cultures promoted by medical specialties and professions. Palliative care promotes a high-context, relational style of caring. Social work practice is also relationship based, looking to locate persons in the context of their lives, to build specific and individual understanding, utilizing awareness of self and other through observation and verbal communication, as well as body language. Biomedical training promotes a low-context culture, synthesizing data-driven information, scientific knowledge into a task-driven system designed to achieve outcomes that are often measureable.

Illness and dying are high-context experiences. There is no universal experience of cancer. A diagnosis exists in the life of a person, with meanings made and changed as illness progresses. Relationships are central to the process. Slowing down enough to share meaning and story enhances connection and a sense of being "in sync" with patients, families, and other providers. This leads to better communication and the space where we can really learn about hopes, wishes, values, and fears—about what is most important to a person. It is at this interface of high-context process and low-context outcomes where important conversations are had across professions to create paths to align institutional needs with the humanity of the work.

LANGUAGE

As editors, we have engaged in iterative reflection about chosen language and the essential importance and challenges of our use of specific phrases. This has been an exhilarating and at times exhausting challenge in seeking to create a cohesive whole out of many different voices. Both in editing the words of authors and in choosing our own words, our goal has been to use thoughtful, respectful, and inclusive language. We recognize the power of words, particularly in how they can reflect and amplify dominant or primary power structures and reinforce existing biases or ideas. We recognize the power of words to create feelings, enhance empathy and relay implicit judgment. In our words, we hope to capture the complexity of this work, to challenge simplicity and bias, and to privilege the experiences and ideas of patients and families that are often diminished in a culture and systems of care that may lack the time, attention, and attunement to truly see or hear.

Throughout this book there are numerous examples of how modeling language, through interactions with colleagues, patients, and families and in documentation, is an intervention itself. As social workers consider the language they use in speaking with patients and colleagues, we invite the same careful and rigorous attention to documentation. Might the language change, if you knew the patient or the family were reading your words? Would the language change if you knew your words might influence whether your patient would receive a treatment that might extend her life?

We have made some specific choices. Writing from and seeking to honor and normalize a feminist perspective, we have chosen "she" as the default pronoun to discuss individuals. In case narratives, a language is used to reflect a range of racial and ethnic backgrounds and identities. In Chapter 10 on "children and older adults," we have chosen not to use the medical terms of "pediatrics" and "geriatrics" in order to underscore the humanity of persons and their families as more than medical subspecialty groups. We choose to use "therapy first language" that does not identify or conflate patients with their diagnoses or treatments (United Spinal Association, 2015). Consequently, language changes from "the patient failed chemotherapy" to "the chemotherapy is no longer working as we had hoped it would"—implying that there is no failure on either the part of the patient or the provider. The "addict" becomes a person with the disease of addiction. This highlights how clinicians can both separate and individualize the person from the medical processes they engage, remove judgmental language, promote clarity, and invite further discovery. There are places within this book where phrases or words can be found common to health care settings and often used interchangeably. This includes "care conference," "case conference," and "family meeting," for example, where we recognize regional and institutional cultures.

As we have considered language, it has led us to think critically about the ways we talk about our work in different settings. We personally avoid words or phrases appearing to align with palliative care or hospice services as an "industry," such as a business or something to sell. Respecting the complex processes that infuse adaptation and decision-making, phrases like "she isn't on board for hospice" simplify the complex nature of these decisions and perhaps also simplify the work that supports these transitions. Additionally, we advocate for not shortening words or phrases, such as "pall care" for palliative care or "dispo planning" for disposition planning—a word defined as "getting rid of something." These abbreviated phrases are associated with health care structures and a culture where whole-person, patient-centered language is not always prioritized. The argots, or private communication and vocabulary of a specific group, such as physicians, create opportunities to privilege the primary power structures within health care and to marginalize those with less power. In health care settings, using this shorthand language serves to bridge a connection to the primary culture while risking a challenge both to identity and to our professional values and ethics.

This book has been a well-intended but imperfect human pursuit; we ask for an allowance on word choices or phrases we have missed or misused. Use your noticing of our errors to inspire shared discussion and learning locally. Our hope has always been to use language conveying the utmost respect and appreciation we have for the persons—professionals, patients, and families—we have the privilege of working with. Language reflecting anything other than this is our responsibility and a reminder that we must always strive to do better.

TEAM: A FOUNDATIONAL CONCEPT

The concept of team is at the heart of palliative care just as it has been a core component of the structure of hospice programs. The intent is for different disciplines to work together with trust and mutual respect to meet the physical, psychosocial, and spiritual needs of patients and their families. The language used to describe teams reflects the aspirations of clinicians, promoting an ongoing reflective process to both study and experiment with various team models aimed toward sustainability and effectiveness. This can be described as multidisciplinary, interdisciplinary, transdisciplinary and interprofessional—each implying a gradual shift from the siloed structure of multidisciplinary to a shared vision, an acceptance of integrated responsibilities and a comfort with role overlap reflected in the transdisciplinary and interprofessional models.

Teams bring together members of varied professions who receive discipline specific training yet little or no training on team process or how to manage dynamics such as competition, hierarchy and power. Members bring their codes of ethics, unique personal histories and that of their disciplines, and often work together in formal teams with an intent to value the contributions of colleagues and share responsibility for common goals. Yet formal teams are in constant process of interface with others. For example a palliative care team may be asked to consult on a hospitalized patient who is cared for by a primary team on the inpatient unit and a dialysis team in the community—thus team negotiations and collaborations move much beyond the nuclear palliative care team. Teams come together, as if an extended family, to collaborate and cooperative in the care of a particular patient and their family.

It is this model of nuclear and extended family team that seems particularly relevant as palliative practices integrate further into health social work.

When working on any established team the care of many patients requires that we stretch beyond boundaries, join with others who are important to the life of a particular patient—build organic teams that form to meet needs and then dissipate as need dissipates. This flexibility and fluidity is reflected in this guide.

CONCLUSION

Taking the best care possible of patients and families living with serious illness, from diagnosis through bereavement, through single encounters or long-term relationships, requires curiosity, creativity, collaboration, courage and heart. As the population ages and medical technology continues to advance, more people will live longer, and many will manage the terrain of serious illness. We are positioned, in numbers across settings, to build a human-centered health care system: a system that honors the individual, within her family and community; a system that listens for values, preferences, and beliefs, for strengths, resilience, and meaning, for worries, fear, and anticipation. This health care system relies on human providers, those of us able to be in our own personhood as we provide care and accompany many through the uncertain and the unknown. Here, in a space often assumed to be sad, lives so much life: connection, belonging, stories, relationships new and old, laughter, tears, and possibility. Here is the simple, the mundane, and the everyday, as well as the transcendent, the inspiring, and the profound.

Our intention is that this book will be a guide and companion into this space. To be familiar with the landscape of palliative care may be to reaffirm the values and vision that led you to health social work. If something piques your interest, study and explore further on your own or with others in your setting. Pick any subject in this book—someone is spending their lives exploring and studying it: find them. This text provides an introduction. We have worked to present material in an accessible and thoughtful way, highlighting specific skills and interventions to help build a foundation of knowledge and understanding. The focus on language and documentation highlights aspects of daily work that can change practice, influence others, and cost nothing. There is much that remains unanswered and unexplored. This resource is intended to encourage ongoing self-reflection and introspection. This work is also an invitation to spark your creativity and curiosity not only about patients and families, but also about the health care systems you work in and the opportunities presented every day to shape them.

REFERENCES

Amstislavski, P., Matthews, A., Sheffield, S., Maroko, A. R. & Weedon, J. (2012) Medication deserts: Survey of neighborhood disparities in availability of prescription medications. *International Journal of Health Geographics, 11*(48), 1–13.

Braveman, P., & Gruskin, S. (2003). Defining equity in health. *Journal of Epidemiology & Community Health, 57,* 254–258.

Bronfenbrenner, U. (1979). *The ecology of human development: Experiments by nature and design.* Cambridge, MA: Harvard University Press.

Center to Advance Palliative Care (CAPC). (n.d.) *Get palliative care.* Retrieved from www.getpalliativecare.org/whatis/.

Christ, G. H., & Sormanti, M. (1999). The social work role in end-of-life care: A survey of practitioners and academicians. *Social Work Health Care, 30,* 81–99.

Connor, S. R., Downing, J., & Marston, J. (2017). Estimating the global need for palliative care for children: A Cross-sectional analysis. *Journal of Pain and Symptom Management, 53*(2), 79–87.

Crenshaw, K. (1993). Mapping the margins: Intersectionality, identity political and violence against women of color. *Stanford Law Review, 43*(6), 1241–1299.

Gomes, B., Calanzani, N., Curiale, V., McCrone, P., Higginson, I. J., & deBrito, M. (2013). Effectiveness and cost-effectiveness of home palliative care services for adults with advanced illness and their caregivers. *Cochrane Database of Systematic Reviews, 6,* 1–279.

Hallenbeck, J. (2006). High context illness and dying in a low context medical world. *American Journal of Hospice & Palliative Medicine, 23*(2), 113–118.

Heiman, H. J., & Artiga, S. (2015). Beyond health care: The role of social determinants in promoting health and health equity. Retrieved from www.kff.org/disparities-policy/issue-brief/beyond-health-care-the-role-of-social-determinants-in-promoting-health-and-health-equity/.

Institute of Medicine. (2015). *Dying in America: Improving quality and honoring individual preferences near the end of life.* Retrieved from www.nationalacademies.org/hmd/Reports/2014/Dying-In-America-Improving-Quality-and-Honoring-Individual-Preferences-Near-the-End-of-Life.aspx.

Marshall, K. J. (2017) Mastry. Breuer Museum audio guide. www.metmuseum.org/exhibitions/listings/2016/kerry-james-marshall/audio-guide. New York, NY.

National Consensus Project for Quality Palliative Care (NCP). (2013). *Clinical practice guidelines for quality palliative care,* 3rd ed. Pittsburgh, PA: NCP.

Payne, M. 2009. Developments in end-of-life and palliative care social work. *International Social Work, 52*(4), 513–524.

Rabow, M., Kvale, E., Barbour, L., Cassel, J. B., Cohen, S., Jackson, V., . . . Weissman, D. (2013). Moving upstream: A review of the evidence of the impact of outpatient palliative care. *Journal of Palliative Medicine, 16,* 1540–1549.

Rogers, M, & Dumanovsky, T. (2017). *How we work: Trends and insights in hospital palliative care.* The Center to Advance Palliative Care and the National Palliative Care Research Center. New York, NY.

Sumser, B., Remke, S., Leimena, M., Altilio, T., & Otis-Green, S. (2015). The serendipitous survey: A look at primary and specialist palliative social work practice, preparation, and competence. *Journal of Palliative Medicine, 18*(10), 881–883.

United Spinal Association. (2015). *Disability etiquette: Tips for interacting with people
with disabilities.* Retrieved from www.unitedspinal.org/pdf/DisabilityEtiquette.
pdf.

World Health Organization (2014). *Strengthening of palliative care as a component of
comprehensive care through the life course.* Retrieved from apps.who.int/gb/ebwha/
pdf_files/wha67/a67_r19-en.pdf.

World Health Organization (2017). *Palliative care fact sheet.* Retrieved from www.who.
int/mediacentre/factsheets/fs402/en/.

The Convergence of Social Work Practice

Integrating Health Social Work and Specialized Palliative Care

COLLEEN M. MULKERIN ■

> The range of what we think and do is limited by what we fail to notice. And because we fail to notice that we fail to notice, there is little we can do to change; until we notice how failing to notice shape[s] our thoughts and deeds.
>
> —R. D. LAING

INTRODUCTION

We are in a dynamic time in social work as we address the evolving convergence in social work practice and the effort to join and integrate primary palliative care into all health care. This chapter will examine both a model of health social work as primary clinicians in palliative care, and the interface with specialized palliative social workers and interprofessional palliative care teams. Social workers, like other members of the interprofessional team, are confronted with a limited specialty palliative care workforce, which has led to the movement to increase primary skills among all members of the health care team (IOM, 2015; Quill & Abernethy, 2013). However, it is essential to challenge the concept that the only purpose of a trained primary team is to address a gap in the specialty workforce. There is an imperative to recognize and be prepared to address all domains of palliative care across all health care teams. The call to action that originates from the deficit model in the specialty workforce misses the opportunity to honor the quality narrative that palliative care is, at its essence, good health care.

Health social workers are ideally aligned with the field of palliative care. The variation in confidence and competence of health social workers to respond to palliative care needs, as well as variable access to consultative palliative care, requires a shared commitment to develop opportunities for education and mentorship. Going beyond a binary model of primary or specialist, the ongoing work rests in creating high-quality reciprocal relationships that are marked by respect, mutuality, and collaboration.

IS PALLIATIVE CARE A SPECIALTY IN SOCIAL WORK?

Palliative care strives to provide "whole-person" care. "Palliative care is an approach that improves the quality of life of patients and their families facing the problems associated with life-threatening illness, through the prevention and relief of suffering by means of early identification and impeccable assessment and treatment of pain and other problems, physical, psychosocial and spiritual" (World Health Organization, n.d.). Palliative care is also defined by the Center to Advance Palliative Care as specialized care for people with serious illness. Through an interdisciplinary team approach, and collaboration with other providers, palliative care focuses on providing expert symptom management and mitigating the stress of a serious illness. A goal is to improve quality of life for both the patient and the family. Palliative care can be provided with disease-modifying therapies for people of all ages (Center to Advance Palliative Care, 2017).

Palliative care, having grown out of the hospice movement, has long been identified as an interdisciplinary practice in medicine. For more than a decade, a primary concern has been defining a social work specialty within the field and on the team. Palliative care teams and social work departments have explored role clarification for both the unique and complementary competencies in the domains within palliative care (Blacker, 2004; Bosma et al., 2009; Christ & Blacker, 2005; Gwyther, 2005; Mitchell et al., 2012; Panel, 2011). Palliative social workers have contributed a unique voice to the interdisciplinary team, as the core values, ethical principles and tenets of the profession of social work and the specialty are naturally aligned. These include service, social justice, dignity and worth of the person, importance of human relationships, integrity, and competence. As palliative social work evolved, the National Association of Social Workers (NASW) published professional standards of practice (National Association of Social Workers, 2004). In collaboration with the National Hospice and Palliative Care Organization (NHPCO), a national credential was developed in hospice and palliative care, tailored to capture the specialized knowledge, skills, and abilities of professional social workers in hospice and palliative care settings (National Association of Social Workers, 2004). Currently there is in development a test-based certification process similar to that of nursing.

Palliative social workers have endeavored to differentiate skills and domains for a social work subspecialty. Social work competencies have been well documented (Bosma et al., 2009; Cadell, Jonston, Bosma, & Wainright, 2010; Gwyther et al., 2005; Sumser, Remke, Leimena, Altilio, & Otis-Green, 2015). *The Oxford Textbook of Palliative Social Work*, the *Journal of Social Work in End of Life Care*, and the Social Work Hospice and Palliative Care Network (SWHPN) are resources that have defined and symbolically established the credibility and authenticity of the specialty. There is now an opportunity to move beyond the question of whether palliative care is a specialty to explore the ways in which patients and families benefit when health social workers recognize palliative care needs and intervene accordingly. As early as 1998, Quinn, a social work educator, advocated palliative care as "an approach that is the responsibility of all professionals whose work brings them into contact with people suffering from a life-threatening illness: it is not the exclusive responsibility of palliative care specialists" (p. 12).

Palliative care teams in hospital settings began to grow rapidly in the first decade of the 2000s. Teams continue to work diligently to establish their role as central to the care of persons living with serious illness, highlighting the team approach to symptom management, goals of care discussions and medical decision making, and providing support through the trajectory of serious illness into bereavement. This ethos, committed deeply to understanding patient values and preferences for care, came at a time when vast strides in medical technology had overshadowed the basic principles of person-centered care (Connors, Dawson, & Desbiens, 1995).

As specialty palliative care teams grew in numbers, it was not uncommon to find that they were staffed without dedicated social workers. Social work advocated for "a seat at the table" during a time of scarce resources and challenging environments (Higgins, 2011; Meier & Beresford, 2008). When palliative care teams did include social workers, some degree of tension and role confusion occurred as disciplines established their roles, identities, and influence, often in the setting of shared inexperience about how to work together as a team. At other times, the tension occurred between the palliative social worker and the rest of the social work department and sometimes the tension was felt between social workers in the care of a shared patient (Meier & Beresford, 2008). These are not just dynamics of the past, as social workers continue to navigate issues related to role delineation while building understanding of the contribution of colleagues. To move beyond these tensions, it is vital to assess and understand the systemic issues contributing to these historical dynamics.

UNDERSTANDING HISTORY LOCALLY

Identifying stakeholders in the creation of the specialty palliative care service gives context to the origin story at every institution. If interdisciplinary leadership was not a part of the planning, the vision and mission may not be understood, and the palliative social worker may face isolation from both the palliative care team and the social work department.

In many settings, for the first dozen or so years, palliative social workers have had to do the clinical, emotional, and cognitive work, both within and beyond the profession, to distinguish the discipline as a specialty. At times, health social workers have been the comparison variable used by palliative social workers to distinguish their work as a specialty. Perhaps an unintended consequence of this effort to establish a scope of practice has been the diminishing of colleagues, rather than a shared effort to affirm health social work skills and build upon them (Sumser et al., 2015). At the same time, and at another point of intersection, palliative care teams were working out relationships with other health care teams, sometimes entering these clinical encounters with a moral superiority and the notion that patients need rescuing from their primary teams (Meier & Beresford, 2007). In locations where palliative care teams are newly established and continue to develop, these patterns may still emerge. This awareness creates an opportunity to frame collaborative processes that mitigate the possibility of repeating historical patterns.

ORGANIZATIONAL HOME

Where a position is housed may represent a structural decision that has implications for practice and collaboration. Some palliative care teams are aligned in an interprofessional fashion within the hospital system in a single department with a single reporting structure. Alternatively, team members may be housed in different departments, united in their assignment to the palliative care team. A dual reporting structure may leave staff accountable to a centralized department such as Social Work and Case Management, while having a full-time clinical assignment in palliative care. Relying on the history and the strength of the dual model of reporting, team members can become trapped in the variation of institutional priorities, culture, and roles. If the social worker on the palliative care team is part of a larger social work department, she may get pulled to staff gaps in unit-based coverage, which may be viewed as the primary mission of the hospital social work department. An authentic commitment to health social work on all teams would aim to avoid putting clinicians in the position of having to straddle conflicting demands.

DISCHARGE PLANNING AND CLINICAL SOCIAL WORK

An important structural aspect of health social work is an understanding of where in the system the discharge planning/case management, assessment and function reside. There has been a tendency to place a higher value on certain social work activities, creating a hierarchical scheme for each role, and diminishing some functions and the skills associated with them. At times, the divide between the primary unit-based social worker and specialty palliative social worker is discharge planning versus what some view as clinical social work. In many settings, staffing pressures have stripped the discharge-planning role of the clinical components that relate to loss, adaptation, and the complex meanings attached to illness-related changes that come uninvited into the lives of patients and families. The primary unit or service line social worker is essential to clinical assessment and may already be supporting medical decision-making, planning family meetings, coordinating communication, attending to loss and grief, negotiating a plan for continuing care needs, capturing the emotional impact, and facilitating care transitions to social work colleagues in other settings.

The specialty palliative social work role is designed for flexibility and fluidity to respond and partner with the health social worker in enriching clinical assessment, patient-family biopsychosocial care, family meetings, and psychosocial support for medical decision-making. As we create awareness of the historic power and privilege at play in a system most comfortable with hierarchy, these dynamics can be observed, depersonalized, and addressed. When social workers on any team are devalued, the system dynamics of power and privilege also contribute to devaluing the people in our care, and those we serve may have mirrored experiences (Saleebey, 2000).

BINARY THINKING

Thinking about health and illness beyond a binary model can enhance our understanding of how health care has evolved and how it influences those living with serious illness. The experiences of feeling "healthy" or "sick," for example, are subjective and fluid, existing in a landscape marked by functioning and biopsychosocialspiritual ease or distress. Many people being cared for across health settings are living with conditions that may not have a cure. Innovations in health care have developed methods of managing and transforming what once was a terminal diagnosis with a short dying trajectory into a chronic condition managed over time. Consider the evolution of managing HIV/AIDS, the range of advanced therapies evolving for heart disease, and the enormous research efforts and innovation in cancer care. As such, palliative care principles and interventions are increasingly relevant to patients and families upstream, as early as the time of diagnosis. The work is relevant to all patients and transcends end-of-life care to include treatment plans that are disease modifying or curative, over time. It is not limited to end-of-life care.

A public health framework has helped to identify factors that interfere with a patient and families' ability to engage with the health care system in an empowered way. This includes low health literacy, the sheer volume of information available about the natural history of diseases, and the tendency to focus on prevention and health promotion rather than living with an advanced illness. Therefore, there are myriad opportunities for ongoing psycho-education related to navigating both the health care system and the evolving experience of illness. It is this imperative that makes palliative care everyone's work within the interprofessional health care community and leads to a special alliance with social work. Social work plays an instrumental role in primary health settings to provide education, reduce barriers to access, and support informed patient choices and advocacy.

Since health and illness are not binary processes, there exists an enormous opportunity to develop and effectively utilize the role of social work from meeting practical needs to crisis intervention and psychotherapeutic assessment and interventions to guide the plan of care (Gwyther et al., 2005; Mitchell et al., 2012). Health social workers are well positioned to reject binary thinking and polarization, entering a person's life when there is a unique opportunity to preserve the patient's voice, through early and ongoing advance care planning. By working to establish goals steeped in the values and preferences of each individual and engaging with medical and nursing colleagues in a process of informed advance care planning, linkages can be made to outcomes such as improvement in end-of-life care, increased patient and family satisfaction, and reduction of stress, anxiety, and depression in surviving relatives. The clinician has impact in the present and extending into the future (Russell, 2015).

The Institute of Medicine (IOM) released specific recommendations health social workers can follow to improve the care of people living with serious illness (IOM, 2015). These not only serve as a guide to quality care, but also can become tools for advocacy and leadership.

Dying in America, IOM Recommendations

Recommendation 1: Delivery of Person-Centered, Family-Oriented Care

Government health insurers and care delivery programs, as well as private health insurers, should cover the provision of comprehensive care for individuals with advanced serious illness who are nearing the end of life.

Recommendation 2: Clinician–Patient Communication and Advance Care Planning

Professional societies and other organizations that establish quality standards should develop standards for clinician–patient communication and advance care planning that are measurable, actionable, and evidence based. These standards should change as needed to reflect the evolving population and health system needs and be consistent with emerging evidence, methods, and technologies. Payers and health care delivery organizations should adopt these standards and their supporting processes, and integrate them into assessments, care plans, and the reporting of health care quality.

Recommendation 3: Professional Education and Development

Educational institutions, credentialing bodies, accrediting boards, state regulatory agencies, and health care delivery organizations should establish the appropriate training, certification, and/or licensure requirements to strengthen the palliative care knowledge and skills of all clinicians who care for individuals with advanced serious illness who are nearing the end of life.

Recommendation 4: Policies and Payment Systems

Federal, state, and private insurance and health care delivery programs should integrate the financing of medical and social services to support the provision of quality care consistent with the values, goals, and informed preferences of people with advanced serious illness nearing the end of life. To the extent that additional legislation is necessary to implement this recommendation, the administration should seek, and Congress should enact such legislation. In addition, the federal government should require public reporting on quality measures, outcomes, and costs regarding care near the end of life (e.g., in the last year of life) for programs it funds or administers (e.g., Medicare, Medicaid, the Department of Veterans Affairs). The federal government should encourage all other payment and health care delivery systems to do the same.

Recommendation 5: Public Education and Engagement
    Civic leaders, public health and other governmental agencies,
    community-based organizations, faith-based organizations, consumer
    groups, health care delivery organizations, payers, employers, and
    professional societies should engage their constituents and provide
    fact-based information about care of people with advanced serious
    illness to encourage advance care planning and informed choice
    based on the needs and values of individuals. (IOM, 2015)

Health social workers, embedded in a variety of settings, are positioned to review
the IOM recommendations to validate and ground current practice while developing continuous learning communities linking with social work leaders and palliative care specialists to fully actualize the key recommendations (Russell, 2015).

RAFAEL

Rafael, age 23, lived in Puerto Rico until the age of 20, when he left with his
younger siblings and mother Flora, whose advocacy and planning had created
access to necessary health care in the United States. Rafael was diagnosed with
type 1 diabetes mellitus at the age of 8. He was a high school graduate, single
and unemployed. He lived with multiple consequences of his diabetes, including neuropathy, retinopathy, hypertensive renal disease, and anemia from
chronic renal insufficiency. He developed cardiac disease, congestive heart
failure, gastroparesis, and a seizure disorder. He lost his vision and lived with
many complex symptoms that affected his quality of life, including nausea, di-
arrhea, sleep disturbances, headache, eye pain, and seizures. His kidney function declined, requiring hemodialysis treatments three times per week.

    His primary care was centered in a tertiary care hospital clinic and he re-
ceived dialysis through a hospital-based program. Rafael required frequent
hospitalizations. Transitions designed to maintain psychosocialspiritual continuity and enhance growth for Rafael and his family were a primary focus of
social workers in each setting.

Interventions: Micro, Meso, Macro

MICRO
Rafael was sincere, direct, and soft-spoken. He had acclimated to many changes
in his life. Diabetes mellitus type 1, magnified by socioeconomic determinants
of health including access to health care, stress, and low income, created chronic
illness unresponsive to common behavioral adaptations prior to moving to the

United States. His mother eventually relocated the family to improve his access to medical care. The teams that cared for Rafael were often in a reactive posture and held strong opinions about what was within his control for closer management of his diabetes. At the same time, some providers felt his disease was so advanced and complex that it would not be possible for him to closely control his diabetes with diet, exercise, and insulin. Rafael's symptom burden was significant and directly affected by any variation in his body, such as infection or complications with dialysis, and required close follow-up and proactive management of headaches, gastric symptoms, and seizures. An ongoing role for social work across settings was to advocate for adequate symptom control and to provide psychosocial history and context to providers (See Chapter 3; "Physical Aspects of Care"). These interventions mediated team distress and frustration and informed deliberations that influenced medication management for pain and other symptoms.

Rafael's dialysis schedule and his near-complete loss of vision left him reliant on Flora. Their relationship was complicated by a developmental drive for independence and individuation and the concurrent need for help which required that he depend on his mother for some aspects of physical care. Rafael worked to negotiate some autonomy from his mother during his mid-twenties. A thread woven throughout Rafael's treatment plan was partnering with community resources to support care organized around his values and preferences, highlighting aspects of his care he could influence and control. His spiritual life was an important part of his coping and meaning-making. His Pentecostal community was a primary source of support, providing connection with other young adults (See Chapter 6; "Spiritual, Religious, and Existential Dimensions of Care"). Three social workers effectively partnered to care for Rafael over settings and time, through primary care, dialysis, and in-patient palliative care consultations. The contiguous themes focused on advocacy for symptom management, family work focused on boundaries around self-scheduling sleep/wake times to maintain meal and insulin needs, iterative advance care planning conversations, and recording a legal advance directive, including appointing a health care representative and completing a living will. These themes supported the developmental needs of a young adult with complex and unpredictable illness.

Meso

Rafael's mother and siblings were an important focus of patient-centered, family-focused care. His younger siblings were impacted by medical crises, witnessing episodes of critically low blood sugar and seizures. Frequently, ambulances came to the home to treat and transport Rafael to the hospital. Flora neglected her own medical care, and all children experienced additional distress as she ignored her own needs, leaving them worried about her well-being over time and therefore, their own. Just as Flora has sought medical care for Rafael, social work intervened to guide her in locating a primary care provider. After assessing together the real pressures and demands of life and responsibilities, suggestions for respite were explored.

Indirect service interventions included support to staff to elicit their concerns, fears, and hopes. Many of the nurses and doctors caring for Rafael were of his generation, and his care teams often valued the opportunity to reflect, express their sadness and frustration with systems as well as patients, and to reconnect with empathy for Rafael and for themselves. A key social work role was to bridge his care teams and identify barriers to the plan of care. Social workers can promote healthy collaboration among the teams caring for the patient and family through role modeling and peer mentoring. Across settings, advocacy focused on culturally and linguistically congruent communication and ensuring, as much as possible, continuity of care at the systems level, so that Rafael did not have a new physician at every hospitalization. Social workers functioned as change agents and advocates, providing continuity in his care as well as iterative assessment and interventions to enhance the psychosocialspiritual well-being of Rafael and his family.

MACRO
When caring for individual patients, challenges quickly accumulate related to the systems at large in which the care occurs. Rafael's need for language translation became an issue. On a macro level, creating interventions to sensitize clinicians to notice and assess communication needs is an essential component of psychosocial care, enhancing the likelihood of culturally congruent care and lessening the burden on family members. Evaluating communication styles and techniques impacts future outcomes and informs learning. For example, did Rafael and his family understand the information provided to them? How does the team understand their decision-making process? What is the standard of care for patients with visual impairments? How can providers encourage cultural humility to create a space for curiosity and inquiry? Rafael and his family needed a system of providers that intervened at all levels to enhance well-being across the domains of care. Social workers' attention, advocacy and collaboration leads to systems change (Damaskos & Gardner, 2015).

SELF-CARE

> One must always be aware, to notice-even though the cost of noticing
> is to become responsible.
>
> —Moss (1994)

Self-care is heralded as a foundation that sustains those who choose to work with seriously ill patients and their families. There is a high degree of concurrence in the social work profession and the field of palliative care about the importance of self-reflective practice and building resilience among clinicians. Many social workers struggle to have an adequate vocabulary or a framework for a self-care practice. One model that provides both a language and a locus of responsibility comes from Renzenbrink, who invokes an Irish expression that substitutes an American expression "take care" with "mind yourself" or "mind how you go." She encourages social workers to "mind how you go" to develop intentional and relentless self-care (Renzenbrink, 2004). How do providers "mind" themselves? An approach to self-care is to move away from a focus on burnout, stress, and compassion fatigue to a focus on resilience and creating compassion satisfaction, developing active approaches to create meaning and fulfillment in the work and in our lives (Pooler, Woolfer, & Freeman, 2013). It is customary practice to routinely reflect on the strengths of patients to sustain hope and discern sources of joy and meaning. The concept of strengths, joy, and meaning-making is not just for those in our care, but can be an approach to finding the joy in our work (Pooler, Woolfer, & Freeman, 2013, Saleebey, 2000).

In Lipsky's important work on trauma stewardship, she introduces a model of *the five directions*: a daily practice of centering self, creating space for inquiry, choosing our focus, finding balance, and creating compassion and community (van Dernoot Lipsky, 2009). Rather than being prescriptive, these ideas add specificity to help move self-care from an ethereal notion to a lived experience. This offers aspects that are personal and individualized and components that are communal and may be incorporated into both workplace culture and practice and our lives beyond our work identity. All aspects of this practice of centering have the potential to be relationship based or to be practiced quite privately. In continuing to reflect on the importance of self-care strategies and promoting resilience, the social work community can both recommit and model attention to creating and sustaining a culture of tangible self-care practices.

CONCLUSION

There are enduring opportunities to infuse palliative care principles into our health care systems. Palliative care needs are ubiquitous; it is a shared obligation to thoughtfully engage these needs in every setting along the continuum. We are called to evolve from a binary approach to this work, characterized by an either/or mentality, thinking about people as "well" or "sick" and treatment parameters as "do everything" or "nothing more to do." Educator/activist Parker Palmer describes the value of entertaining the ideas that come from "both/and" thinking. We often talk in palliative care about holding more than one reality simultaneously. This moves us away from ideas that limit our thinking of "either/or" and moves us to consider "both/and." Paradoxical approaches to the most complex issues of mortality and meaning will deepen and broaden our efficacy (Parker, 2017). As social work and palliative care continue to develop a consensus that defines palliative care skills for all health social workers, we will evolve exponentially from binary thinking. This will enhance interprofessional quality care for all living with serious illness, which will naturally address issues in the workforce. The field of palliative care will benefit from expansive vision and ingenuity to continue to grow and change. Creativity and commitment will be at the center of this process.

LEARNING EXERCISES

1. Primary and Specialist: Imagine you work on a busy inpatient service in an academic medical center with frequent rotations of medical colleagues. There is very little time or ability for your changing team dynamics to accommodate shared processing or discussion of the emotional impacts of the work. What opportunities or rituals might you create to optimize self-care inside and outside of work? Knowing yourself, what steps could you take to enhance compassion satisfaction, and resilience in the self, or, if you prefer, what suggestions might you make for another?

2. Consider the origin story of the department or service that you work with. Interview staff who worked to build the service, noting those processes that built coherence, commitment, and integration and those that reinforced hierarchy and separation. What, if any, are the continuing remnants of this origin story? Consider paths to remediating the disruptive factors, if any, that continue to impact the quality of the work.

3. Research and review the competencies informing health social work and palliative care, noting where they overlap and where they may differ.

REFERENCES

Altilio, T., & Otis-Green, S. (2011). *Oxford textbook of palliative social work.* New York: Oxford University Press.

Blacker, S. (2004). Palliative care and social work. In J. Berzoff & P. Silverman (Eds.), *Living with dying* (pp. 409–423). New York: Columbia University Press.

Bosma, H., Johnston, M., Cadell, S., Wainwright, W., Abernethy, N., Feron, A., ... Nelson, F. (2009). Creating social work competencies for practice in hospice and palliative care. *Palliative Medicine, 24*(1), 1–9. doi:10.1177/0269216309346596.

Cadell, S., Johnston, M., Bosma, H., & Wainright, W. (2010). An overview of contemporary social work practice in palliative care. *Progress in Palliative Care, 18*(4), 205–211. doi:10.1179/096992610X12775428636700.

Center to Advance Palliative Care. (2017). What is palliative care. Retrieved from Get Palliative Care: getpalliativecare.org/whatis/.

Christ, G., & Blacker, S. (2005). Setting an agenda for social work in end-of-life and palliative care: An overview of leadership and organizational initiatives. *Journal of Social Work in End-of-Life & Palliative Care, 1*(1), 9–22. doi:10.1300/ J457v01n01_02.

Connors, A. F., Dawson, N. V., & Desbiens, N. A. (1995). A controlled trial to improve care for seriously ill hospitalized patients: The Study to Understand Prognoses and Preferences for Outcomes and Risks of Treatments (SUPPORT). *JAMA, 274*(20), 1591–1598. doi:10.1001/jama.1995.03530200027032.

Damaskos, P., & Gardner, D. S. (2015). Cultivating a culture of mentorship in palliative social work. *Journal of Social Work in End-of-Life Care, 11*(2), 101–106. doi:10.1080/ 15524256.2015.1074138.

Gwyther, L. A. (2005). Social work competencies in palliative and end-of-life care. *Journal of Social Work in End-of-Life & Palliative Care, 1*(1), 87–120. doi:10.1300/ J457v01n01_06.

Higgins, P. (2011). Guess who is coming to dinner? The emerging identity of palliative social workers. In T. Altilio & S. Otis-Green (Eds.), *Oxford textbook of palliative social work* (pp. 31–42). New York: Oxford University Press.

IOM. (2015). *Dying in America: Improving quality and honoring individual preferences near the end of life.* Washington, DC: The National Academies Press.

Meier, D. E., & Beresford, L. (2007). Consultation etiquette challenges palliative care to be on its best behavior. *Journal of Palliative Medicine, 10*(1), 7–11. doi:10.1089/ jpm.2006.9997.

Meier, D. E., & Beresford, L. (2008). Social workers advocate for a seat at the table. *Journal of Palliative Medicine, 11*(1), 10–14. doi:10.1089/ jpm.2008.9907.

Mitchell, P., Wynia, M., Golden, R., McNellis, B., Okun, S., Webb, C. E., ... Von Kohorn, I. (2012). *Core principles & values of effective team-based health care.* Washington, DC: Institute of Medicine. Retrieved from www.nationalahec.org/pdfs/vsrt-team-based-care-principles-values.pdf.

Moss, T. (1994). *Thylias moss.* Retrieved from www.poemhunter.com/thylias-moss/.

National Association of Social Workers. (2004). NASW Standards for palliative and end of life care. Washington, DC: NASW Press.

Panel, I. E. (2011). *Core competencies for interprofessional collaborative practice: Report of Interprofessional Education Collaborative expert panel.* Washington, DC: Interprofessional Education Collaborative.

Parker, P. J. (2017, January 7). A friendship, a love, a rescue. (T. Gillis, Ed.) Retrieved from On Being: onbeing.org/blog/a-friendship-a-love-a-rescue/

Pooler, D., Woolfer, T., & Freeman, M. (2013). Finding joy. *Health Section Connection.* Washington, DC: NASW Specialty Practice Sections. Retrieved from NASW: www. socialworkers.org/assets/secured/documents/sections/health/newsletters/2013%20 Health%20Newsletter%20-%20Winter.pdf.

Quill, T. E., & Abernethy, A. P. (2013). Generalist plus specialist palliative care creating a more sustainable model. *New England Journal of Medicine, 368*(13), 1173–1175.

Quinn, A. (1998). Learning from palliative care: Concepts to underpin the transfer of knowledge from specialist palliative care to mainstream social work settings. *Social Work Education, 17*(1), 9–19. doi:10.1080/02615479811220021.

Renzenbrink, I. (2004). Relentless self-care. In J. Berzoff & P. Silverman (Eds.), *Living with dying: A handbook for end-of-life healthcare practitioners* (pp. 848–861). New York: Columbia University Press.

Russell, J. (2015). Effects of constraints and consequences on plan complexity in conversations about end-of-life care. *Journal of Social Work in End-of-Life & Palliative Care, 11*(3), 323–345. doi:10.1080/15524256.2015.1111286.

Saleebey, D. (2000). Power in the people: Strengths and hope. *Advances in Social Work, 1*(2), 127–136.

Sumser, B., Remke, S., Leimena, M., Altilio, T., & Otis-Green, S. (2015). The serendipitous survey: A look at primary and specialist palliative social work practice, preparation and competence. *Journal of Palliative Medicine, 18*(10), 1–3.

Van Dernoot Lipsky, L. (2009). *Trauma stewardship: An everyday guide to caring for self while caring for others.* San Francisco: Berrett-Koehler.

World Health Organization. (n.d.). *WHO definition of palliative care.* Retrieved from www.who.int/cancer/palliative/definition/en/.

Structure and Processes of Care

ANNE KELEMEN AND REGINA TOSCA ■

I feel like I'm an observer in my life.
—A 45-YEAR-OLD PATIENT DESCRIBING HER ONGOING TREATMENT
FOR CANCER

INTRODUCTION

Health social workers play a vital role in ensuring that patient and family needs, perspectives, and preferences are reflected in medical care and treatment planning. With a clinical focus on psychosocial and spiritual assessment and knowledge of service networks, insurance, reimbursement policies, and community resources, social workers use an ecological lens to understand challenges and enhance patient self-determination. This empowerment-based approach is consistent with palliative care's focus on the whole person and family. This is enhanced by ensuring that patients and families have access to critical health information about illness, prognosis, and treatment options, as well as available sources of practical assistance and psychosocial support. Through partnerships with primary and specialty teams, there is a shared learning which enriches understanding, informs care plans and supports patient and family decision-making. This psychoeducation about the impact of illness on emotional and social functioning has been shown to improve mood, reduce stress, and increase a sense of personal agency (Lukens & McFarlane, 2004).

TEAM ASSESSMENT

Assessment forms the foundation of health social work practice and serves as the blueprint for the development of an intervention plan. Assessment incorporates information from a variety of sources, including discussions with patients and families, medical record review, and consultation with primary and specialty services.

Social work assessment is informed by input from other team members, which might include other social workers, physicians, advanced practice professionals, nurses, pharmacists, physical therapists, case managers, and chaplains, to create an interdisciplinary, holistic plan of care. The assessment includes basic demographic data about patients and families, understanding of the medical condition and treatment options, communication preferences, decision-making style, and hopes, wishes and worries regarding treatment, quality of life, and what the future might hold. Comprehensive assessment evolves over time, in relationship to changing physical, social, psychological, and spiritual circumstances. The social work assessment adds an important dimension to the medical evaluation by illuminating social determinants of health and informing coordinated care plans. This promotes care planning grounded in the lived reality of each patient and family, adapting to changing needs as illness evolves.

Initial assessment looks to understand history. This includes previous illness experience, conversations, and documents that might relate to treatment preferences. Advance care planning helps patients and families envision medical probabilities as an illness progresses and provides opportunities for conversation and decision-making, guided by patient and family values, before a crisis occurs. Often this process includes discussion of preferences for care at end of life, such as attempts at cardiopulmonary resuscitation, intubation, artificial nutrition, antibiotics for infections, dialysis for kidney failure, and, importantly, hospice services. Patient preferences for care along the course of illness are often recorded in a legal document known as an advance directive, or in a physician's order that becomes part of the medical record. Social workers, discharging and receiving patients, share in the responsibility of ensuring that these documents transition with patients from one care setting to another (See Chapter 9; "Legal and Ethical Aspects of Care"). No matter the practice setting and regardless of role, social workers can promote effective care planning that is proactive, integrating what has been learned into transitions between settings and health care services.

Table 2.1 lists the domains of palliative care, a sampling of the components that inform those domains, with questions that can begin to guide assessment and listening, bringing palliative care principles into daily practice. Open-ended

Table 2.1 CROSSWALK

Domain	Components: A Sampling	Open-Ended Questions
Process of care	Patient & family goals Prognosis Safety Team collaboration Transitions/care plan Understanding of illness	One of our hopes is that your health care reflects your values. Can you share a little about what is most important to you? to your family? What do we need to know about you as a person to give you the best care possible? Often the doctors have a sense of what the future might look like. Would you want to know about that? What have the doctors shared about your illness?
Physical	Functional status Issues related to medications Nausea/vomiting Pain Shortness of breath	How are you feeling physically? How have things changed for you physically over the last weeks/months? How is your sleep? Are there things you do to manage any pain/sleep/breathing, etc.
Psychological	Adaptation/coping strategies Anticipatory grief Anxiety/depression Bereavement risk Delirium/altered mental status Stress	How is/are your mood/spirits? Are you sad or depressed? How are you doing emotionally? Any recent losses? How have you taken care of yourself when things were tough? What helps you to keep going?
Social	Caregiver well-being Family friend support Financial concerns Health literacy Home life/safety	Has your illness affected your relationships, work, home life? How do you think family are doing? Do you need help with paperwork or logistical questions or concerns? Anything at home you are worried about? Whom do you go to when things are tough?

(continued)

Table 2.1 Continued

Domain	Components: A Sampling	Open-Ended Questions
Spiritual	Existential questions/ concerns Forgiveness Hopes & fears Reconciliation Spiritual, religious belief system	Are you spiritual or religious? If yes, is that comforting? Do you feel at peace? Are you at peace?[b] What are you hoping for? worried about? What gives you strength?
Cultural	Communication style Dietary preferences Experience of health care system Family structure Preferred language Role of ritual	What is your preferred language? How can the team best provide information to you & your family? Who in your family should we be talking with? Are there any rituals that are important to you?
End of life	Bereavement risk Education & normalization End-of-life preferences & values Legacy work Prognosis	Some people feel it's helpful to know what to expect at the end of life. Would that information be helpful? When you think about the end of your life what comes to mind? Have you had conversations about hopes or preferences related to end-of- life care?
Ethics	Advance directives Decisions related to code status Informed consent Surrogate decision-maker	If you are unable to talk with us, who can help with health care decisions? Have you completed papers to identify that person? Would you like more information on thinking ahead about your future care? Or how decisions might be made if you could not participate?

(Kelemen, Tosca & Sumser)

[a] Chochinov, M. (2012). *Dignity therapy: Final words for final days*. New York, NY: Oxford.

[b] Steinhauser, L., Volis, C., Clipp, E., Bosworth, H., Christakis, N., & Tulsky, J. (2006). Are you at peace? One item to probe spiritual concerns at end of life. *Archives of Internal Medicine, 166*(1), 101–105.

questions facilitate rapport building while allowing patients and families to direct the conversation, supporting space for more or less intimacy and distance from the situation at hand. The questions that follow are merely suggestions that will be customized to the therapeutic style, the nature of the relationship, and the clinical focus of the encounter.

NARRATIVE EXAMPLES

The following two narratives describe social work practice within the context of the ecological framework and consider multiple domains of personal and family functioning. These examples illustrate the complex factors affecting patients and families facing serious illness, and demonstrate the role and potential of social work to advance care that is patient centered, family focused, culturally sensitive, and strengths based. They highlight collaboration across teams and the opportunity to engage specialists in efforts to improve care and attend to patient, family and clinician distress.

Malcolm

Malcolm is a 42-year-old African-American male with advanced heart failure, hypertension, pulmonary hypertension, and diabetes. He had an implantable cardioverter defibrillator placed five years earlier. He is admitted to the hospital with shortness of breath, abdominal distention, pain, and bilateral lower-leg swelling. He has been in the hospital four times in the previous year for similar symptoms, a consequence of heart failure.

Malcolm lives with his mother Frances, having moved into her home as he became more ill and had to stop working. She is his primary caregiver. The increased dependence on his mother, for financial support and caregiving assistance, weighs heavily on him, magnifying his sense of helplessness in the face of his progressing illness. His three teenage nieces also live in the home. Their mother (his sister) died of heart failure in 2011. Malcolm has a girlfriend, two adult children, and extended family who visit him in the hospital but, according to Frances, do not contribute much to his care at home.

Malcolm describes a tough persona that helps him survive in his neighborhood, stating, "no one messes with me." He shares growing up in an environment characterized by frequent violence and expresses pride in being a survivor. These well-honed survival strategies prove ineffective against his heart failure, which is a source of anguish and panic for Malcolm, exacerbating his feelings of loss of control.

Prior to meeting Malcolm, the social worker learns that he has been evaluated for a type of heart device, placed surgically, which has the potential to extend his life by several years. After an exhaustive workup, the medical team makes the hard decision not to offer this treatment, due in part to Malcolm's "non-compliance." There are significant psychosocial concerns related to device placement given the intensive self-management at home, coupled with regular clinical follow-up. He is deemed to be high risk from a psychosocial perspective. Malcolm's medical record documents multiple missed clinic appointments and difficulty following his home medication regimen. In addition, Malcolm's hospitalizations for complications of his heart failure indicate to his medical team that he is not following the cardiac diet his doctor has prescribed.

During the initial meeting with Malcolm, he is understandably sad and worried. These feelings are compounded by a sense of frustration and anger as medical decisions that influence his life expectancy are outside of his control. He is guarded in interactions, questioning the motivations of clinicians entering his room. He often lashes out at staff. Over the course of his admissions, he has received a clear message that his "behaviors" have worsened his heart failure and have made him ineligible for a heart device. Malcolm references this judgment time and again, asserting, "you people are just going to let me die" and "you've given up on me."

The social worker focuses on building a relationship with Malcolm using supportive counseling to explore his emotions and concerns about his illness and to help ground her interventions. Together, they identify that Malcolm has inherent skills for adapting to changing circumstances and that there are aspects of his care he can control, such as beginning the process of advance care planning. In communication with the cardiac team, she and the social worker responsible for discharge planning frame Malcolm's accusations as expressions of anger, grief, and anxiety about facing the end of his life.

The social worker checks in regularly with Malcolm; sometimes he is receptive and other times he declines her visits. Taking the lead from him, her goal in their growing relationship is to offer a safe container for the great range of his feelings and thoughts.

Malcolm is placed on continuous intravenous cardiac medications that could extend his life by several months. The medical team agrees to reassess the possibility of device placement if Malcolm "demonstrates he is able to comply" with medical recommendations by keeping future appointments and controlling his diet. Social work interventions focus on identifying barriers to Malcolm attending appointments and controlling his diet, as well as collaborative problem solving, which helps promote Malcolm's agency and role within the plan of care. Malcolm also agrees to meet with the outpatient cardiac social worker during visits to his cardiologist.

During the next six months, Malcolm is admitted to the hospital three times with complications of heart failure. The outpatient medical record reflects missed clinic appointments, and inpatient nurses report that Malcolm openly consumes large quantities of fluids, which are restricted from his diet. These behaviors reinforce the medical team's concern that Malcolm cannot manage a cardiac device. Malcolm's emotional appeals become couched in charges of racism: "You won't treat me because I am African-American."

The cardiology team continues to struggle with the reality that they cannot offer a medical device to extend his life. To ensure they have considered every perspective, they ask the bioethics consult service to weigh in on their decision in an effort to acknowledge and mediate the distress of some clinicians. They have expanded deliberations beyond their nuclear team and created an extended team—temporary though it might be—to obtain an objective view. The ethics committee meeting with providers is a setting for the social worker to discuss her assessment, focusing on Malcolm's strengths, the challenges he faces in managing a cardiac device, and highlighting his concerns about the evaluation process. The ethics team supports the conclusion that the psychosocial challenges to the effective management of the device preclude this as an option for Malcolm. To do otherwise could place Malcolm at unacceptable medical risk.

The conflict between Malcolm and the medical team escalates following the bioethics consultation. Malcolm feels at the mercy of the cardiology team. This is aggravated when his request for a second opinion and treatment at another cardiac program out of state is thwarted by insurance limitations. The social workers channel their distress into the therapeutic work of collectively supporting Malcolm and his family, exploring the impact of his illness related issues on family as a unit and as individuals and reinforcing the treatment options available. Concurrently, they share a full psychosocial assessment in discussions with the cardiology team, emphasizing how social determinants of health, including racism, unemployment, and stress, have influenced Malcolm's perspective, experiences, and ability to manage progressive disease. While not changing the decisions, these perspectives temper judgment with empathy, a kind of education that occurs in the day to day work of reciprocal learning across teams.

Over the next months, Malcolm's health continues to decline, despite maximal medical and pharmacologic therapies. Providing continuity across transitions between inpatient and outpatient settings, the social workers engage external supports for Malcolm, his nieces, and Frances, whose second adult child is now dying of heart disease. The social worker joins with Malcolm in his hope for a second opinion, while also using psychoeducation to introduce hospice services, as this resource could support Malcolm with care in the community while he explores the possibility of evaluation by another cardiac team.

While Malcolm continues to state his intention to pursue a second opinion, his health declines and he concurrently agrees to home hospice care, as symptom management and time with his family become clear priorities. Malcolm dies at home.

ANALYSIS

Malcolm's narrative highlights the challenging intersection of medical illness and racial, socioeconomic, and institutional disparities that have influenced his access to care, illness experience, and outcomes. The ecological perspective (Bronfenbrenner, 1979), an environmental approach to assessment that forms the foundation of social work practice, provides opportunities for intervention across multiple domains. This lens facilitates the assessment of patients and families based on personal and environmental factors that serve to either enable or inhibit opportunity and growth. Social workers use these assessments to help shape the delivery of care, reflecting individual patient and family needs, values, strengths, circumstances, preferences, and experiences.

Micro

Beginning at the micro level, learning about Malcolm's relationship to his illness forms a critical foundation for development of an intervention plan. To understand and facilitate his coping and medical decision-making, it will be crucial to explore how this illness and its expected trajectory affect Malcolm's self-concept, perspectives on living, plans for his future and reflections on his sister's death as he anticipates his own dying. Working from the lens of intersectionality— which recognizes that oppression is inherent in all formalized social systems— affirming Malcolm's wisdom and strengths provides a counterbalance to a health-care system that has left Malcom feeling marginalized (Crenshaw, 1989). Given Malcolm's statements about how his race affects his health-care options, exploring Malcolm's experiences and perceptions of racism and conveying his perspective to the medical team provides important context. This may mitigate judgment of his behavior, reduce conflict, and promote empathy.

Eiser and Ellis (2007) assert that the role of mistrust is an important aspect of the African-American experience of medical care due to ongoing and persistent health disparities along racial and ethnic lines. In Washington, D.C., African Americans are more likely to be unemployed, are less likely to graduate from high school, and are more likely to rely on Medicaid for their health care. African-American men in the District live on average 15 years less than their white counterparts. In the area of the District where Malcolm lived, there are no grocery stores, no specialty hospitals, and nearly one-fifth of African-American residents are unemployed (Georgetown University School of Nursing and Health Studies, 2016).

Phenomenological variant of ecological systems theory (PVEST) can also offer a framework for assessing how Malcolm's specific life experiences have influenced his ability to manage his illness (Spencer, 2008). PVEST posits that a person's coping process can only be fully understood in relationship to his or her environmental and developmental context. PVEST eschews standard definitions of behavior as either adaptive or maladaptive, and instead views functioning from an individual standpoint.

Through the lens of PVEST, we could view Malcolm's anger as a means of coping with his fear of dying, and imagine his anger as a protective strategy used in other aspects of his life. Malcolm's statement about how others perceive him ("no one messes with me") suggests that he views his anger as a tool for survival. In the world of the hospital, however, interacting in this way serves to undermine Malcolm's hopes and compounds his isolation and distress. Social workers who are able to view Malcolm's anger as useful, even necessary, elsewhere in his life can affirm its value while helping him explore alternatives that may best facilitate his goals with the medical team. Framing Malcom's anger as a valuable survival strategy historically, the social worker could help draw a connection between this coping strategy and Malcolm's current "fight for survival" against heart failure, increasing the team's understanding of his experience.

Malcolm's relationships also influence and are affected by his illness. Malcolm is both a partner and a father. These aspects of his identity can be acknowledged by exploring how they are impacted by his health and increased dependence. Exploring his experience of loss—past, present and anticipated—may help to understand Malcolm's sadness and anger. Diving deeper, the social worker can also explore how the death of Malcolm's sister has influenced his thoughts, worries, and feelings about his illness. This can create an opportunity to further uncover skills and beliefs that Malcolm used to cope with his sister's death, which may serve him now. This process could also reveal that her death has left him with fears and assumptions about access to care which may be mitigated in the shared work of anticipating Malcolm's end of life. Additionally, this family is about to experience a second process of decline and death from cardiac disease, an invitation to assess bereavement risk and provide resources to mitigate complex grief reactions within the family.

Much research has been conducted on locus of control as it relates to coping with illness. It proposes that action-focused coping helps patients maximize influence on health outcomes, while emotion-focused coping is more adaptive in low-control circumstances (Park, Sacco, & Edmondson, 2012). This research suggests that Malcolm's attempts to influence factors outside his control only intensify his frustration, anger, and sadness, as he feels increasingly helpless. A life review could be especially powerful for Malcolm as a way to help him reflect on his accomplishments, important relationships, and significant milestones, highlighting the ways in which his life has had meaning. A social worker could explore Malcolm's roles within the family, what is meaningful for him now, and what legacy he hopes to leave for his family and his community. Intervening in this way can support Malcolm's sense of self as a whole person, not solely a patient with a diagnosis, and perhaps inform legacy work that might enrich the lives of his surviving children and family.

Important at any stage of the illness is discussion of concerns patients may have about intimacy and sexual expression. This can be a sensitive issue for some and it is often necessary to both normalize this aspect of an assessment and highlight its importance as part of the whole-person approach to care. The social worker can reassure Malcolm by universalizing the reality that illness affects intimacy for many patients, and this is a common and reasonable concern that often intensifies loss and loneliness for partners. Discussing the ways intimacy might be supported and maintained, such as hand-holding, sharing the bed, massage, hugging, and provision of personal care enhances connection with an intimate partner (Kelemen, Cagle, & Groninger, 2016).

Meso

As a meso-level intervention, inclusion of the bioethics team brings objectivity to the decision-making process, particularly in situations where patients and families question the recommendations of the medical team, or when there is distress among clinicians. Social workers who develop relationships with hospital bioethics programs can ensure their proper use in shared educational processes and as arbiters of patient rights in situations where program policies and practices may use inexact criteria to limit patients' access to treatments or procedures.

In Malcolm's situation, a comprehensive approach would consider issues of justice, autonomy, beneficence, and non-maleficence from a multicultural perspective. Koenig (1997) notes, "within the bioethics community, little attention has been paid to questions of ethnic or cultural diversity" (p. 369). As an advocate for Malcolm, the social worker would raise questions about the origins of a bioethical framework and any inherent biases that may disadvantage certain patients subject to its application.

With regard to enhancing the quality of care delivery, the social worker can support medical outcomes by insuring that Malcolm and his family receive information in a format that is understandable. Cooper (2004) notes, "professional jargon forces clients to adopt a position of dependency and mystifies the power-over nature of such a relationship . . . [and] hinders a client's ability to express their version of their needs and supports the stance of paternalism taken by some professions" (p. 149). From a social justice perspective, facilitating patient access to important medical information enables decision-making from a position of power and autonomy, rather than dependency.

Additional interventions might include linking Malcolm with peer support to help promote a sense of affiliation, as well as provide a safe outlet for his feelings and thoughts. Joon and colleagues (2010) indicate that peer support during times of serious illness has been shown to reduce feelings of isolation through opportunities for interpersonal engagement and connection. They go on to say that peers can offer each other not only practical support, but also strategies for coping with serious illness (Joon, Kraus, Jowsey, & Glasgow, 2010).

Psychoeducation focused on the role and benefits of hospice care and exploring values and spiritual beliefs related to end-of-life decisions potentially enhance Malcolm's sense of control over important aspects of his care. Partnering with other hospital and community-based social workers can ensure referral and access to helpful services and information for Malcolm and his family.

Macro
At the macro level, social workers can maintain awareness of the broader social and cultural forces shaping the lives of patients and families. By adopting a stance of humility, openness, and sincere inquiry, social workers can learn how patients and families view themselves in relationship to these forces. Further, elevating this knowledge to the level of team and institutional leadership can encourage collaboration with patients and families to enhance communication and develop systems and practices that affirm their strengths, rituals, beliefs, and wisdom. As advocates for systems change, partnering with families to co-construct illness narratives that are validating, empowering, and reflective of their realities can reinforce the shared humanity of experiences. To promote institutional practices and policies that are inclusive of diversity, social workers can participate on advisory committees, institutional review boards, quality improvement efforts, and in program and service planning, while advocating for treatment decision-making standards that are unbiased and support equal access for all patients.

Lisa

Lisa is a 30-year-old Chinese-American female with HIV and end-stage renal disease (ESRD) who is admitted to the intensive care unit (ICU) with a serious heart infection. The surgery team determines that she is not a "candidate" for surgery due to her active substance use and history of "noncompliance." Lisa admits to current cocaine use, which helps her "feel better." She previously has been treated for depression and bipolar disorder.

Lisa grew up in Northern California in a traditional Chinese-American home. As a child, Lisa moved frequently between several cities on the West Coast and reported that no place ever felt like "home." She graduated from high school and left college before graduating. Lisa describes making a series of "bad choices" as a young adult, leading to the use of drugs and alcohol. In a cascade of events leaving Lisa feeling out of control and powerless, she became pregnant, was diagnosed with HIV, and lost her job and apartment. Her parents were given custody of her son, Eric, shortly after he was born.

Lisa has not been receiving antiretroviral therapy for her HIV as she does not have stable housing or transportation to access care. She no longer has a relationship with Eric, who is 8 years old. She sees her mother occasionally, but has a contentious relationship with her father, as he feels she has brought shame to the family. Lisa helps support her son with benefits she receives from the Temporary Aid to Needy Families (TANF) program. This is meaningful because it is currently the only way she stays connected to her son and provides for him—supporting that essential aspect of her identity as a mother.

During the initial social work visit in the ICU, Lisa presents with pressured speech and does not open her eyes during the conversation. She reports significant pain, asking the social worker to come back later. During the second, visit Lisa presents with a flat affect, but is engaged, with her eyes open, and shares easily. She reports her pain is better controlled and acknowledges her reluctance to ask for pain medications as she does not want to be labeled as drug-seeking. Through frequent admissions to the hospital, Lisa recognizes that staff are worried about her cocaine use and are cautious in prescribing opioids. They ask frequent questions about her relationship to specific medications and are vigilant in checking the prescription-monitoring program to understand the pattern of prescribing, a consciousness focused on ensuring her safety and that of her prescribers yet with the unintended consequence that she feels delegitimized by these inquires. (See Chapter 3; "Physical Aspects of Care".)

Lisa shares regrets about "bad choices" she has made in her life. Lisa understands she could die soon; however, she is making plans to educate other young adults on how to "stay off the streets." This is part of the legacy she wants to leave. Lisa asks for assistance in reconnecting with her family. As part of preparing Lisa for both the potential benefits and challenges of an attempted reconciliation, the social worker explores the nature of her past relationships with family which includes report of past abuse by her father. Lisa is able to integrate the potential benefits and risks of reaching out to family and eventually asks for help locating her parents to then discover her father died within the last few months. Sharing the news with Lisa, she becomes profoundly upset, crying and asking, "How is this possible?" The social worker sits in silence for a long time, recognizing Lisa's need for space to experience the myriad of complex emotions related to the death, its meaning and her hopes for a potential reunion.

Prior to this hospitalization, Lisa had been unemployed, living periodically with friends and other times spending the night at homeless shelters. Her unstable living situation precluded the option of dialysis. During this hospitalization, she begins to realize she may be nearing the end of her life and is often distressed, crying and describing feelings of being overwhelmed: "I'm so exhausted I can't even cry anymore." After discussions about the possible benefits of stabilizing her mood and mitigating some of her depressive symptoms, the team requests a psychiatry consultation (See Chapter 4; "Psychological Aspects of Care").

Her medical condition eventually stabilizes and she is transferred out of the ICU. The physical therapist recommends discharge to a skilled nursing facility for continued rehabilitation, but it has been documented that "patient is refusing skilled nursing facility placement." Having just left the intensive care unit and the familiar staff, she is now asked to anticipate a future move to an unknown setting. Social work organizes an interdisciplinary care conference to provide an opportunity for Lisa to align her hopes and wishes with the options for care so the team can make the best recommendation moving forward. Lisa describes having spent private time processing her thoughts and feelings about treatment options and she would like to continue dialysis and learn about supports in the community to maintain the treatment schedule. She commits to taking her antiretroviral medication. Lisa shares her worry that by transitioning to a skilled nursing facility she will lose her disability check and therefore her ability to contribute financially to her son's care, a threat to identity and purpose in her life. This conversation illuminates Lisa's priorities and worries, and the team can work toward a responsive discharge plan. While the language in Lisa's chart reflects her "refusing to be discharged to a skilled nursing facility," by listening to Lisa's narrative and understanding the root of her reluctance, providers may respond from compassion rather than judgment.

Lisa eventually transfers to a community program offering housing to homeless individuals with serious illness, which supports her treatment preferences. In collaboration with Lisa, the social worker connects with colleagues in both the dialysis and community housing program to enhance support across transitions and to reinforce the "team of creation" that is evolving to support Lisa into the community.

ANALYSIS

Micro

The ecological model provides a framework for understanding Lisa's relationship to her circumstances, including her illness, and developing interventions to help support her functioning. Beginning at the micro level, Lisa's regret over her life choices provides an opportunity to intervene using medical crisis counseling (MCC) and narrative therapy. Through the use of narrative therapy, the social workers can engage Lisa in a review and retelling of her life to gain insight into her regrets and feelings of shame. Narrative therapy has been shown to be effective for individuals with substance use history and uses techniques such as journaling, creating memory books, and letter writing (Caldwell, 2005; Gardner & Poole, 2009).

The social worker might weigh with Lisa an intervention which focuses on writing a post-death letter to her father about the things she had hoped to discuss with him before his death. This would recreate a connection with her father and begin to address the complicated emotional dynamics within the relationship (Bowen, 1978). As Lisa enjoyed the process of writing, she was encouraged to journal. This reflective time promoted the externalization of thoughts and feelings, helping to gain insight into her early experience with family, the choices she had made, and perhaps the life she wishes to create.

MCC focuses on three primary areas: illness, coping, and family relationships. MCC can be used at initial diagnosis, prior to discharge from the hospital, at the time of increasing symptoms, or at reoccurrence of disease (Pollin & Kanaan, 1995). As opposed to traditional crisis intervention that is integrated at one point in time, MCC is an ongoing intervention used throughout the duration of a serious illness. It addresses patient fears about illness and the disruptions in the patient's life, elicits adaptive coping strategies, complementing the strengths-based and ecological approach (Koocher, Curtiss, Pollin, & Patton, 2001; Pollin & Kanaan, 1995).

Meso

At the meso-level of intervention, the social worker might explore with the team the terms used to describe Lisa: "difficult, drug seeking and refusing." Facilitated discussion could focus on data about Lisa's pain, etiology and treatment plan as well as the challenges of homelessness and addiction, inviting further critical thinking and minimizing the helplessness in staff (see Table 2.2). Her lack of social support places greater pressure on Lisa to advocate for her own needs at a time of enhanced vulnerability. Understanding Lisa's social experience in respect to intersectionality honors the dynamics at play through her identity as a Chinese-American woman, a mother separated from her son, and a homeless person living with HIV and substance abuse (Crenshaw, 1989).

Macro

Lack of access to treatment options for homeless persons presents micro- and meso-level challenges for Lisa within a macro framework. This population often has chronic medical conditions and dies younger as compared to the general population (Sumalinog, Harrington, Dosani, & Hwang, 2017). Data show that individuals who are homeless worry about medical mistreatment, lack of control regarding decisions, dying alone, and undergoing treatment without proper consent—concerns that might be mitigated through effective listening, sharing information in an accessible way and advance care planning (Song, 2007; Tobey et al., 2017). While individuals who are homeless are less likely to have an advance directive, Song et al. (2008) found when given the opportunity, many will complete advance directives, and after doing so, their worries about dying decrease (Sumalinog et al., 2017). Many were also more willing to write down and talk about their wishes (Song et al., 2008). Advance care planning might have helped alleviate some of Lisa's fears around end of life, pain management, and worries about her family. It could also help assure her of care she would receive over time. Due to the nature of homelessness, providing medical care, advance care planning, and end-of-life services can be challenging. Social workers who work together across settings to address mistrust of the health care system might use this data to enhance outreach and advocacy to bring medical care and evidence-informed services into the community.

LANGUAGE

> If patients become, in the minds of their doctors, complainers, liars, or failures, then therapeutic care will surely imitate language.
> —MONROE, *Holleman and Holleman (1992, p. 47)*

The experiences of Lisa and Malcolm highlight routine and demeaning language that might reflect distress, judgment, and worry in clinicians and may affect how patients are treated and the care received. In medicine, patients are often referred to by their diagnoses, or behaviors, rather than as whole human beings who exist beyond their illnesses (Altilio, 2011; Altilio & Lyon Leimena, 2013). Monroe et al. (1992) suggest that "abstract language, used exclusively, abstracts the person out of the case" (p. 49). Clinicians may use common clinical jargon without awareness of the unintended consequences and the impact on clinician attitudes and patient and family care. Using descriptors such as "failing treatment," "battling cancer," and "noncompliant" often encourages what Bedell, Graboys, Bedell, and Lown (2004) refer to as "therapeutic bias." This bias can lead to misguided interpretations of medical information. For example, in reading Lisa's chart, one might see language of "drug-abuser" and believe she is only pursuing care at the hospital for "drugs." Bedell et al. (2004) also argue that physicians use "terror" language to urge patients to become more "compliant." Physicians urged Lisa to change her code status by saying that resuscitation attempts would "break her ribs," among other frightening potential outcomes rather than acknowledging her unique context and individualizing the decision and its outcomes to her diagnosis, prognosis and values related to her life and goals.

Social workers who reserve judgment and explore why clinicians might choose language and a coercive communication style come to recognize that the difference in roles and responsibilities may be one dynamic; for example, social workers do not participate in resuscitation efforts. Perhaps doctors and nurses having participated in multiple unsuccessful attempts to resuscitate patients will express distress through "terror language" in an effort to protect self from moral distress and patient from anticipation of harm. It is important to approach the hurtful language from a nonjudgmental place in order to gain better understanding of why this language is used. Patient descriptors are often an invitation to explore the observations of colleagues to inform further social work assessment and understanding of the challenges of patients and families and providers. Language can be modeled that minimizes judgments and enhances empathy. Some comments and questions that might encourage shared reflection include the following:

- I am worried how these descriptors influence relationship and treatment options. What are you seeing that worries you?
- When I hear you say "breaking ribs," I am wondering if you are worried about doing harm and causing unnecessary suffering. Can you imagine any value an attempt at resuscitation might have for this patient or family?

In Malcolm's story, being labeled as "noncompliant" may truncate further assessment and divert the support that could enable him to participate and potentially meet the medical requirements for advanced therapies to extend his life. For Lisa, the language used to document her substance use disorder and multiple admissions to the hospital labeled her "drug abusing" or "drug seeking," behaviors which warranted an addiction evaluation. When in pain, she feared asking for medications in an effort to avoid labels of "drug seeking." As a consequence, she endured unmanaged pain, a source of significant distress. Rather than creating a treatment plan responsive to both pain and a substance use disorder, provider's worry about keeping both Lisa and themselves safe allowed innuendo to surround her care and infuse relationships.

One way for clinicians to be more sensitive with their language is using narrative and "healing" language (Bedell, Graboys, Bedwell, & Lown, 2004; Monroe et al., 1992). "Healing language is also silent; it includes a pause during which the patient can quietly consider the physician's explanations and suggestions" (Bedell et al., 2004, p. 1367). When communicating about end-of-life values and goals, it is often preferable to use a "therapy first" approach, as in "the chemotherapy is no longer working," instead of a "patient first" approach, as in "the patient is failing chemotherapy." This helps remove blame from the patient and enables clinicians to join with patients and families in the realization that the expected outcome of a treatment was not achieved (Kelemen & Groninger, 2017). Table 2.2 includes examples of language that may be both diagnostically significant and create an opportunity to clarify or change the tone surrounding the care of patients. Listening for judgment and assumption—language that may commonly shut down conversation—when observed and engaged, can alternatively invite further discussion. The second column of Table 2.2 suggests language that social workers might use in discussions with colleagues and in documentation to help foster curiosity, acknowledging the

Table 2.2 LANGUAGE FROM DOCUMENTATION

Language Inviting Further Exploration	Language to Invite Curiosity, Report Observations & Defer Judgment
Behavioural descriptors	Patient descriptors
Speech was loud with an angry tone	She presented with
Appeared poorly groomed	Shares feelings of overwhelm
Uncooperative, difficult	Is concerned about
Refusing to answer; to be discharged	Expresses, states, reports
Complains	Describes multiple barriers to . . . .
References to clinician judgments & observations	Language to avoid assumption & encourage curiosity
Failed treatments	Treatments have not had the expected outcome
Not a candidate, will not offer	Cannot access medical/psychosocial supports
Noncompliant, nonadherent	Treatment does not support patient hopes
	Patient has questions, concerns re:current medications
Drug abuser, behaviour disorder	
Poor insight, denial	She has a history of substance abuse to be assessed
Poor historian, memory problems	Working to integrate the significance of medical information
	Noted cognitive challenges, need to explore baseline cognitive function

importance of observations and exploration, and allowing space for change and understanding to evolve.

CONCLUSION

This chapter provides insight into the structure and process domain of palliative care. It affirms and promotes the adoption of palliative interventions as a routine part of health social work practice to advance quality, patient-centered, family-focused care across teams, settings and diagnoses. Social work assessment is a tool for practice within an ecological framework, which explores personal and environmental factors that affect care, and informs the development of interventions.

The patient narratives demonstrate how micro, meso, and macro factors shape patient and family interaction with systems of care, and affect both access to and receipt of health care services. The narratives further describe the social worker's role as an advocate for patients and families, and ways in which interventions at multiple levels and at various points in the trajectory of illness facilitate medical decision-making that is patient-centered, culturally informed, and reflective of patient and family values and needs. Finally, a section on language highlights how words can shape clinician perspectives, promote bias, and impact treatment options for patients. Suggestions for more empowerment-based, patient-centered language are provided.

In summary, the chapter seeks to affirm and promote the integration of palliative principles in the practice of health social work to enhance care across systems and through transitions. The alignment between the whole-person approach of palliative care and the person-in-environment philosophy of social work practice suggests that health social workers are poised to play an integral role in infusing palliative principles across settings.

LEARNING EXERCISES

1. In Boxes 2.1 and 2.2 there are samples of documentation one might find in an electronic medical record—documentation that is permanent and that follows patients. Consider your thoughts, feelings, and perceptions as you read. Consider how you could (a) rewrite this as a model for documentation; and (b) explore with the writer his or her concerns/worries about the patient.

Box 2.1

A Model for Documentation

Ms. A is a 40-year-old homeless, unemployed Irish-American female with end-stage HIV/AIDS, contracted 20 years ago from IV drug abuse. She is noncompliant with her medications. She has been verbally abusive with staff throughout her admission, complaining that her pain is not well managed.

Box 2.2

A Model for Documentation

Ms. A is a 40-year-old Irish-American female who has been on dialysis for the last five years. Today she describes multiple barriers to receiving treatment for HIV. She also has expressed frustrations throughout her hospital stay, feels unheard, and reports a high level of pain, both physically and psychologically distressing.

Plan: Collaborate with medical and nursing to further understand pain and related distress; explore barriers to treatment access in community.

REFERENCES

Altilio T. (2011). The power and potential of language. In T. Altilio & S. Otis-Green (Eds.), *Oxford textbook of palliative social work* (pp. 689–694). New York: Oxford University Press.

Altilio T., Lyon Leimena, M., & Li, Y. (2013). Attention and intention: An invitation to reflection on language. *AAPHM Quarterly, 14*(4), 14–17.

Bedell, S. E., Graboys, T. B., Bedell, E., & Lown, B. (2004). Words that harm, words that heal. *Archives of Internal Medicine, 164*(13), 1365–1368. doi:10.1001/archinte.164.13.1365.

Bowen, M. (1978). *Family therapy in clinical practice.* New York: Aronson.

Bronfenbrenner, U. (1979). *The ecology of human development: Experiments by nature and design.* Cambridge, MA: Harvard University Press.

Caldwell, R. (2005). At the confluence of memory and meaning—Life review with older adults and families: Using narrative therapy and the expressive arts to re-member and re-author stores of resilience. *The Family Journal, 13*(2), 172–175. doi:10.1177/1066480704273338.

Cooper, D. E. (2004). *Ethics for professionals in a multicultural world.* Upper Saddle River, NJ: Prentice Hall.

Crenshaw, K. (1989). Demarginalizing the intersection of race and sex: A black feminist critique of antidiscrimination doctrine, feminist theory and antiracist politics. *The University of Chicago Legal Forum, 140*(1), 139–167.

Eiser, A. R., & Ellis, G. (2007). Cultural competence and the African American experience with health care: The case for specific content in cross-cultural education. *Academic Medicine, 82*(2), 176–183. doi:10.1097/ACM.0b013e31802d92ea.

Gardner, P., & Poole, J. M. (2009). One story at a time: Narrative therapy, older adults and addictions. *Journal of Applied Gerontology, 28*(5), 600–620. doi:10.1177/0733464808330822.

Georgetown University School of Nursing and Health Studies. (2016). The health of the African American community in the District of Columbia: Disparities and recommendations. Retrieved from www.georgetown.edu/sites/www/files/The%20Health%20of%20the%20African%20American%20Community%20in%20the%20District%20of%20Columbia.pdf#_ga=2.99727326.1573850186.1497270516-1454094264.1480960495.

Joon, Y. H., Kraus, S., Jowsey, T., & Glasgow, N. (2010). The experience of living with chronic heart failure: A narrative review of qualitative studies. *BMC Health Services Research, 10*(77), 3–9.

Kelemen, A. M., Cagle, J. G., & Groninger, H. (2016). Screening for intimacy concerns in a palliative care population: Findings from a pilot study. *Journal of Palliative Medicine, 19*(10), 1102–1105. doi:10.1089/jpm.2016.0092.

Kelemen, A. M., & Groninger, H. (2017). Therapy first, not the patient? *Journal of Social Work in End-of-Life and Palliative Care, 13*(1), 9–12. doi:10.1080/15524256.2017.1282918.

Koenig, B. (1997). Cultural diversity in decision making about care at end of life. In M. J. Field & C. K. Cassel (Eds.), *Approaching death: Improving care at the end of life* (pp. 363–383). Washington, DC: National Academies Press.

Koocher, G. P., Curtiss, E. K., Pollin, I. S., & Patton, K. E. (2001). Medical crisis counseling in a health maintenance organization: Preventive intervention. *Professional Psychology: Research and Practice, 32*(1), 52–58.

Lukens, E., & McFarlane, W. (2004). Psychoeducation as evidence-based practice: Considerations for practice, research and policy. *Brief Treatment and Crisis Intervention, 4*(3), 205–225. doi:10.1093/brieftreatment/mhh019.

Monroe, W. F., Hollerman, W. L., & Holleman, M. C. (1992). Is there a person in this case? *Literature and Medicine, 11*(1), 45–63.

National Center for Child Traumatic Stress. (2004). How to implement trauma-focused cognitive behavioral therapy, 1–70. Retrieved from www.nctsn.org/resources/how-implement-trauma-focused-cognitive-behavioral-therapy-tf-cbt-implementation-manual

National Consensus Project for Quality Palliative Care. (2009). Clinical practice guidelines for quality palliative care. Retrieved from www.nationalconsensusproject.org/guideline.pdf.

Park, C. L., Sacco, S. J., & Edmondson, D. (2012). Expanding coping goodness-of-fit: Religious coping, health locus of control, and depressed affect in heart failure patients. *Anxiety Stress Coping, 25*(2), 137–153. doi:10.1080/10615806.2011.586030.

Pollin, I., & Kanaan, S. B. (1995). *Medical crisis counseling: Short-term therapy for long-term illness.* New York, NY, US: WW Norton & Co.

Song, J., Bartels, D. M., Ratner, E. R., Alderton, L., Hudson, B., & Ahluwalia, J. S., (2007). Dying on the streets: Homeless persons' concerns and desires about end of life care. *Journal of General Internal Medicine, 22*(4), 435–441. doi:10.1007/s11606-006-0046-7.

Song, J., Ratner, E. R., Bartels, D. M., Alderton, L., Hudson, B., & Ahluwalia, J. S. (2007). Experiences with and attitudes toward death and dying among homeless persons. *Journal of General Internal Medicine, 22*(4), 427–434. doi:10.1007/s11606-006-0045-8.

Song, J., Wall, M. W., Ratner, E. R., Bartels, D., Ulvestad, N., & Gelberg, L. (2008). Engaging homeless persons in end of life preparations. *Journal of General Internal Medicine, 23*(2), 2031–2045. doi:10.1007/s11606-008-0771-1.

Spencer, M. B. (2008). Phenomenology and ecological systems theory: Development of diverse groups. In W. Damon & R. Lerner (Eds.), *Child and adolescent development: An advanced course* (pp. 696–769). Hoboken, NJ: John Wiley & Sons.

Steinhauser, K., Voils, C., Clipp, E., Bosworth, H., Christakis, N., & Tulsky, J. (2006). Are you at peace? One item to probe spiritual concerns at the end of life. *Archives of Internal Medicine, 166*(1), 101–105.

Sumalinog, R., Harrington, K., Dosani, N., & Hwang, S. (2017). Advance care planning, palliative care, and end-of-life care interventions for homeless people: A systematic review. *Palliative Medicine, 31*(2), 109–119. doi:10.1177/0269216316649334.

Tobey, M., Manasson, J., Decarlo, K., Ciraldo-Maryniuk, K., Gaeta, J., & Wilson, E. (2017). Homeless individuals approaching the end of life: Symptoms and attitudes. *Journal of Pain and Symptom Management, 53*(4), 738–744. doi:10.1016/j.jpainsymman.2016.10.364.

Physical Aspects of Care

TERRY ALTILIO AND MEAGAN LYON LEIMENA ∎

I did not know what happened to me; I felt like I was broken into a million pieces.

—A 53-YEAR-OLD PATIENT DESCRIBING THE IMPACT
OF UNCONTROLLED RECTAL PAIN

INTRODUCTION

Social workers across health care settings engage with persons experiencing symptoms, many of which disrupt their lives and prompt contact with clinicians of varying disciplines and skills. Symptoms are multidimensional— based perhaps in the body—yet they are linked to culture, mind, emotions, spirit, and socioeconomics. Similarly, diagnosis and management converge science, ethics, public policy, and psychosocialspiritual aspects of personhood. Therefore, interventions extend much beyond the medical, and social workers have a vital role to play—a role that is adapted and modified to the setting and context of the clinical relationship.

This chapter will link specific symptoms in specific diagnoses to prevalence data, potential impact on patients and families, and treatments, and will identify opportunities for social workers in health care to assess, advocate, and intervene. For some, the sheer numbers of patients affected heightens the ethical mandate driving a desire to intervene. While data drive some, others have witnessed patients and families living with symptoms causing intense suffering, compromising autonomy and threatening our commitment to beneficence and the prevention of unnecessary harms. On a micro level, this work complements medical management to enhance the care of persons through direct interventions. On a macro level, health social workers are poised to improve the political, socioeconomic, cultural, and ethical environment in which pain occurs and is managed. For example, the undertreatment of pain in vulnerable populations including, but not limited to, older adults, the marginalized, people of color, and children threatens the commitment to social justice, an ethical value central to social work (Anderson, Green, & Payne, 2009; Blacksher, 2001; Brennan, Carr, & Cousins, 2007; LeResche, 2011; Paice & Ferrell, 2011; Tait & Chibnall, 2014; Tarzian & Hoffman, 2004).

Complicating the management of symptoms such as pain, dyspnea, or anxiety are the public health concerns related to the abuse and misuse of prescribed medications. Some of the most effective medications for pain, anxiety, or shortness of breath are controlled substances. In the United States these medications are regulated by the Drug Enforcement Agency and are under increased scrutiny by legislators and public health officials in an effort to enhance safe use (Sehgal, 2012). In some countries, pharmaceutical ads in the media graphically describe both the benefits and potential side effects of medications, creating a complicated macro environment when combined with public health concerns. These interrelated influences may surreptitiously impact the trust and confidence of patients and families in both prescribing clinicians and the medications themselves, which when properly used may provide primary benefits. Medications also, for some, have attributed meaning. For example, some believe morphine is used to hasten death; for others, the prescribing of methadone to manage pain may be misinterpreted by patients and family to mean that the patient is also diagnosed with the disease of addiction. Deaths caused by abuse of prescribed medications have left many patients and families frightened and reluctant to use effective medications—an example of the intimate, intersecting relationship between macro and micro factors (Alexander, Barbieri, & Kiang, 2017). When patients and families choose not to use medications as prescribed, they may be reflecting fears and preconceptions that require intervention by skilled clinicians—as does the assessment of addiction, misuse, or abuse of substances.

PAIN: A MOST STUDIED AND PREVALENT SYMPTOM

Pain is unique in the world of symptoms, as it is a shared and essentially universal experience and a focus of clinicians, researchers, ethicists, educators, and policy advocates. Important to survival, pain signals danger and thus allows for self-protection. For example, when we touch something very hot, we protect ourselves from further injury because pain signals move quickly to the brain and we respond by withdrawing from the source of the heat. Those persons born without pain signals are at high risk of hurting themselves (US National Library of Medicine, 2012).

The International Association for the Study of Pain (IASP) defines pain as an unpleasant sensory and *emotional* experience associated with actual or potential tissue damage or described in terms of such damage. It is always *subjective* (International Association for the Study of Pain, 2010). This definition links the physiology of pain to emotions and affirms the subjectivity of the experience. The absence of objective pain-measurement instruments (such as thermometers or blood tests) can create discomfort for clinicians who are most familiar with the objective representation of physical findings and less certain of subjective descriptors. Social work begins with the subjective, and thus it is natural to our practice to begin with the patient's report of pain, though assessment does not end there. Other variables that both enrich and complicate exchanges related to the management of pain include the cultural, spiritual, and family values that have infused, consciously or not, perceptions and beliefs related to pain and that, at times, color the responses of patients and families as well as clinicians.

While pain may be unique as a shared universal symptom, the link between symptoms and suffering generalizes beyond pain. Fatigue, anorexia, nausea, insomnia, constipation, and confusion can cause great distress for patients and families, threaten dignity and self-esteem, and contribute to suffering, depression, and anxiety. Social work advocacy for excellence in symptom management emanates from an awareness of the multidimensional aspects of symptoms and the many ways in which they impact the lives of patients, caregivers, and families (Dugan, 2012).

Symptoms, such as pain or shortness of breath, often have symbolic significance and may be harbingers of disease progression. Persons whose pain is overwhelming may express a desire for death, a preferable choice in the setting of clinician helplessness to treat expertly and emergently. For some, the symptoms are side effects or toxicities associated with necessary treatments, such as some chemotherapies. Yet in other situations, pain is predictable and is caused by health care providers in the process of helping, as in procedural pain related to the debridement of pressure sores. Cognitive impairment may prevent a person from understanding why clinicians are "hurting them," creating a poignant vulnerability that speaks to the need for compassionate and expert care, including preemptive pain management. Pain associated with diagnostic procedures or caused by treatments designed to benefit patients may have an added layer of emotional and cognitive complexity, as patients often hope that consenting to a potential hurt will create a benefit that outweighs the pain. They are sometimes profoundly disappointed. Thus, the meaning of symptoms is unique to the patient, the diagnosis, and the etiology, and is an avenue for exploration. All of these complexities are an invitation for social workers to advocate, assess, and intervene, impacting a patient's care and well-being. The nature and extent of interventions will depend on the setting and the available time for establishing relationships. Critical thinking will guide priorities established in consultation with team members, patients, and families.

Physical symptoms can reflect a complicated interaction of physical, social, emotional, spiritual, and practical concerns, aptly described as "total pain" (Saunders, 1996; Twycross & Wilcock, 2001). The concept of total pain suggests that optimal management requires team members with differing expertise to work together to understand and address multiple factors impacting not only the symptom, but also the person living with the symptom.

A related concept of suffering is defined as distress related to the threat of the loss of intactness or integrity of a person; it is a consequence of personhood—subjective and reflects a convergence of individual factors (Cassell, 1991). For example, while pain interfering with ambulation may cause considerable distress in one person, the cognitive changes that may accompany pharmacotherapy may be the source of intense suffering in another who values cognitive function and clarity above physical function. While this threat to personhood may involve pain and symptoms, people can experience pain without suffering, and suffering may likewise exist separate from any symptom burden. A primary task of the social worker is to join with patient and family to understand their multidimensional experience and unique sources of suffering, as an essential component in fulfilling the ethical responsibility to offer quality care and symptom management (Oliver, Wittenberg-Lyles, Washington, & Sehrawat, 2009). As clinicians move from physical pain to explore other aspects of the symptom experience, patients often require reassurance that expressed interest in their thoughts and feelings is not a denial of their physical pain. Rather, it is an invitation to understand the impact of any symptom on their whole person, including their thoughts, emotions, function, relationships, and quality of life (Altilio & Eskra-Tropeano 2015; Cagle & Altilio, 2011; Mendenhall, 2003; Moss, 2017). For example, pain may cause reciprocal distress within the meso system of family if economics are impacted by a patient's symptom-related disability. This threat to family structure and stability may create a consequent need to interface with a macro system such as public assistance or Social Security. Beyond the stress of working with bureaucracies, the symbolic meaning of disability—its relationship to illness progression and the need to ask for help—can threaten a sense of self for some patients. This merging of micro, meso, and macro dynamics is one example of many interfaces where social work assessment and intervention focus at the level of the individual and the family system, where equilibrium is challenged and families are asked to reorganize.

INTERSECTIONALITY: INFLUENCES ON PHYSICAL SYMPTOMS

Further complicating the lived experience and management of physical symptoms of illness, including pain, is the social location of the patient. Through a lens of intersectionality, constellations of social forces (such as socioeconomic status, access to health care, health insurance coverage, healthy food, education, safe housing, as well as marginalization, power, and privilege) and aspects of personhood (such as sexuality, ethnicity and race, culture, gender, gender identity, religion and spirituality, psychosocial functioning) interact to directly influence health and illness. The experience of physical symptoms, such as shortness of breath or difficult-to-control pain, might have cultural meaning not obvious to a provider, yet when understood has great value to informing a treatment plan (Lasch, 2000). Similarly, religious or spiritual values might strongly influence the meaning attached to physical suffering and the ability to cope. If a person is socially vulnerable and marginalized, and/or feels compromised or disempowered, she may be unable to advocate for her needs, struggle to report the burden of her symptoms, or actively explore options for treatments and medications with her providers (Green et al., 2003; Lohman, 2010). Those who identify with a group that historically has been silenced or discredited might have great difficulty describing symptoms or believing that providers will honor and respond to their reports of pain. Beyond the implications for provider–patient relationships, resource-limited communities often experience structural barriers, including fewer providers and more limited pharmacological options, such as opioid access in neighborhood pharmacies (Green, Khady Ndao-Brumblay, West, & Washington, 2005).

The active consideration of intersectionality when assessing and intervening to ameliorate physical symptoms is important in caring for the whole person (Lasch, 2000; Narayan, 2010). Creating awareness and fostering sensitivity among teams to these potential influences on pain and physical symptoms can improve therapeutic relationships and create avenues for greater understanding and responsiveness to the patient's subjective experience of suffering.

LINKING SYMPTOM PREVALENCE AND IMPACT TO INTERVENTION

Table 3.1 links a symptom, pain, to specific diagnoses and potential impacts on patients and families and serves to guide critical thinking, inquiry, and interventions. The intent is to assist social workers to appreciate the available evidence that, along with practice wisdom, helps to inform assessments and interventions in the everyday practice of health social work. A patient and family

Table 3.1 PAIN CROSSWALK

Disease	Prevalence Ranges	Impact on Patient & Beyond	Assessment Questions & Tools to Guide Thinking & Listening
Cancer	30%–94%	Moderate to severe pain associated with poor quality of life, impacting mood & activity level, & causing fatigue (Haumann, 2017); coping strategies essential to managing pain (behavioral, spiritual, psychosocial) (Deng, 2011); advanced disease & specific cancers associated with high rates of pain, episodic & chronic, impacting psychological well-being & treatments (Paice, 2011)	How does pain affect your everyday life (activities, routine, mood)? What helps to manage your pain? Does it ever feel out of control? What makes your experience of pain better or worse? What is most important to you right now?
End-stage renal disease (ESRD)	11%–83%	Moderate to severe pain associated with depression, insomnia, & thoughts of discontinuing dialysis; severe irritability, anxiousness, & inability to cope with stress more common in persons with pain (Davison, 2005)	What has been the impact of pain on your mood; patience with yourself or others; your thoughts about dialysis; worries about the future?
Chronic obstructive pulmonary disease (COPD)	21%–77%	Persistent & episodic pain leads to impaired function, anxiety, & depression in conjunction with other disabling symptoms (Nakken, 2016); disease progression creates risk of exacerbating symptoms, fluctuating pain, & unstable management (Blinderman, 2009)	Have you any strategies for coping with persistent pain & when pain flares? What thoughts & feelings evolve when your pain worsens or flares?
Congestive heart failure (CHF)	41%–78%	Common & misunderstood, pain often occurs with other symptoms (dyspnea, depression, fatigue, edema), complicating assessment & treatment (Cagle, 2017); can contribute to patient's fears, including fear of a painful death (Adler, 2009; Nordgren, 2003)	How distressing is pain compared to your other symptoms? What worries you most about your illness, symptoms, & the future?

(continued)

Table 3.1 CONTINUED

Disease	Prevalence Ranges	Impact on Patient & Beyond	Assessment Questions & Tools to Guide Thinking & Listening
Dementia	14%–63%	Acute & chronic pain prevalent; unrecognized pain frequently underlies behavioral changes, leading to misdiagnosis & treatment with antipsychotics rather than pain medications (Achterberg, 2013); accurate assessment is challenging, requiring expertise & sensitivity (Hunt, 2015)	Enhance possibility of self-report through continuity of staff, using assessment tools specific to dementia (PAINAD); engage caregiver & family observations of changed behaviors; compensate for visual or hearing impairments; assess environmental, physical contributors
Parkinson's disease	42%–85%	Pain often underreported; causes distress, disability, morbidity; understanding pain etiology & biopsychosocial aspects can enhance treatment plan (e.g., physical therapy) (Fil, 2013); severe pain associated with depression & poorer quality of life; worsens over disease course (Valkovic, 2015)	What is most important to you right now? Does pain interfere? What meaning does pain have for you, for your family? Have you any worries, now or for the future? What are you hoping or wishing for?
Motor neuron disease (MND) such as amyotrophic lateral sclerosis (ALS)	52%–76%	Pain can be episodic or prolonged & associated with worsening quality of life; pain descriptors are complex & include exhaustion/tiring (Pagnini, 2012)	How does pain affect your life? Which symptoms are most troubling to you & your family?
Multiple sclerosis (MS)	68%	Pain intensity impacted by catastrophizing (Osborne, 2007), pain beliefs such as attitude, acceptance, fears (sign of further damage or disease progression) (Harrison, 2014); associated with disability, depression, & anxiety (Drulovic et al., 2015)	What are your beliefs, thoughts, feelings or worries about your pain? How do you cope with the pain? Are you depressed, anxious, nervous?

narrative follows, exploring layers of distress and efforts to construct meaning in the context of an illness trajectory within a personal ecology, providing an illustration of the complex work integral to pain and symptom management.

While there are many definitions for pain, Table 3.1 will enhance the IASP definition with Harrison's Principles of Internal Medicine:

The function of the pain sensory system is to protect the body and maintain homeostasis. It does this by detecting, localizing, and identifying potential or actual tissue-damaging processes. Pain is an unpleasant sensation localized to a part of the body. It is often described in terms of a penetrating or tissue-destructive process (e.g. stabbing, burning, twisting, tearing, squeezing) and/or of a bodily or emotional reaction (e.g. terrifying, nauseating, and sickening). Furthermore, any pain of moderate or higher intensity is accompanied by anxiety and the urge to escape or terminate the feeling. These properties illustrate the duality of pain: it is both sensation and emotion. When it is acute, pain is characteristically associated with behavioral arousal and a stress response consisting of increased blood pressure, heart rate, pupil diameter and plasma cortisol levels. In addition, local muscle contraction (e.g. limb flexion, abdominal wall rigidity) is often present. (Rathmell & Fields, 2012, Chapter 18)

Mary

It's hard to get lost when you are coming home from work. When you have a job, and a paycheck, the road is set right out in front of you: a paved highway with no exits except yours. There's the parking lot, the grocery store, the kids' school, the cleaners, the gas station and then your front door.

—MOSLEY (2007, *p. 3*)

Mary is a 50-year-old Italian American woman newly diagnosed with stage three lung cancer, the presenting symptom of which was back pain. She has managed a restaurant for the past 10 years and shares an apartment with her husband of 30 years. She has three married children and five grandchildren. Shortness of breath, back pain, and fatigue have forced her to resign, and she is faced with filing for disability. Her husband works infrequently as he is chronically ill. As she mourns her role as primary breadwinner, she is fearful about the future—the financial and emotional implications as illness and disability not only shrink financial resources, but also limit the energy and social connections

generated through the work that fed her soul and stimulated her mind. Mary
has a strong Christian faith and overcomes physical challenges to attend Sunday
services. Attendance at church and trips to the clinic for treatment are now the
only times she leaves her apartment. The pleasure and activity related to work
served as a source of pride and a validation of personal strength and accomplishment. She now feels "useless" and "lazy" and misses her coworkers and
contact with the public as she lies on the couch, immobilized by fatigue, pain,
shortness of breath, and, perhaps, depression. Mary has resisted taking opioid
medications suggested for her pain and the shortness of breath that limit her
activity.

Mary speaks with her pastor and asks for his prayers. He tells her God is
testing her strength and will, and physical pain on Earth is part of the promise of
a better life in Heaven. She prays for strength and wonders if taking medications
to diminish symptoms is a sign of weakness and lack of faith in the providence
of God. She tries to remain stoic and often underreports the intensity and frequency of her pain to both the medical team and to family, as she does not
wish to worry them. As she refuses the offers of prescription medication from
her physicians, she struggles with another conflict, as she has been taught in
her family and culture to respect authority figures and she is unsure how to
negotiate the differing perspectives of her pastor and her physicians. Her private worries focus on their financial future, the care of her husband should
she die, and the suffering of her children. At a recent clinic visit, her doctor
and nurse suggested referral for home care, an idea that, while intended to be
helpful, further threatens her sense of self-efficacy. Perceived as an invasion of
her private self and private space, she wonders if this suggestion is an implicit
judgment of her family and their adequacy in providing care. She refuses home
care, indicates that she intends to continue disease-modifying treatments, but
forgoes pain medications and antidepressants as she will continue to put her
faith in God for "healing from her pains."

MOVING FROM ASSESSMENT TO INTERVENTIONS; MICRO, MESO, AND MACRO

Social workers practicing in health settings will meet Mary and her family at
all different stages along the continuum of illness and will listen for the threads
that weave together micro, meso, and macro dynamics. Mary presents myriad
opportunities to assess and intervene through an ecological lens at the complex
intersection of serious illness, pain, and shortness of breath. The impacts of
disease and symptoms infuse aspects of personhood—social, emotional, and
spiritual—flowing from the micro environment of self to the meso environment
of work, family, and church, to the macro environment of medical settings and

entitlement agencies. The application of an ecological framework invites social workers to hold Mary's multiple realities, prioritize related distress, and construct a shared plan of care (Bronfenbrenner, 1979). The following summary explores conceptual frameworks and hypotheses that create opportunities to assist Mary and her family. Interventions and clinical decisions are informed by the nature of each unique clinical relationship, setting specific opportunities and limitations, and, most critically, by timing. Timing is perhaps the most important and elusive component, reflecting the emotional and cognitive readiness of Mary and her family.

Beginning at the micro level, the assessment of pain, dyspnea, depression, and fatigue, their impacts and meaning, will begin to engage Mary in a process that triages symptom-related distress and informs psychoeducation, pharmacologic, and psychological interventions. Grief, often unidentified, emanates from a range of losses—actual, perceived, or anticipated (See Chapter 4; "Psychological Aspects of Care"). Readily identified is grief associated with the loss of the healthy self, employment, financial security, and value assigned to Mary's role as breadwinner and caregiver for husband. Less obvious but equally important is the impact of losses linked to assaults to identity and self-esteem and a social isolation that may further destabilize Mary and her family structure. By co-investigating the pain and illness-related losses, perceived and actual, with Mary, priorities can be co-constructed. Asking, "What about your illness, or pain, is causing you the most distress?" is one path to empower Mary to recover a sense of agency as her priorities guide a plan of care.

The anticipated changes forced by illness and the potential of foreshortened life may mean an altered living environment, as well as an adaptation in the assumptive future that Mary imagined for herself and her family. Implicit in these losses, immediate and impending as disease progresses, is the potential for adaptation, support of strengths, preserving of personhood, and an enriched legacy created by Mary and her family as they are assisted through this illness experience.

Mary's self-worth and identity may be most threatened by the forced accommodations consequent to pain and new diagnosis. At the same time that one honors the many aspects of her identity, both within and beyond work and her role as a breadwinner, a gentle reframing may invite her to consider that her worth also extends to such roles as wife, mother, and grandmother and to loving relationships within family and community. New meaning may come to Mary and her family from a suggestion that this illness experience, while uninvited, may prove to be a path to continue to teach how families come together during adversity to adapt and support each other. Identifying and normalizing the range of emotions involved in integrating disease, living with symptoms, and allowing others to provide care may invite family to express their individual feelings and thoughts, thus creating an intimacy of shared experience. While precipitated by the experience of illness, developmentally this crisis provides all involved the prospect of stepping into new and important roles.

Mary's experience of pain and dyspnea are intimately linked to a life-threatening diagnosis and to aspects of personhood, including self-concept, role within family and society, self-worth, and spiritual values and beliefs. Disease and related symptoms converge and result in loss of work and social isolation and may be contributing to depression or demoralization, requiring assessment to ensure comprehensive person-centered care. The religious interpretation as a test from God attributes meaning that may create additional distress. Clinicians will encourage the use of medications to mitigate symptoms and enhance function with a hope to relieve suffering, preserve integrity of self, and support coherence in identity beyond the illness experience (Antonovsky, 1979). Understanding the meaning and interrelationship of pain, suffering, and spirituality brings important meaning to Mary's ambivalence about accepting medications and moves clinicians beyond labels of "help rejecting" or "nonadherent" to interventions that engage the pastor, honoring beliefs while inviting negotiations. Psychoeducation and prioritizing hopes and values might allow Mary to integrate medications to support aspects of personhood such as enhancing function, mood, and engagement in all aspects of her life, including the spiritual. For example, the pastor might help Mary to balance religious attributions to pain and suffering with God's desire for Mary to be comfortable enough to attend church, diminish the worry of her family, and spend meaningful time with grandchildren (See Chapter 6; "Spiritual, Religious, and Existential Dimensions of Care"). Interventions that support negotiation and problem-solving begin at the micro level, and include supportive counseling and psychoeducation about pain, partializing aspects of Mary's thoughts, emotions, and experience, negotiating and reframing the use of medications as a tool to support aspects of self, rather than remaining a symbol of loss and weakness. Exploring the etiology of stoicism or fatalism broadens perspectives and, when done with respect and humility, has the potential to introduce new meanings and achieve negotiated outcomes (Cagle & Altilio, 2011). Reaching out to social and spiritual networks blends the micro and meso, enhancing communications and building a platform linking medical and community. This connection honors an aspect of Mary's life preceding illness and might be a source of future support to her family—an aspect of legacy that continues to extend her sense of self beyond her contributions as "breadwinner."

Assessment of depression and demoralization contributes to a treatment plan ensuring that pain and fatigue do not mask other diagnoses that may warrant pharmacologic, psychological, or practical interventions. Psychoeducation focused on the relationship of pain, mood, and function is a micro intervention that extends to family and involves medical collaboration to ensure proper diagnosis and management (See Chapter 4; "Psychological Aspects of Care").

Concurrent with the management of symptoms and interventions focused on myriad levels of loss, the practical challenges of Mary's experience link micro, meso, and macro aspects of illness. While applying for disability is consequent to a forced resignation, the threat to self-esteem may be mitigated by viewing disability as an earned benefit and an ongoing way of contributing to family. Over time, with careful thought and sensitive clinical timing, there may be a reframing, suggesting that this is a time for Mary to allow herself to be cared for. However, premature reframing can leave her feeling isolated and not well understood. Perhaps her husband's health status also requires consideration of a disability application, which can threaten the balance in this dyad, yet also minimize the anxiety related to her husband's future financial security. Anticipatory guidance preparing Mary for the "work and challenge" of applying for disability or Social Security might engage family to assist and feel helpful—all intended to support her agency, as she struggles with complex feelings related to accepting help, a proxy for acceptance of a changed life.

The potential loss of her apartment and consequent need to move to a different, and likely less desirable, housing situation could be devastating to her pride, experienced as a loss of the financial legacy she has worked to create for her family, which could be deeply destabilizing. Exploring the meaning of home and the history of this shared space with family will help a social worker better understand Mary's personal narrative and the place of illness in that narrative (See Chapter 5; "Social Aspects of Care"). Asking questions such as, "What does your home mean to you? What might it mean if you have to leave your home? What of your current home is most essential to you and your family—memories, objects, and such?" can create a dialogue that moves from hypothesis and assumption to Mary's unique experience capturing what is lost and what remains through a transition to different space. This therapeutic inquiry is not intended to minimize related suffering, but rather to identify aspects of family and space that might become a source of stability and continuity through major, and forced, changes. Engaging a process of meaning-making, from addressing macro issues such as financial pressures to micro issues such as her perceived and actual losses of aspects of identity, can be useful in assisting Mary to identify and preserve aspects of self, values, beliefs, and hopes that are generative and that can be maintained in the face of serious illness.

Figure 3.1 highlights Mary's story from assessment to intervention through the ecological framework. By extracting the narrative context, we are able to isolate potential clinical interventions that are informed by setting and the nature of the clinical relationship, and that prove pertinent across many aspects

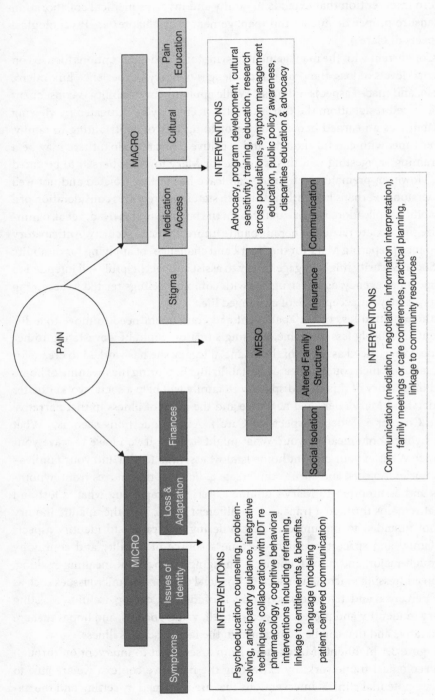

Figure 3.1. Ecological model applied: Pain.

of disease- and symptom-related concerns. For example, anticipatory guidance and psychoeducation could be a useful intervention in addressing grief, finances, or engagement of children and grandchildren who are observing the suffering and distress within the family. As such, suggested interventions are not limited to micro, meso, and macro aspects of assessment, but will often find relevance across an ecological framework.

CONCLUSION

This chapter uses an ecological lens to explore the challenges and opportunities for social workers when working with individuals experiencing pain and symptoms that have rippling impacts. Deconstructing issues into micro, meso, and macro creates space to both impact public policy and examine the range of forces and factors that influence the assessment and management of symptoms across settings, specialties, and disease trajectories. This is a framework to sort through the many influences, beliefs, and feelings shaping an individual's narrative related to pain and other symptoms, an invitation to social workers to maximize their contributions to patients and their families as they negotiate these multifaceted experiences. Mary's illness narrative demonstrates the incredible richness and potential for meaningful intervention when timing, skill, and therapeutic relationship are harmonious. There is significant variation in the ways social workers will interact with patients who are symptomatic, and the assessment and selected interventions will be moderated by setting and by the depth and focus of the relationship. Through careful listening, curiosity, and informed thoughtfulness about the nature of disease and its relationship to symptoms, there is endless potential for social workers to increase expertise and make a positive impact on the lives of patients and families, whether meeting them in crisis or over many months of a serious illness.

LEARNING EXERCISES

1. Imagine you work in a health center located in a neighborhood where pharmacies routinely do not carry many of the medications, including opioids, that your patients are prescribed. You know this is an established hardship for your patients. What could you do? Where could you begin?
2. A patient with metastatic lung cancer and a history of addiction to heroin has been in recovery for five years. She has significant pain from disease that has spread to bones, yet is reluctant to consider

opioid medication as she fears relapse which would threaten her
recovery, an essential aspect of her identity. Research the standard
of care for managing pain in persons with cancer and coexisting
diagnosis of addiction. Create a care plan to both manage pain and
enhance safe prescribing for patient as well as prescribers.

RESOURCES

Assessment Tools and Links

- City of Hope Pain and Palliative Care Resource Center:
  Clearinghouse to disseminate information and resources to assist in
  improving the quality of pain management and end-of-life care; central
  source for a variety of materials, including pain-assessment tools,
  patient education materials, quality assurance materials, end-of-life
  resources, research instruments, and other resources. prc.coh.org/
- Fast Facts and Concepts—Palliative Care Network of Wisconsin
  (PCNOW):
  Over 200 Fast Facts, a PDA version, and a discussion blog. www.
  mypcnow.org/fast-facts
  - Cultural Aspects of Pain Management
  - Establishing Pain Relief Goals
  - Insomnia Assessment and Treatment
  - Pain Assessment in the Cognitively Impaired
  - Pain, Suffering, and Spiritual Assessment
  - Pediatric Pain Assessment Scales
- Home Health Pain Management Flow Sheet—University of Wisconsin
  Hospitals and Clinics, Madison, Wisconsin:
  - A one-page pain management flow sheet for use in the home care
    setting. prc.coh.org/pdf/HH-pain-mgmt.pdf
- Pain Management—US Department of Veterans Affairs (VA): Provides
  centralized access to clinical tools and resources for the provision
  of pain services within the VA healthcare system. www.va.gov/
  PAINMANAGEMENT/Resources.asp
- Pain Scales in Multiple Languages:
  - The British Pain Society has produced a series of pain scales
    in multiple languages (Albanian, Arabic, Bengali, Chinese
    [simplified], Chinese [traditional], Greek, Gujurati, Hindi, Polish,
    Punjabi, Somali, Swahili, Turkish, Urdu, Vietnamese, and Welsh).
    www.britishpainsociety.org/british-pain-society-publications/
    pain-scales-in-multiple-languages/

- Psychosocial Pain Assessment Form—City of Hope, Duarte, California:
  - Developed by Shirley Otis-Green, MSW, LCSW, this eight-page assessment and guided interview measures the impact of pain on five domains: economics, social support, activities of daily living, emotional problems, and coping behaviors as perceived by the interviewer, patient, and significant other. Available for adults, children, and adolescents in Spanish. www.midss.org/content/psychosocial-pain-assessment-form-ppaf
- State-of-the-art review of tools for assessment of pain in nonverbal older adults: /prc.coh.org/PAIN-NOA.htm

ADDITIONAL READINGS

Altilio, T., Cagle, J., Coombe, K., Pasquale Doran, M., Sim Gim Hong, A., Kohn, J., & Isac Tsambe, I. (2016). International association for the study of pain curriculum outline for pain in social work. Retrieved from www.iasp-pain.org/Education/CurriculumDetail.aspx?ItemNumber=495

Altilio, T., & Pasquale Doran, M. (2013). Pain. *Encyclopedia of social work.* Retrieved from socialwork.oxfordre.com/view/10.1093/acrefore/9780199975839.001.0001/acrefore-9780199975839-e-276.

Altilio, T., Pasquale Doran, M., & Lyon Leimena, M. (2016). Pain management. *Oxford bibliographies.* Retrieved from www.oxfordbibliographies.com/view/document/obo-9780195389678/obo-9780195389678-0242.xml.

REFERENCES

Achterberg, W. P., Pieper, M. J., Van Dalen-Kok, A. H., De Waal, M. W., Husebo, B. S., Lautenbacher, S., . . . Corbett, A. (2013). Pain management in patients with dementia. *Clinical Interventions in Aging, 8,* 1471–1482.

Adler, E. D., Goldfinger, J. Z., Kalman, J., Park, M. E., & Meier, D.E. (2009). Palliative care in the treatment of advanced heart failure. *Circulation, 120,* 2597–2606.

Alexander, M., Barbieri, M., & Kiang, M. V. (2017, May 15). Opioid deaths by race in the United States, 2000–2015. Retrieved from osf.io/preprints/socarxiv/jm38s.

Altilio, T., & Eskra Tropeano, L. (2015). Pain and symptom management. In G. H. Christ, C. Messner, & L. Behar (Eds.), *Handbook of oncology social work: Psychosocial care of the patient with cancer* (pp. 239–246). New York: Oxford University Press.

Anderson, K. O., Green, C., & Payne, R. (2009). Racial and ethnic disparities in pain: Causes and consequences of unequal care. *The Journal of Pain, 10*(12), 1187–1204.

Antonovsky, A. (1993). The structure and properties of the Sense of Coherence Scale. *Social Science & Medicine, 36*(6), 725–733.

Blacksher, E. (2001). Hearing from pain: Using ethics to reframe, prevent, and resolve the problem of unrelieved pain. *Pain Medicine, 2*(2), 169–175.

Blindeman, C. D., Homel, P., & Portenoy, R. K. (2009). Symptom distress and quality of life in patients with advanced COPD. *Journal of Pain and Symptom Management,* *38*(1), 115–123.

Brennan, F., Carr, D. B., & Cousins, M. (2007). Pain management: A fundamental human right. *Anesthesia & Analgesia, 105*(1), 205–221.

Bronfenbrenner, U. (1979). *The ecology of human development: Experiments by nature and design.* Cambridge, MA: Harvard University Press.

Cagle, J., & Altilio, T. (2011). The social work role in pain and symptom management. In T. Altilio & S. Otis-Green (Eds.), *Oxford textbook of palliative social work* (pp. 271–287). New York: Oxford University Press.

Cagle, J. G., Bunting, M., Kelemen, A., Lee, J., Terry, D., & Harris, R. (2017). Psychosocial needs and interventions for heart failure patients and families receiving palliative care support: A systematic review. *Heart Failure Reviews, 22*(5), 556–580.

Cassell, E. J. (1991). Recognizing suffering. *Hastings Center Report, 21*(3), 24–31.

Davison, S. N., & Jhangri, G. S. (2005). The impact of chronic pain on depression, sleep, and the desire to withdraw from dialysis in hemodialysis patients. *Journal of Pain and Symptom Management, 30*(5), 465–473.

Deng, D., Fu, L., Zhao, Y. X., Wu, X., Zhang, G., Liang, C., . . . Zhou, Y. F. (2011). The relationship between cancer pain and quality of life in patients newly admitted to Wuhan Hospice Center of China. *American Journal of Hospice and Palliative Medicine, 29*(1), 53–59.

Drulovic, J., Basic-Kes, V., Grgic, S., Vojinovic, S., Dincic, E., Toncev, G., . . . Pekmezovic, T. (2015). The prevalence of pain in adults with multiple sclerosis: A multicenter cross-sectional survey. *Pain Medicine, 16*(8), 1597–1602.

Dugan, D. M. (2012). Interdisciplinary hospice team processes and multidimensional pain: A qualitative study. *Journal of Social Work in End of Life & Palliative Care, 8*(1), 53–76.

Fil, A., Cano-de-la-Cuerda, R., Muñoz-Hellín, E., Vela, L., Ramiro-González, M., & Fernández-de-las-Peñas, C. (2013). Pain in Parkinson disease: A review of the literature. *Parkinsonism & Related Disorders, 19*(3), 285–294.

Green, C. R., Anderson, K. O., Baker, T. A., Campbell, L. C., Decker, S., Fillingim, R. B., . . . Vallerand, A. H. (2003). The unequal burden of pain: Confronting racial and ethnic disparities in pain. *Pain Medicine, 4*(3), 277–294.

Green, C. R., Khady Ndao-Brumblay, S., West, B., & Washington, T. (2005). Differences in prescription opioid analgesic availability: Comparing minority and white pharmacies across Michigan. *Journal of Pain, 6*(10), 689–699.

Harrison, A. M., Bogosian, A., Silber, E., Mccracken, L. M., & Moss-Morris, R. (2014). "It feels like someone is hammering my feet": Understanding pain and its management from the perspective of people with multiple sclerosis. *Multiple Sclerosis Journal, 21*(4), 466–476.

Haumann, J., Joosten, E. B. A., & Van Den Beuken-Van, M. H. (2017). Pain prevalence in cancer patients: Status quo or opportunities for improvement. *Current Opinion in Supportive and Palliative Care, 11*(2), 99–104.

Hunt, L. J., Covinsky, K. E., Yaffe, K., Stephens, C. E., Miao, Y., Boscardin, W. J., & Smith, A. K. (2015). Pain in community-dwelling older adults with dementia: Results from the national health and aging trends study. *Journal of the American Geriatrics Society, 63*(8), 1503–1511.

International Association for the Study of Pain. (2010). Annual Report. Retrieved from www.iasppain.org/files/Content/ContentFolders/AboutIASP/IASPAnnualReport_2010.pdf.

Lasch, K. E. (2000). Culture, pain, and culturally sensitive pain care. *Pain Management Nursing, 1*(3), 16–22.

LeResche, L. (2011). Defining gender disparities in pain management. *Clinical Orthopaedics and Related Research, 469*(7), 1871–1877. doi.org/10.1007/s11999-010-1759-9.

Lohman, D., Schleifer, R., & Amon, J. J. (2010). Access to pain treatment as a human right. *BMC Medicine, 8*(1), 8.

Mendenhall, T. (2003). Psychosocial aspects of pain management: A conceptual framework for social workers in pain management teams. *Social Work in Health Care, 36*(4), 35–51.

Morrison, R. S., Wallenstein, S., Natale, D. K., Senzel, R. S., & Huang, L. L. (2000). "We don't carry that": Failure of pharmacies in predominantly nonwhite neighborhoods to stock opioid analgesics. *New England Journal of Medicine, 342*(14), 1023–1026.

Mosley, W. (2007). *Blond faith.* New York: Little, Brown.

Moss, A. H. (2017). Integrating supportive care principles into dialysis decision-making: A primer for palliative medicine providers. *Journal of Pain and Symptom Management, 53*(3), 656–662.

Nakken, N., Janssen, D. J., Bogaart, E. H., Vliet, M. V., Vries, G. J., Bootsma, G., . . . Spruit, M. (2016). Patient versus proxy-reported problematic activities of daily life in patients with COPD. *Respirology, 22*(2), 307–314. doi:10.1111/resp.12915.

Narayan, M. (2010). Culture's effects on pain assessment and management. *The American Journal of Nursing, 110*(4), 38–47.

Nordgren, L., & Sorenson, S. (2003). Symptoms experienced in last six months of life in patients with end-stage heart failure. *European Journal of Cardiovascular Nursing, 2*, 213–217.

Oliver, P. D., Wittenberg-Lyles, E., Washington, K., & Sehrawat, S. (2009). Social work role in pain management with hospice caregivers: A national survey. *Journal of Social Work in End of Life Palliative Care, 5*(1), 1–12.

Osborne, T., Jensen, M., Ehde, D., Hanley M., & Kraft, G. (2007). Psychosocial factors associated with pain intensity, pain-related interference, and psychological functioning in persons with multiple sclerosis and pain. *Pain, 27*(1), 52–62.

Pagnini, F., Lunetta, C., Banfi, P., Rossi, G., Fossati, F., Marconi, A., . . . Molinari, E. (2012). Pain in amyotrophic lateral sclerosis: A psychological perspective. *Neurological Sciences 33*(5), 1193–1196.

Paice, J., & Ferrell, B. (2011). The management of cancer pain. *CA: A Cancer Journal for Clinicians, 6*(1), 157–182.

Rathmell, J. P., & Fields, H. L. (2012). Pain: Pathophysiology and management. In T. R. Harrison & L. L. Longo (Eds.), *Harrison's principles of internal medicine* (Chapter 18). New York. McGraw-Hill.

Saunders, C. (1996). Hospice. *Mortality, 1*(3), 317–322.

Sehgal, N., Manchikanti, L., & Smith, H. S. (2012). Prescription opioid abuse in chronic pain: A review of opioid abuse predictors and strategies to curb opioid abuse. *Pain Physician, 15*(3), ES 67–92.

Tait, R., & Chibnall, J. (2014). Racial/ethnic disparities in the assessment and treatment of pain: Psychosocial perspectives. *American Psychologist, 69*(2), 131–141.

Tarzian, A., & Hoffman, D. (2004). Barriers to managing pain in the nursing home: Findings from a statewide survey. *Journal of the American Medical Directors Association, 5*(2), 82–88.

Twycross, R., & Wilcock, A. (2001). *Symptom management in advanced cancer: Pain relief.* Oxford: Radcliff Medical Press.

US National Library of Medicine. (2012). Congenital insensitivity to pain. In *Genetics home reference.* Retrieved from ghr.nlm.nih.gov/condition/congenital-insensitivity-to-pain.

Valkovic, P, Minar, M., Singliarova, H., Harsany, J., Hanakova, M., Martinkova, J., & Benetin, J. (2015). Pain in Parkinson's disease: A cross sectional study of its prevalence, types, and relationship to depression and quality of life. *PLoS One, 10*(8), e0136541.

Vermylen, J., Szmuilowicz, E., & Kalhan, R. (2015). Palliative care in COPD: An unmet area for quality improvement. *International Journal of COPD, 10,* 1543–1551.

Zaza, C., & Baine, N. (2011). Cancer pain and psychosocial factors: A critical review of the literature. *Journal of Pain and Symptom Management, 24,* 526–542.

Psychological Aspects of Care

CHRISTOPHER ONDERDONK AND KATHRYN THORNBERRY ■

Compassion is not a relationship between the healer and the wounded. It's a relationship between equals. Only when we know our own darkness well can we be present with the darkness of others. Compassion becomes real when we recognize our shared humanity.

—PEMA CHODRON

INTRODUCTION

The diagnosis of a serious or life-threatening disease can reveal a patient and family's strong adaptive coping skills, or it can expose difficulties in their ability to maintain psychological equilibrium (Kelly, McClement, & Chochinov, 2006; Zabora, 2011). At any point in the disease process, from diagnosis to death, patients and families may experience psychological distress on a continuum from mild fear and sadness to more profound and severe conditions such as anxiety and depression (Crunkilton & Rubins, 2009; Holland et al., 2010). This same continuum extends following the death through the bereavement period as families navigate their grief experience (Hall, 2014; Mancini, Beyza, & Bonanno, 2011). Psychological suffering can threaten a patient and family's ability to adaptively cope with the often complex stresses and demands associated with chronic or serious illness and death (Zabora, 2011). This chapter highlights the continuum of psychological functioning associated with serious illness and how health social workers can utilize their awareness of the micro, meso, and macro forces to enhance patient and family functioning and quality of life.

The ecological vision of mental health and well-being, as articulated by Joubert and Raeburn (1998), provides a clear picture of what an optimal quality of life may look like for patients and families working to adjust to the demands of living with a serious or chronic illness. In this vision, mental health is defined as "the capacity of each and all of us to feel, think, and act in ways that enhance our ability to enjoy life and deal with the challenges we face. It is a positive sense of emotional and spiritual well-being that respects the importance of culture, equity, social justice, interconnections and personal dignity" (Joubert & Raeburn, 1998, p. 16). This definition provides health social workers with signposts to gauge patient and family coping and adjustment. It also provides reference points for the relative effectiveness of the interventions that health social workers employ as they collaborate with patients and families to help them achieve their goals.

On a micro level, health social workers provide direct therapeutic interventions, such as cognitive-behavioral therapy (CBT), anticipatory guidance, and behavioral interventions for symptoms, to relieve psychological and emotional distress (Cagle & Altilio, 2011; Pollin & Kanaan, 1995). On a meso level, health social workers facilitate family meetings and enhance communication within families and between patients and their medical providers to inform care plans and alleviate suffering (Fineburg & Bauer, 2011). Additionally, partnering with community organizations such as local hospices improves access to psychological services such as bereavement care. Collecting and utilizing outcome data to advocate for policy, structural, and process changes in community institutions such as hospitals and clinics make these settings more patient and family centered and responsive to psychological needs, such as implementing trauma-informed care (Crunkilton & Rubins, 2009; Feldman, Sorocco, & Bratkovich, 2014; Ivanko, 2011). On a macro level, by assisting patients and families in navigating the health care system, entitlements, and insurance companies, distress can be reduced. Social workers are uniquely positioned to advocate for underserved populations who are subject to larger sociopolitical forces of discrimination and racism by partnering with local, state and federal policy advocates to make health and social systems more responsive to their needs (See Chapter 2; "Structure and Processes of Care").

Cultivating knowledge and awareness of the intersecting sociopolitical mechanisms that may impact patient and family psychological functioning is necessary to mitigate stress while addressing possible disparities. Social categories do not operate independently of one another (Cole, 2009; Novotney, 2010). We encounter patients and families who by virtue of their age, class, culture, education, ethnicity, gender identity and expression, immigration status, language, race, religion, and sexual orientation are more likely to have experienced and/or are currently experiencing multiple and simultaneous forms of oppression, such as sexism and discrimination, impacting identity formation and overall health and well-being (Cole, 2009). Social workers combine awareness of this intersectionality with clinical skill to uncover the nuance and diversity of individual patients and families. Ultimately, drawing upon the knowledge and awareness of micro, meso, and macro forces impacting psychological adaptation in the setting of serious illness informs intervention strategies. The goal is to reduce psychological distress, enhance coping, and assist patients and families in achieving their goals.

PSYCHOLOGICAL FACTORS IN SERIOUS ILLNESS

Resilience and Meaning-Making

The construct of resilience is an important factor, along with coping and adaptation, in the examination of mental health and well-being. Resilience has been defined as "a dynamic process wherein individuals display positive adaptation despite experiences of significant adversity or trauma" (Luthar & Cicchetti, 2000, p. 2). The construct of resilience also complements the central theoretical underpinning of the social work profession's strengths perspective—a perspective that is often at odds with the medical model's focus on individual deficits, diagnosis, and pathology (Emlet, Tozay, & Raveis, 2010; Gould, 2016; Saleeby, 2001).

Being aware of the differences in perspectives between the strengths approach and the medical model is particularly important when health social workers consider illness-related psychological factors. Recent research on the role of resilience in response to trauma and loss, often associated with serious illness, has found that most people do not experience protracted, extensive suffering in response to these events, but instead, more often than not, demonstrate resilience (Bonanno, 2004; DeShields, Tibbs, Fan, & Taylor 2006; Ganz et al., 2004). The research also highlights the almost limitless diversity in how people demonstrate resilience in the face of trauma and loss (Bonanno, 2004).

Research points to the importance of recognizing and highlighting resilience in patients and families in order to build on existing strengths and further reinforce the process of coping and adaptation. The American Psychological Association emphasizes common resilience behavior in the following way:

It involves the capacity to:

- Make realistic plans and take steps to carry them out
- Have a positive view of yourself and confidence in your strengths and abilities

- Use skills in communication and problem solving
- Engage the capacity to manage strong feelings and impulses. (American Psychological Association, n.d.)

A related and equally important construct in capturing people's strengths is Antonovsky's (1987) "sense of coherence," which he defines as possessing the "pervasive, enduring though dynamic, feeling of confidence that life is . . . comprehensible . . . , manageable . . . and meaningful" (p. 19). A sense of coherence particularly highlights the importance of finding meaning in response to stressful life circumstances (See Chapter 5; "Social Aspects of Care"). The process of "meaning-making" is strongly correlated with positively impacting psychological functioning in the context of serious illness (Breitbart, Gibson, Poppito, & Berg 2004; Chochinov, 2006). In considering the variety of sources of biopsychosocialspiritual suffering, meaning-making has the potential to reduce distress across all of these domains (Breitbart et al., 2004; Chochinov, 2006; Crunkilton & Rubins, 2009).

While it is important to recognize and support an individual's resilience and meaning-making, it is also critical for social workers to remain vigilant about those patients who may be at risk for more severe psychological distress. Patients and families come to us with psychological histories and experience, which might include complex trauma, which may manifest in more severe psychological symptoms such as prolonged distress, aberrant drug-taking behavior, and/or social isolation. While many people find meaning in their illness experience, still others find themselves losing their sense of purpose and meaning, leading to potentially significant psychological and existential distress.

Denial

It's not unusual in a medical setting to hear from colleagues that a patient "is in denial" when the patient doesn't respond with openness and acceptance to the information related to her illness. It is important to be precise with our language and to be mindful of labels that are dismissive and uninformed. "True denial," such as completely refusing to acknowledge the diagnosis or the need for treatment, is not widespread (Rabinowitz & Peirson, 2006; Salander & Windhal, 1999). More common is avoidance, a conscious strategy to deliberately avoid potentially emotionally distressing information (Rabinowitz & Peirson, 2006; Salander & Windhal, 1999). Yalom (2008) equates this process to looking at the sun, where people can only stare at death in very short intervals. This is an acknowledgment that on some days and at some moments, a patient or family member is able to acknowledge with varying degrees of directness that the patient is coming to the end of her life, while at other moments she is not. It is critical to person-centered care that social workers travel alongside patients and families as they find their way.

The most important clinical questions related to denial and avoidance that need to be considered are the following: (1) Is this a problem? (2) If so, for whom? (3) If it is a problem, why? (Hardy & Kell, 2009). These questions help social workers consider if the behavior is adaptive or maladaptive and to look closely at whose distress, theirs or ours, needs to be addressed (Rabinowitz & Peirson, 2006). For instance, for some people with an end-stage diagnosis, denial or avoidance may be a way to minimize their anxiety and grief in order to get through each day. For others, their denial and avoidance may lead to delaying treatment, worsening symptoms, and interfering with important life goals (Rabinowitz & Peirson, 2006). By clearly differentiating adaptive and maladaptive denial and avoidance, social workers help patients avoid being labeled unnecessarily and help providers change their perspective and approach in their interactions with these patients and families.

COMMON FORMS OF PSYCHOLOGICAL DISTRESS IN SERIOUS ILLNESS

Psychic distress associated with chronic and serious illness can take many forms. This chapter will focus on delirium, anxiety, grief and loss, demoralization, and depression, with a particular focus on depression through the introduction of a narrative and application of the ecological approach for understanding the themes emerging in the setting of serious illness.

Delirium: The Role of the Health Social Worker

Delirium is "an acute change in mental status that may fluctuate and has underlying physiological causes" (Irwin, Pirrello, Hirst, Buckholz, & Ferris, 2013). Clinician awareness of delirium is important when conducting a psycho-social assessment. A patient with a serious physical illness is at higher risk of impaired brain and cognitive functioning (Crunkilton & Rubins, 2009). The symptoms of delirium can mimic symptoms of other psychiatric disorders, including anxiety and depression. Patients who are hyperactively delirious might be labeled by providers as agitated and anxious (Pessin, Rosenfeld, & Breitbart, 2002). Patients with hypoactive delirium are frequently ignored, as they present as withdrawn or pleasantly confused. Symptoms may include subtle changes in emotional expression and communication, often noticed by social workers because these aspects of relationship are central to practice. Bringing attention to and raising questions about observed changes may inform medical management. A study in 2013 showed that when patients' delirium was aggressively treated, they described how much suffering they had endured while delirious (Irwin et al., 2013).

Social workers can serve as advocates for appropriate pharmacology when delirium is identified and can work with staff to provide in-the-moment interventions to empower families to soothe the patient. These interventions include calming voice and words, introducing yourself before approaching or touching, frequent reorientation to surroundings, maintaining normal day–night light exposure, using hearing and visual aids, providing cognitively engaging activities, and following sleep protocols by providing a quiet, dark environment and rescheduling medication and laboratory tests to avoid sleep disruption (Irwin et al., 2013). For a discussion of terminal delirium assessment and management, please refer to Chapter 8, "Care of Patients and Families at the End of Life."

Anxiety

It is not uncommon for patients and families to report anxiety as they navigate the often-uncertain course of serious illness (Crunkilton & Rubins, 2009; Holland et al., 2010). Anxiety also frequently accompanies other types of distress, most commonly depression, for which the primary symptom is anxiety and/or agitation (Delgado-Guay, Parsons, Li, Palmer, & Bruera, 2009). Pain and shortness of breath can also trigger anxiety (See Chapter 3; "Physical Aspects of Care"). A patient with cancer and a history of panic disorder might find herself at home with acute pain, triggering an anxiety attack. This physiological response includes a racing heart, increased blood pressure, tightness in the chest, and difficulty breathing, which can lead to a further exacerbation of pain and symptoms, causing a negative feedback loop (Crunkilton & Rubins, 2009; Pessin et al., 2002).

Teaching behavioral approaches such as relaxation training, mindfulness, and guided imagery, as well as cognitive-behavioral interventions, may interrupt this feedback loop and reduce patient and family anxiety (Jacobsen & Jim, 2008). When possible, recording these teaching sessions on patient and family cell phones provides an easily accessible relaxation tool that can serve as a transitional object linking patient to clinician and a resource to mitigate future anxiety episodes. Other anxiety-reducing strategies include working toward an environment that is predictable and responsive to patient needs, with access to medications in the home and a concrete plan to address acute episodes of pain and anxiety. Providing anticipatory guidance about next steps and treatment expectations can address fears and concerns about the future (Altilio, Otis-Green, & Dahlin, 2008).

Grief and Loss

The experience of grief and loss is universal (Hall, 2014). The diagnosis of serious illness and the life that follows is often marked by losses—loss of functioning, roles, and an imagined future (Brennan, 2001; Crunkilton & Rubins, 2009). Grief symptoms might include physical exhaustion, loss of appetite, difficulty concentrating, confusion, anger, sadness, fear, existential distress, withdrawal, and isolation (Bonanno, 2004; Periyakoil et al., 2005; Shear, 2011). There is also considerable diversity in the experience and the expression of grief, loss, and mourning that is embedded in a person's cultural identity (See Chapter 7; "Cultural Aspects of Care"). In some cultures, people internalize their distress with stoicism, while in others there may be an expectation of a public display of emotion in the form of wailing. Health social workers need to demonstrate cultural humility, an approach that positions the social worker as an open and curious cultural learner, when encountering cultural diversity in grief and loss (Gerbino & Raymer, 2011).

Persons living with normal grief and loss experience fluctuations in their mood states, oscillating between moments of distress and moments of emotional equilibrium and stable day-to-day functioning (Bonanno, 2011; Periyakoil et al., 2005; Stroebe & Schut, 2001). Grief reactions can be quite powerful and may be misinterpreted by medical providers who equate intensity with pathology. For this reason, patients may be labeled as depressed or needing counseling when in fact their reaction is normal, adaptive, and does not require intervention (Periyakoil et al., 2005; Shear, 2011). Similar to cultural differences, gender differences may inform adaptive responses to loss. For many women, the response may be intuitive or more focused on emotions, and may be expressed through weeping and tears, whereas many men may be more focused on their thoughts and intellect, or may be instrumental, where doing something is a way of responding to the loss (Doka & Martin, 2011). Identifying risk as well as protective factors in patient and family response aids in clarifying clinical needs related to grief and loss.

In assessing grief and loss, a powerful approach is to listen attentively, using simple reflective statements, while validating feelings and normalizing the process: "You're grieving this loss. I work with many people like you who share similar feelings of sadness" (Neimeyer, 2012). Many people find sharing their experience with someone close to them is helpful. For those who are instrumental processors, who find expression through art or doing something, activities such as journaling, creative art including photography, painting, sewing, working in the soil, or building things, large and small, can be outlets for their grief (Doka & Martin, 2011; Neimeyer, 2012).

Demoralization

Demoralization is a syndrome that can also be experienced in the setting of chronic or serious illness. Boscgalia and Clarke (2007) describe demoralization as characterized by helplessness, hopelessness, existential despair, and loss of purpose and meaning to life. After a prolonged illness and/or difficult treatments, patients may begin to start feeling better, and may be told a treatment is having an expected benefit, only to then be faced with worsening physical symptoms and news that the treatment has ceased to have the intended outcome (Clarke, Kissane, Trauer, & Smith, 2005). These types of setbacks can cause understandable psychological distress and illustrate how a loss of meaning and coherence in the course of the disease process can be debilitating for some people. Despite the possible intensity of this distress, it does not constitute a psychiatric disorder (Clarke et al., 2005).

It is not uncommon for patients exhibiting these types of reactions to be labeled as depressed. However, anhedonia, or the total loss of pleasure, is not present in demoralization, and therefore a diagnosis of depression does not fit. Depression is persistent and pervasive, whereas with grief and loss and demoralization there are rays of light where the patient's mood may brighten when visited by close family and friends or in response to improvement in physical symptoms (Boscaglia & Clarke, 2007).

An important approach for helping the demoralized patient is to assess and address symptoms, which can lead to an improvement in mood. Concurrently, cognitive-based approaches can reframe experience by identifying limiting and repetitive thoughts. Within a collaborative clinical relationship, it can be helpful to set manageable goals and to schedule easily attainable and pleasurable activities to be checked off on a day-to-day basis in order to address feelings of subjective incompetence (Clarke et al., 2005). For instance, it may be possible to schedule a day that includes activities such as taking a shower, going outside, watching a movie, and meditating at bedtime. Checking off these tasks can increase feelings of subjective competence and control, instilling hope about the possibility of regaining meaning and purpose in their day-to-day lives. Finally, inviting people to reflect on their past sources of meaning and how they might apply those perspectives to their current situation may also help reconnect to parts of themselves that have been temporarily lost through multiple treatment setbacks or simply by the assumed role of "patient."

Depression

Depression is a psychiatric diagnosis defined in the *Diagnostic Statistical Manual of Mental Disorders*, fifth edition (DSM-5), as the presence of five or more of the symptoms listed in Table 4.1 during the same two-week period that interfere with routine daily activities (Uher, 2014).

However, many of the physical symptoms of depression in psychiatric populations do not translate to those with a serious illness because the underlying disease can often cause similar symptoms such as loss of appetite, weight loss, fatigue, and psychomotor retardation (Periyakoil et al., 2005). Depression is common, but not a given, in the context of life-threatening illness. Estimates of prevalence vary with 15%–50% of patients at end of life experiencing depressive symptoms and 5%–20% of patients meeting criteria for major depressive disorder (Rosenstein, 2011; Warm & Weismann, 2015). For this reason, assessment and diagnosis primarily rely on the first two items as a screening for depression: "Are you depressed?" and "In the last two weeks what's brought you joy?" (Chochinov, 1997; Crunkilton & Rubins, 2009; Kelly et al., 2006; Payne et al., 2007; Periyakoil et al., 2005). The presence of anhedonia, the absence of pleasure, and feelings of hopelessness can signal the presence of depression and warrant serious attention and care (Crunkilton & Rubins, 2009; Rodin et al., 2007).

It is frequently helpful to assist patients and families to distinguish the fleeting feeling of depression versus the clinical diagnosis of major depression or dysthymia (Block, 2006; Periyakoil et al., 2005). Depression in more severe forms

Table 4.1 DSM-5 CRITERIA FOR MAJOR DEPRESSIVE DISORDER

Major Depressive Disorder
Five or more of nine symptoms (including at least one of depressed mood and loss of interest or pleasure) in the same two-week period; each of these symptoms represents a change from previous functioning

- Depressed mood (subjective or observed)
- Loss of interest or pleasure
- Change in weight or appetite
- Insomnia or hypersomnia
- Psychomotor retardation or agitation (observed)
- Loss of energy or fatigue
- Worthlessness or guilt
- Impaired concentration or indecisiveness
- Thoughts of death or suicidal ideation or suicide attempt

(American Psychiatric Association, 2013)

can become all-consuming, robbing patients and families of quality of life, and in some cases where treatment adherence or participation in rehabilitation are vital to survival, depression can be life-threatening (Block, 2006; Crunkilton & Rubins, 2009; Hare, Toukhsati, Johansson, & Jaarsma, 2014).

Depression can also lead to suicidal behaviors and requests for hastened death, often rooted in the intersection of physical suffering, hopelessness, loss of control, and increased dependence, as well as loss of purpose and meaning (Block, 2006; Breitbart et al., 2000; Chochinov, 1995; Crunkilton & Rubins, 2009; Rodin et al., 2007). Health social workers can assist in disentangling sources of distress, skillfully and compassionately exploring the feelings and thoughts behind these statements. Social workers also assist in uncovering past sources of hope and meaning, bringing neglected strengths and coping strategies to bear on present struggles. Consulting with other clinicians, potentially specialists in psychiatry or palliative care, can ensure that the necessary social, ethical, and legal aspects of care are integrated into a plan of care, including interventions and referrals (Breitbart et al., 2000; Chochinov, 1995; Crunkilton & Rubins, 2009).

Given the profound impacts of untreated depression, a collaborative, interdisciplinary approach is critical. If depression is assessed, evidence-informed treatment may involve both pharmacologic and integrative approaches combining pharmacology and psychotherapy, along with in-the-moment connection, empathy, and behavioral approaches, such as encouragement to spend time outside or to engage in physical activity, sometimes in serious illness still possible through the use of meditation and visual imagery (Block, 2006; Crunkilton & Rubins, 2009; Rodin et al., 2007; Roeland et al., 2010).

Countertransference

Working with patients and families living with serious illness can bring up a range of feelings and reactions for clinicians. Social workers are trained to attend to their own thoughts and feelings, as well as those of patients and families, during clinical encounters. Transference describes the thoughts and feelings the client has toward the clinician, while countertransference refers to the feelings and reactions the practitioner has toward the patient or client (Sadock, Sadock, & Ruiz, 2015). At times, countertransference can be a useful clue to clinical information—feelings the patient is not expressing that may need to be brought into the clinical encounter. However, the practitioner's thoughts and feelings can also be rooted in childhood family dynamics and culture and serve no clinical purpose in the encounter with patients and families (Gibbons, Murphy, & Joseph, 2011; Sadock et al., 2015).

Warning signs of countertransference in the medical culture that could impede standard of care include providers avoiding certain patients or, without reason, going above and beyond for others. This may be the case when patients are particularly grateful for the work and they make providers feel good about themselves. The practitioner may think about this patient frequently after hours, and may even cross the line from thinking about to wanting a personal friendship. The practitioner may disclose personal information not clinically relevant. The reverse of these positive emotions is also true. The labeling of patients as "noncompliant" or "crazy" is a clue that countertransference may be impacting clinical judgment. When unaware of countertransference, it is not unusual to blame clients or patients when the interventions aren't helpful (Munson, 2012). Clinicians who suspect that countertransference may be impeding good quality care are expected to seek out clinical supervision (NASW, 2008). In many interdisciplinary teams, the social worker has more training in recognizing countertransference and is uniquely situated to highlight these issues in order to consistently advocate for the shared goal of high-quality standard of care for all.

Douglas

Douglas is a 64-year-old African-American male with congestive heart failure (CHF), following a cardiac arrest one year ago, who presents to the emergency room with shortness of breath, fatigue, pain, and increased lower extremity edema. He is obese and a lifelong smoker, and according to his spouse, Donna, has "never listened to me all these years," referencing her efforts to help him to lose weight and stop smoking. Douglas and Donna were told three days ago that he is "not a candidate" for advanced heart therapies. During an initial assessment in the emergency room, Douglas presents with a sad affect, not volunteering much information, and allowing Donna to do much of the talking. For the past 15 years, Douglas has worked as a history professor in a community college, and Donna blames his health behaviors and work stress for leading to his cardiac event. The couple live alone and have four adult children and nine grandchildren. Douglas struggles to identify what brings him joy, but agrees with Donna, who interjects that he has "always said giving back and helping people" brought him happiness.

Douglas is described by Donna as the patriarch at the center of a close-knit family. Since his cardiac arrest he says he "just doesn't have the energy" to leave the house to attend birthday parties or church. Donna comments that he "hasn't been himself" since his heart attack, citing angry exchanges with family and spending more and more time alone in his "man cave." The family encourages him to "pray to God for strength." "We've all been saying for a year he just needs to snap out of this and get back to his old self."

A lay pastor at his local Christian church, Douglas hasn't functioned in that role in over six months. The primary breadwinner, he hasn't worked in months. Donna talks of feelings of loss related to their retirement plans, which depend on Douglas working for two more years. Douglas looks over to Donna and says, "I am so sorry." Donna looks down and remains silent. Upon admission to a cardiac unit, in a private interview Douglas shares profound feelings of guilt and shame for having "caused all of this," referring to his inability to quit smoking or follow through with his diet. He speaks harshly about himself and his inability to "resist temptations." He feels worthless as a husband and father and increasingly isolated from Donna, who he believes is intensely angry at him for not following through with promises. Wondering if she can ever forgive him, Douglas worries he will have to go through the next days and months without her support.

Douglas feels frustrated by his visits to the cardiac clinic, remarking how "it's always the same. I leave feeling just as bad as when I came in." He voices relief that the inpatient cardiac team are "giving me enough pain medication so I can get through this nightmare." Over the last several days Douglas has been requesting increased pain medication. In an effort to enhance his sense of control and more effectively manage pain, patient-controlled analgesia (PCA) was started. While doses have been increased, there has been no sustainable improvement in reports of pain, data which leads to a re-assessment. The cardiac team feels ineffective, wonders about substance abuse, and feels increasingly pressured, as they are hoping to discharge Douglas soon.

DISCUSSION

Douglas and his family are experiencing a range of psychological responses to the life-threatening nature of his heart condition and subsequent decline. By applying the ecological framework, a comprehensive treatment and care plan can be developed that acknowledges the complex interplay among physical, emotional, social, cultural, and spiritual aspects of their suffering.

Beginning by actively listening to Douglas and Donna tell their story and providing grief and loss counseling to encourage expression of feelings such as shock, anger, and sadness can facilitate their anticipatory grieving process. Douglas's statements, as well as his behaviors, warrant further exploration to clarify their meaning and place them within the context of his personal history and the present experience of illness. While reluctant to volunteer details in the joint interview with Donna, meeting with him privately provides an opportunity to use motivational interviewing skills to elicit clarifications. Reflective statements, often using Douglas's own words, demonstrate understanding, which strengthens rapport and deepens the interaction—"You feel you've caused all of this," or "It feels as if they don't understand how hard it is" (Pollak, Childers, & Arnold, 2011). Summarizing, a related skill, can also be powerful in moving the interaction forward toward acknowledging hopes and setting goals: "So, even though you see all of what's happening as being your fault, you are still hoping to feel better and it's been frustrating your clinic visits haven't achieved that. Now you are here in the hospital hoping to somehow feel better to get through this nightmare. Do I have that right?" These simple yet powerful skills convey understanding and connection and increase trust through the assessment process and into the intervention phase (Pollak, Childers, & Arnold, 2011).

As Douglas feels seen and heard, essentially starting where he is, there is opportunity to gather information about the life he has lived and the life he might imagine in the future. The busy nature of health care settings can often lend itself to assuming rather than clarifying thoughts and feelings. By avoiding assumptions, time spent may enhance the validity of the assessment and the value of the interventions that follow.

Douglas may struggle to remember the last time he felt truly happy or was able to enjoy normal activities, such as family gatherings or church functions, perhaps stretching as far back as before his heart attack. His isolating behaviors may stem, in part, from his reluctance to acknowledge the psychic pain of his shame, loss of self-worth, and the significance of a religious interpretation of being unable to "resist temptation." In addition, the cultural stigma existing around mental illness in the African-American culture may further compound Douglas's isolation. African-American men have prescribed cultural role expectations of resilience, which may influence the family mantra to "snap out of it" (Plowden, Adams, & Wiley, 2016). It is sometimes more acceptable to express feelings of depression through physical symptoms of pain, exhaustion, and lack of energy. These masked expressions of depression can result in providers misapplying medical interventions, such as opioids, to psychological symptoms. When these interventions don't work, providers may label patients as "failing the treatments," an inappropriate use of language that reinforces the patient's feelings of failure, the provider's helplessness, and ultimately leading to a loss of faith in the provider's ability to mitigate suffering (Block, 2006).

Increasing pain medicines has not improved Douglas's pain relief, leading to reassessment and a concern that he may be using the opioids to self-medicate or chemically cope with what he has referred to as a "nightmare."

Further assessment would include a personal or family history of substance abuse, mental illness, or trauma and psychosocialspiritual aspects of distress that might influence his experience and expression of pain and use of medications. Douglas freely indicates the medication helps him to sleep and he would like to "check out right now." As he acknowledges anhedonia, helplessness, and a desire to escape, there can be a shared acknowledgment of the depth of his struggle, as well as an assessment for suicidality. During this reassessment phase, the social worker can name and mirror the dynamics related to chemical coping, helping Douglas "see" a more accurate sense of self. He then has an opportunity to begin to change his behavior to align more closely with the adaptive range on the coping continuum. Psychoeducation about the frequency of depression in patients following a heart attack normalizes his experience and potentially mitigates the stigma and sense of isolation that may accompany this diagnosis. Affirming depression as a treatable condition reframes what it could mean to "feel better" and invites Douglas to extend his focus beyond physical symptoms to a recognition that improving psychological symptoms will also enhance his quality of life. The connection between improved psychological functioning and feeling better and more like himself may enhance Douglas's receptivity to interventions that he may view as stigmatizing, such as psychiatric consultation. Sharing the observation that increased use of opioids has been ineffective in improving his pain contributes to a recognition of the complexity of his experience. There may be a hint of hopefulness in the realization that effectively treating depression may improve his physical symptoms of pain, lack of energy, and exhaustion. Though in the past psycho-pharmacology would take weeks to determine benefit, recent promising research has demonstrated the efficacy of faster-acting treatments such as Ketamine (Iglewicz et al., 2015).

Using the patient's language and statements about his hopes is one way of assessing and validating what is most important. With Douglas it might sound like, "If you were feeling better what would you hope your day-to-day life would look like?" This question is intended to elicit person-centered goals, Douglas's unique hopes and aspirations about the future in the face of his serious illness. This may involve feeling well enough to participate in family and church functions, to reclaim or possibly redefine his identity as the family patriarch despite declining functional status, and perhaps most important, to resolve the tension existing between him and Donna.

Extending to the meso level, Douglas has pointed to the tensions between him and Donna as a significant source of distress. Although intervention may be warranted to address the tension between them, the hospital admission is not likely the time or place for these tensions to be opened up and explored. However, impacting the family system may involve planting seeds to help them to view each other's behavior differently. Reframing Douglas's perception of Donna's anger as a normal emotional response may help to gently challenge his belief that these emotions will color the rest of their relationship. This is a form of instilling hope by raising alternatives to hopeless thinking, which can distort Douglas's appraisals of the future. Prior to discharge, considering referral to social workers in the community, such as cardiac clinic or a behavioral health specialists, may allow for relational work started in the hospital to become ongoing.

In settings where a private meeting with Donna is possible, a first step may be to normalize and validate feelings of anger, while assessing her openness to connect with other feelings such as loss, fear, or sadness, which may underlie her anger. Understanding Donna's thoughts and feelings and whether they are frozen or fluid helps determine whether her anger simply needs to be accepted in the moment and the relationship issues deferred, with a possible referral to outpatient counseling. If she is able to extend her emotional range, this may create an opportunity to connect with feelings of love and concern for Douglas, which, when reflected, may lay the groundwork for healing interactions in the future.

Family Meetings and Transitions of Care
Family meetings can help families find the words to describe their experiences, beginning to name, partialize, and prioritize their concerns, and to create a safe place for honest expression. Social work presence enhances meetings by encouraging a safe environment where emotional and psychological experience is explored and honored, enhancing the understanding by all participants of the dynamics at play for patients and families. The presence of important members of the treatment team, as well as critical members of the patient's circles of support, helps ensure that the outcome is a shared acknowledgment of patient-centered goals that will guide the next steps in care. It is only with the presence of the medical experts that Douglas might receive an answer to his pervasive wondering about the judgment that he is "not a candidate" for further cardiac interventions. Health social workers can then provide practical support with anticipatory guidance, helping patients and families envision, with their permission, what the next days and weeks may hold (Altilio, Otis-Green, & Dahlin, 2008). In the case of Douglas and Donna, the health social worker would likely schedule a family meeting to mutually clarify Douglas's goal to return home and to provide anticipatory guidance, with patient and family assent, about what dying at home might

involve, possibly coordinating an informational visit with hospice. Table 4.2 reflects how continuity of care with Douglas and Donna may unfold beyond the hospital environment.

Douglas and Donna

Douglas has identified multilevel impacts of cardiac disease on his sense of self, his role in the family and community, and his relationship with Donna. In a hospital setting, where time is limited, the primary task is to identify these themes and to help this couple partialize and prioritize concerns, intervening accordingly. Table 4.2 outlines a longer trajectory where social workers, whether practicing in a hospice or cardiac clinic, continue the clinical work begun in the hospital setting.

Ecological Framework of Douglas's Depression

This ecological flowchart follows Douglas's challenges with depression in the context of his end-stage congestive heart failure (CHF). This framework outlines the process of assessment through intervention and how synthesizing his unique story into clinical themes leads to a variety of different strategies for helping Douglas, his family, and health providers. An intervention like psychoeducation can be applied, as in Figure 4.1, to the micro, meso, and macro aspects of the assessment. This helps Douglas and his family understand his depression in the context of illness, while collaborating with providers to identify chemical coping and depression as well as evidenced-informed approaches to addressing these issues.

Narrative Documentation Table

Table 4.3 represents documentation intended to contribute to shared care planning in an inpatient cardiac center where an interdisciplinary team includes an attending physician, fellow physician, nurse practitioner, health social worker, pharmacist, and dietician. Health social work documentation in the inpatient setting is often relegated to more obscure areas of the electronic medical record, presenting the challenge of finding creative ways to ensure that assessment and interventions are seen and integrated into the care plan. For example, creating a form where the interdisciplinary plan of care is documented acknowledges the contribution and accountability of each discipline. Participating in team rounds with Douglas and his family and meeting in individual and joint sessions create varied opportunities to address psychosocial, spiritual, and practical elements of his care, treatment, and related adaptations. Table 4.3 presents examples of documentation through the hospital admission, intended to represent the critical thinking, interventions, and expected outcomes in the context of a time-limited therapeutic relationship. It is written with a dual consciousness: What

Table 4.2 Follow-up Crosswalk

Time after Discharge	Interval Events	Assessment & Intervention
One week	Discharged home with hospice care, Douglas is much weaker now than two weeks ago. He insisted that his recliner, where he spends the majority of time, be set up in his "man cave," which is cluttered & with limited access to a bathroom. He chooses not to use a bedside commode & insists on making the 30-foot walk to the hall bathroom. Donna thought it safer for his recliner to be in the living room, next to the hall bathroom, where family can more easily visit & "keep an eye on him." She says, "Just like always, he doesn't listen to me."	Douglas & Donna are struggling to adjust to his declining functional status & the impact on safety in the home, wrestling with the tension between safety & self-determination, complicated by their existing tension & Douglas's ongoing struggles with depressed mood & social withdrawal. The social worker can use the safety & practical challenges posed by his decline as an opening to explore the underlying emotional & social dynamics, facilitating communication so both feel "seen & heard." Douglas acknowledges the validity of Donna's worry for his safety & the caring it represents; Donna acknowledges Douglas's need for control & the feelings of loss associated with his decline. They negotiate a compromise. Douglas needs his privacy now. He will stay in his "man cave" & use the bedside commode. The social worker affirms their ability to listen to one another's needs & effectively come to an agreement: "I imagine this isn't the first time the two of you have had to make a compromise."
Three weeks	Douglas's functional status continues to decline, & his breathing is more labored, making speaking difficult. Donna & Douglas volunteer they had "heart to heart talks," easing their tensions. At Douglas's request the family bought another recliner for the living room, which he uses as church members, his adult children, & grandchildren come to visit him. His mood has begun to brighten. He is enjoying being with family & sharing stories, despite his physical changes.	The connection Douglas & Donna made during their negotiation has brought them closer to equilibrium in their relationship, a shift likely to mitigate Douglas's greatest fear of distance & isolation from Donna through his dying process. His negative thoughts & fears are replaced with reconnection to those most important to him. The shift in mood & participation precludes the need for additional counseling & invites clinical work focused on legacy, perhaps through the use of life review or interventions such as Dignity Therapy, a structured, evidenced-based approach using specific questions in a recorded interview to be transcribed & bound to become a family legacy document, especially meaningful to Douglas, a history teacher.

(*continued*)

Table 4.2 CONTINUED

Time after Discharge	Interval Events	Assessment & Intervention
Six weeks	Douglas is coming to the end of his life. He is sleeping more, with brief periods of wakefulness in a hospital bed in the living room. The transcribed Dignity document is openly displayed in the living room. Over the last week Donna has increased her activity around the house, cooking, doing laundry, sweeping, & re-sweeping the floors. Her children remark that she "can't seem to sit still."	Donna is experiencing anticipatory grief, & as her awareness of Douglas's imminent death increases, so does her sadness. Staying busy, an instrumental form of grieving, is helping her maintain her emotional balance. During periods of wakefulness, Donna might be encouraged to sit or lie with Douglas & share thoughts, feelings, & memories, which can enhance legacy & facilitate the grieving process. Psychoeducation might focus on the value of silent presence, the suggestion that Douglas might hear even when he cannot speak & the value of sharing authentic emotions, which might include love, gratitude, & forgiveness. The document may be acknowledged the document as a transitional object that will be "passed on" generation to generation. Finally, the social worker can invite reflection on the mutual growth & shared caring reflected in the family.

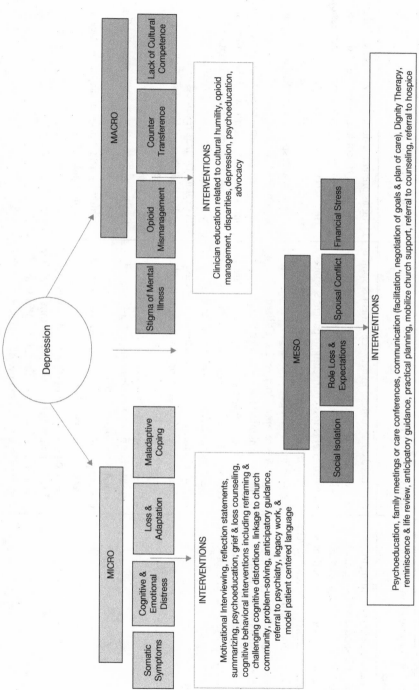

Figure 4.1. Ecological model applied: Depression.

Table 4.3 Interdisciplinary Documentation

Timing & Purpose of Social Work Contact	Interventions Provided	Outcome & Plans
Initial assessment responding to patient & spouse receiving news that patient is coming to the end of his life; exploration of patient & spouse reaction to this news, psychosocialspiritual history & current functioning, medical understanding, sources of support & strength, meaning of patient behavior around opioids, & identification of practical needs that may impact next steps in care.	Facilitated communication between patient & spouse to elicit hopes, worries, & goals. Patient presented as less animated in the presence of his spouse. Provided grief & loss counseling to patient & spouse, normalizing their feelings of shock & facilitating expression of thoughts & feelings. Douglas was receptive to meet 1:1. Utilized motivational interviewing to elicit thoughts, feelings, hopes, & worries related to end-of-life concerns. Patient stated his goals are "to feel better, spend more quality time with family at home, & resolve conflict & recover closeness with spouse." Screened for depression: patient confirmed feeling depressed with limited joy for some time. Provided psychoeducation about depression & cardiac disease, its potential role in his increasing use of opioids without pain relief. Offered psychiatry referral for further assessment & treatment of depression. Validated patient concerns about spousal conflict. Used cognitive behavioral interventions to reframe his negative belief about the future. Offered to meet privately with spouse. Also suggested family meeting to further explore goals & plan next steps.	Douglas presented during 1:1 as more verbal & animated. He confirmed feelings of depression. Alluded to using PCA to cope with depression. He is receptive to psychiatry consultation; will expedite referral; agrees to my meeting privately with spouse & to a family meeting within 24–48 hours. Donna presents as acutely grieving, expressing shock as well as anger toward the patient. She volunteers feelings of loss of assumptive future & her anger is distressing to patient. Will explore Donna's readiness to meet individually to further explore feelings of anger, grief, & loss. Plan for provider meeting with family to further clarify patient & family goals & offer anticipatory guidance to prepare patient & family for next steps in anticipation of leaving the hospital.

Private meeting with spouse to further assess grief & loss reaction & explore relational issues with patient.	Listened, validated, & normalized feelings of anger & helplessness in response to patient & illness. Assessed spouse's openness/readiness & received permission to explore range of feelings. Encouraged exploration of grief & loss & facilitated expression of sadness. Spouse also able to share her feelings of love & concern for patient. Reflected & normalized the range of emotions. Introduced the option of seeking outpatient counseling or church support, weighing issues of confidentiality should couple feel a need for additional assistance with coping.	Spouse expanded her range of feelings beyond anger, sharing her love & concern for patient. Evidence for possibility of future healing with Douglas. Provided spouse with counseling resources & encouraged accessing church support as needed.

information do others need to do their work, and how would Douglas and Donna respond were they to read your words?

CONCLUSION

A health social worker may encounter a vast range of coping styles when tasked with helping patients and families address the psychological aspects of living with serious and/or chronic illness. This chapter has outlined the application of evidence-informed assessment and interventions through an ecological lens to respond to psychological phenomena. Douglas's struggle highlights the complex interplay of intrapersonal, interpersonal, cultural, and systems-level factors that can both obscure and reveal the significant sources of strength, resilience, and support. Careful and thoughtful assessment and skillfully timed interventions can elicit person-centered goals, and even in a time-limited therapeutic relationship, can facilitate meaningful changes in patient and family coping and adaptation. These meaningful changes may occur in the course of an ongoing therapeutic relationship or, as is often the case in the inpatient hospital setting, after discharge, over time, in response to the health social worker "planting seeds." This chapter has highlighted how health social workers can uniquely impact psychological functioning in medical settings by considering the person-in-environment perspective and acting upon the micro, meso, and macro forces at play in order to improve patients and family's quality of life and quality of time spent together.

LEARNING EXERCISE

1. Using documentation (Table 4.3), select aspects of assessment and interventions that you might modify to any setting and time frame. Imagine you are writing in a setting where patients and families, with consent, have access to their medical record through an Internet portal. Would you be comfortable with the documentation in this chapter? What would you change and how?

ONLINE RESOURCES

Columbia University Loss, Trauma, and Emotion Lab. www.tc.columbia.edu/ltelab/
Fast Facts and Concepts #7: Assessing Depression in Advanced Cancer. www.mypcnow. org/blank-hn0yj

Fast Facts and Concepts #43: Is It Grief or Depression? www.mypcnow.org/blank-rc5hu

Fast Facts and Concepts #146: Screening for Depression in Palliative Care. www.mypcnow.org/blank-qlws1

Fast Facts and Concepts #186: Anxiety in Palliative Care—Causes and Diagnosis. www.mypcnow.org/blank-zh5tm

Fast Facts and Concepts #319: Existential Suffering Part 1—Definition and Diagnosis. www.mypcnow.org/copy-of-fast-fact-318

Fast Facts and Concepts #320: Existential Suffering Part 2—Clinical Response and Management. www.mypcnow.org/copy-of-fast-fact-319

ICU Delirium and Cognitive Impairment Study Group. www.icudelirium.org/

Promoting Mental Health. World Health Organization. www.who.int/mental_health/evidence/MH_Promotion_Book.pdf

REFERENCES

Altilio, T., Otis-Green, S., & Dahlin, C. M. (2008). Applying the national quality forum preferred practices for palliative and hospice care: A social work perspective. *Journal of Social Work in End-of-Life & Palliative Care, 4*(1), 3–16.

American Psychiatric Association. (2013). Diagnostic and Statistical Manual and Statistical Manual of Mental Disorders (DSM-5), Fifth edition.

American Psychology Association. (n.d.). The road to resilience. Retrieved from www.apa.org/helpcenter/road-resilience.aspx

Antonovsky, A. (1987). The salutogenic perspective: Toward a new view of health and illness. *Advances, 4*(1), 47–55.

Brennan, J. (2001). Adjustment to cancer—coping or personal transition?. *Psycho-Oncology: Journal of the Psychological, Social and Behavioral Dimensions of Cancer, 10*(1), 1–18.

Block, S. D. (2006). Psychological issues in end-of-life care. *Journal of Palliative Medicine, 9*(3), 751–772.

Bonanno, G. A. (2004). Loss, trauma, and human resilience: Have we underestimated the human capacity to thrive after extremely aversive events? *American Psychologist, 59*(1), 20.

Bonanno, G. A., Westphal, M., & Mancini, A. D. (2011). Resilience to loss and potential trauma. *Annual Review of Clinical Psychology, 7*, 511–535.

Boscaglia, N., & M Clarke, D. (2007). Sense of coherence as a protective factor for demoralisation in women with a recent diagnosis of gynaecological cancer. *Psycho-Oncology, 16*(3), 189–195.

Breitbart, W., Gibson, C., Poppito, S. R., & Berg, A. (2004). Psychotherapeutic interventions at the end of life: A focus on meaning and spirituality. *The Canadian Journal of Psychiatry, 49*(6), 366–372.

Breitbart, W., Rosenfeld, B., Pessin, H., Kaim, M., Funesti-Esch, J., Galietta, M., . . . Brescia, R. (2000). Depression, hopelessness, and desire for hastened death in terminally ill patients with cancer. *JAMA, 284*(22), 2907–2911.

Cagle, J. G., & Altilio, T. (2011). The social work role in pain and symptom management. In T. Altilio & S. Otis-Green (Eds.), *Oxford textbook of palliative social work* (pp. 271–286). New York: Oxford University Press.

Chochinov, H. M., Wilson, K. G., Enns, M., & Lander, S. (1997). Are you depressed? Screening for depression in the terminally ill. *American Journal Psychiatry, 154*(5), 674–676.

Chochinov, H. M., Wilson, K. G., Enns, M., & Mowchun, N. (1995). Desire for death in the terminally ill. *The American Journal of Psychiatry, 152*(8), 1185.

Clark, D. M., Kissane, D. W., Trauer, T., & Smith, G. C. (2005). Demoralization, anhedonia and grief in patients with severe physical illness. *World Psychiatry, 4*(2), 96–105.

Cole, E. R. (2009). Intersectionality and research in psychology. *American Psychologist, 64*(3), 170.

Crunkilton, D. D., & Rubins, V. D. (2009). Psychological distress in end-of-life care: A review of issues in assessment and treatment. *Journal of Social Work in End-of-Life & Palliative Care, 5*(1–2), 75–93.

Delgado-Guay, M., Parsons, H. A., Li, Z., Palmer, J. L., & Bruera, E. (2009). Symptom distress in advanced cancer patients with anxiety and depression in the palliative care setting. *Supportive Care in Cancer, 17*(5), 573–579.

Deshields, T., Tibbs, T., Fan, M. Y., & Taylor, M. (2006). Differences in patterns of depression after treatment for breast cancer. *Psycho-Oncology, 15*(5), 398–406.

Doka, K. J., & Martin, T. L. (2011). *Grieving beyond gender: Understanding the ways men and women mourn*. New York: Routledge.

Emlet, C. A., Tozay, S., & Raveis, V. H. (2010). I'm not going to die from the AIDS: Resilience in aging with HIV disease. *The Gerontologist, 51*(1), 101–111.

Feldman, D. B., Sorocco, K. H., & Bratkovich, K. L. (2014). Treatment of posttraumatic stress disorder at the end-of-life: Application of the stepwise psychosocial palliative care model. *Palliative & Supportive Care, 12*(3), 233–243.

Fineberg, I. C., & Bauer, A. (2011). Families and family conferencing. In T. Altilio & S. Otis-Green (Eds.), *Oxford textbook of palliative social work* (pp. 235–249). New York: Oxford University Press.

Ganz, P. A., Kwan, L., Stanton, A. L., Krupnick, J. L., Rowland, J. H., Meyerowitz, B. E., . . . Belin, T. R. (2004). Quality of life at the end of primary treatment of breast cancer: First results from the moving beyond cancer randomized trial. *Journal of the National Cancer Institute, 96*(5), 376–387.

Gerbino, S., & Raymer, M. (2011). Holding on and letting go: The red thread of adult bereavement. In T. Altilio and S. Otis-Green (Eds.), *Oxford textbook of palliative social work* (pp. 319–338). New York: Oxford University Press.

Gibbons, S., Murphy, D., & Joseph, S. (2011). Countertransference and positive growth in social workers. *Journal of Social Work Practice, 25*(1), 17–30.

Gould, N. (2016). *Mental health social work in context*. New York: Routledge.

Hall, C. (2014). Bereavement theory: Recent developments in our understanding of grief and bereavement. *Bereavement Care, 33*(1), 7–12.

Hardy, R., & Kell, C. (2009). Understanding and working with the concept of denial and its role as a coping strategy. *Nursing Times, 105*(32–33), 22–24.

Hare, D. L., Toukhsati, S. R., Johansson, P., & Jaarsma, T. (2014). Depression and cardiovascular disease: A clinical review. *European Heart Journal, 35*(21), 1365–1372.

Holland, J. C., Andersen, B., Breitbart, W. S., Compas, B., Dudley, M. M., Fleishman, S., . . . Hoofring, L. (2010). Distress management. *Journal of the National Comprehensive Cancer Network, 8*(4), 448–485.

Iglewicz, A., Morrison, K., Nelesen, R. A., Zhan, T., Iglewicz, B., Fairman, N., . . . Irwin, S. A. (2015). Ketamine for the treatment of depression in patients receiving hospice care: A retrospective medical record review of thirty-one cases. *Psychosomatics, 56*(4), 329–337.

Irwin, S. A., Pirrello, R. D., Hirst, J. M., Buckholz, G. T., & Ferris, F. D. (2013). Clarifying delirium management: Practical, evidenced-based, expert recommendations for clinical practice. *Journal of Palliative Medicine, 16*(4), 423–435.

Ivanko, B. (2011). Quality improvement and organizational change. In T. Altilio & S. Otis-Green (Eds.), *Oxford textbook of palliative social work* (pp. 745–752). New York: Oxford University Press.

Jacobsen, P. B., & Jim, H. S. (2008). Psychosocial interventions for anxiety and depression in adult cancer patients: Achievements and challenges. *CA: A Cancer Journal for Clinicians, 58*(4), 214–230.

Joubert, N., & Raeburn, J. (1998). Mental health promotion: People, power and passion. *International Journal of Mental Health Promotion, 1*(1), 15–22.

Kelly, B., McClement, S., & Chochinov, H. M. (2006). Measurement of psychological distress in palliative care. *Palliative Medicine, 20*(8), 779–789.

Luthar, S. S., & Cicchetti, D. (2000). The construct of resilience: Implications for interventions and social policies. *Development and Psychopathology, 12*(04), 857–885.

Mancini, A. D., Sinan, B., & Bonanno, G. A. (2015). Predictors of prolonged grief, resilience, and recovery among bereaved spouses. *Journal of Clinical Psychology, 71*(12), 1245–1258.

Munson, C. (2012). *Handbook of clinical social work supervision.* New York: Routledge.

National Association of Social Workers (NASW). (2008). *NASW code of ethics: Guide to the everyday professional conduct of social workers.* Washington, DC: NASW.

Neimeyer, R. A. (2012). *Techniques of grief therapy: Creative practices for counseling the bereaved.* New York: Routledge.

Novotney, A. (2010). Appreciating differences. *American Psychological Association, 41*(9), 44. Retrieved from www.apa.org/monitor/2010/10/differences.aspx.

Payne, A., Barry, S., Creedon, B., Stone, C., Sweeney, C., O'Brien, T., & O'Sullivan, K. (2007). Sensitivity and specificity of a two-question screening tool for depression in a specialist palliative care unit. *Palliative Medicine, 21*(3), 193–198.

Periyakoil, V. S., Kraemer, H. C., Noda, A., Moos, R., Hallenbeck, J., Webster, M., . . . Yesavage, J. A. (2005). The development and initial validation of the Terminally Ill Grief or Depression Scale (TIGDS). *International Journal of Methods in Psychiatric Research, 14*(4), 203–212.

Pessin, H., Rosenfeld, B., & Breitbart, W. (2002). Assessing psychological distress near the end of life. *American Behavioral Scientist, 46*(3), 357–372.

Plowden, K. O., Adams, L. T., & Wiley, D. (2016). Black and Blue: Depression and African American Men. *Archives of Psychiatric Nursing, 30*(5), 630–635.

Pollak, K. I., Childers, J. W., & Arnold, R. M. (2011). Applying motivational interviewing techniques to palliative care communication. *Journal of Palliative Medicine, 14*(5), 587–592.

Pollin, I., & Kanaan, S. B. (1995). *Medical crisis counseling: Short-term therapy for long-term illness*. New York: W. W. Norton.

Rabinowitz, T., & Peirson, R. (2006). Nothing is wrong, doctor: Understanding and managing denial in patients with cancer. *Cancer Investigation, 24*(1), 68–76.

Rodin, G., Lloyd, N., Katz, M., Green, E., Mackay, J. A., Wong, R. K., & Supportive Care Guidelines Group of Cancer Care Ontario Program in Evidence-Based Care. (2007). The treatment of depression in cancer patients: A systematic review. *Supportive Care in Cancer, 15*(2), 123–136.

Roeland, E., Mitchell, W., Elia, G., Thornberry, K., Herman, H., Cain, J., . . . Von Gunten, C. F. (2010). Symptom control in stem cell transplantation: A multidisciplinary palliative care team approach. Part 2: Psychosocial concerns. *The Journal of Supportive Oncology, 8*(4), 179–183.

Rosenstein, D. L. (2011). Depression and end-of-life care for patients with cancer. *Dialogues in Clinical Neuroscience, 13*(1), 101.

Sadock, B. J., Sadock, V. A., & Ruiz, P. (2015). *Kaplan and Sadock's synopsis of psychiatry: Behavioral sciences/clinical psychiatry* (11th ed.). Philadelphia: Wolters Kluwer.

Salander, P., & Windahl, G. (1999). Does "denial" really cover our everyday experiences in clinical oncology? A critical view from a psychoanalytic perspective on the use of "denial." *Psychology and Psychotherapy: Theory, Research and Practice, 72*(2), 267–279.

Saleebey, D. (2001). *Human behavior and social environments: A biopsychosocial approach*. New York: Columbia University Press.

Shear, M. K., Simon, N., Wall, M., Zisook, S., Neimeyer, R., Duan, N., . . . Gorscak, B. (2011). Complicated grief and related bereavement issues for DSM-5. *Depression and Anxiety, 28*(2), 103–117.

Stroebe, M. S., & Schut, H. (2001). Models of coping with bereavement: A review. In M. S. Stroebe, R. O. Hansson, W. Stroebe, & H. Schut (Eds.), *Handbook of bereavement research: Consequences, coping, and care* (pp. 375–403). Washington, DC: American Psychological Association.

Uher, R. (2014). Persistent depressive disorder, dysthymia, and chronic depression: Update on diagnosis, treatment. Retrieved from www.psychiatrictimes.com/special-reports/persistent-depressive-disorder-dysthymia-and-chronic-depression.

Warm, E., & Weissman, D. (2015). *Fast facts and concepts #7: Assessing depression in advanced cancer*. Retrieved from www.mypcnow.org/blank-hn0yj.

Yalom, I. D. (2008). Staring at the sun: Overcoming the terror of death. *The Humanistic Psychologist, 36*(3–4), 283.

Zabora, J. R. (2011). Screening, assessment, and a problem-solving intervention for distress. In T. Altilio & S. Otis-Green (Eds.), *Oxford textbook of palliative social work* (pp. 169–180). New York: Oxford University Press.

Social Aspects of Care

KARRA BIKSON ■

It really boils down to this: that all life is interrelated. We are all caught in an inescapable network of mutuality, tired into a single garment of destiny. Whatever affects one destiny, affects us all indirectly.

—MARTIN LUTHER KING, *Jr.*

INTRODUCTION

Palliative care provides essential advocacy for individuals and their families at some of the most critical junctures in their lives. It embodies the values of *dignity and worth of the person* and the ethical principle of *self-determination* (NASW, 2008). Saunders's (1978) *total pain* approach to palliative care incorporates a person-in-environment ecosystems perspective as it integrates the physical, emotional, social, and spiritual aspects of experience (Bronfenbrenner, 1979; Gitterman & Germain, 2008; Kondrat, 2008). Foundational to palliative care is a comprehensive interdisciplinary assessment identifying biopsychosocialspiritual needs, goals, and strengths in the context of life-threatening or serious illness (National Consensus Project, 2013). This assessment functions alone or in tandem with the care conference in creating an interdisciplinary care plan (National Quality Form, 2006). The thrust of palliative care remains the same across diagnoses and locations of care: to address pain and suffering using an interdisciplinary approach, maximizing effective communication and shared decision-making that is respectful of unique patient and family context.

An interdisciplinary team is at the core of palliative care, collaborating to assess and implement interventions to maximize well-being. Across health care settings, teams may evolve organically, occurring both formally and informally. A team at a dialysis center might include a medical director, nurse, and nephrology social worker. A team at a small skilled nursing facility might be the nurse manager and a health aide. Teams might have formal structure with established membership, policies, and roles, or may be more fluid, adding and subtracting members and expertise as the work with patients and families evolves and transitions occur.

Social workers are integral team members and are uniquely positioned by training and expertise to lead in the social aspects of care. Often providing the story of the patient, family, and their life outside of illness, social workers can inform the context for a socioculturally sensitive care plan. The expertise in communication and group work also creates a natural role as facilitators of family meetings or care conferences with patients, families, and other providers.

STANDARDS AND PRACTICES

As the field of palliative care has developed, so has the foundation for the social aspects of the illness experience, setting standards and preferred practices for social work assessment and intervention across settings. The National Association of Social Workers' *Standards for Social Work Practice in Health Care Settings* (NASW, 2016) provides a comprehensive overview of the required knowledge and skills for medical social work. Further, understanding the need for standards specific to palliative care, NASW also established *Standards for Palliative and End of Life Care* (2004), defining the knowledge and skills needed for working with patients and families "facing acute or long-term situations involving life-limiting illness, dying, death, grief, and bereavement" (p. 7). These ethical and practice standards buttress and inform the social work approach to patient- and family-centered care, blending both the primary and specialist perspectives.

Keeping in mind that employing palliative care principles can take a variety of forms, the following social aspects are considered through an interdisciplinary lens, illustrated by the National Consensus Project's *Clinical Practice Guidelines for Quality Palliative Care* (Domain 4, NCP, 2013) in Table 5.1.

Drawing upon these clinical guidelines, the National Quality Forum in their *National Framework and Preferred Practices for Palliative and Hospice Care* identified two preferred practices specific to the social aspects of palliative care, described in Table 5.2.

Table 5.1 SOCIAL ASPECTS OF PALLIATIVE CARE

Social aspects of care (Guideline 4.1)
The interdisciplinary team facilitates and enhances
• Patient-family understanding of, and coping with, illness and grief
• Support for patient-family decision-making
• Discussion of the patient's and family's goals for care
• Provision of emotional and social support
• Communication within the family and between patient-family and the interdisciplinary team
Person-centered interdisciplinary assessment (Guideline 4.2)
The interdisciplinary team assesses and documents
• Family structure and function: roles, communication, and decision-making patterns
• Strengths and vulnerabilities: resiliency; social and cultural support networks; effect of illness on intimacy and sexual expression; prior experiences with illness, disability, and loss; risk of abuse, neglect, or exploitation
• Changes in family members' schooling, employment, or vocational roles, recreational activities, and economic security
• Geographic location, living arrangements, and perceived suitability of the living environment
• Patient's and family's perceptions about caregiving needs, availability, and capacity
• Needs for adaptive equipment, home modifications, transportation
• Access to medications (prescription and over the counter) and nutritional products
• Need for and access to community resources, financial support, and respite
• Advance care planning and legal concerns

SOURCE: National Consensus Project (2013).

Table 5.2 PREFERRED PRACTICES

Care Conference (Preferred Practice 18)
• Conduct regular patient and family care conferences with physicians and other appropriate members of the interdisciplinary team to provide information, to discuss goals of care, disease prognosis, and advance care planning, and to offer support.
Social Care Plan (Preferred Practice 19)
• Develop and implement a comprehensive social care plan that addresses the social, practical, and legal needs of the patient and caregivers, including but not limited to relationships, communication, existing social and cultural networks, decision-making, work and school settings, finances, sexuality/intimacy, caregiver availability/stress, and access to medicines and equipment.

SOURCE: National Quality Forum (2006); © [2018] National Quality Forum.

ASSESSMENT TOOLS

The Social Work Assessment Tool (SWAT), developed by the Social Work Outcomes Task Force of the National Hospice and Palliative Care Organization, is an instrument covering psychosocialspiritual issues identified as essential areas of assessment (NHPCO, 2008). Elements of this tool highlight important components of the patient and family experience. SWAT is used to assess and document outcomes after each visit; patient and caregiver are scored separately. The areas of social assessment covered by SWAT are listed in Table 5.3. Validated in research conducted by Reese et al. (2006), this tool importantly allows for monitoring and documenting changes in well-being over time and can be used as an organizing framework for narrative charting.

Additionally, the PEACE Project Review of Clinical Instruments for Hospice and Palliative Care identified 39 tools found to demonstrate a strong evidence base and to be clinically useful for assessing multiple domains of palliative care (Hanson, Scheunemann, Zimmerman, Rokoske, & Schenck, 2010). Two of these focus specifically on social support and bereavement: The Duke-UNC Social Support Scale is an eight-item instrument that assesses functional social

Table 5.3 SOCIAL WORK ASSESSMENT TOOL (SWAT)

Assessment areas rated for both patient *and* primary caregiver:
1. End-of-life decisions consistent with their religious and cultural norms
2. Patient thoughts of suicide or wanting to hasten death
3. Anxiety about death
4. Preferences about environment (e.g., pets, own bed, etc.)
5. Social support
6. Financial resources
7. Safety issues
8. Comfort issues
9. Complicated anticipatory grief (e.g., guilt, depression, etc.)
10. Awareness of prognosis
11. Spirituality (e.g., higher purpose in life, sense of connection with all)
Scoring: 1 = Not well at all, 2 = Not too well, 3 = Neutral, 4 = Reasonably well, 5 = Extremely well

SOURCE: NHPCO (2008).

support for medical patients more broadly and can be used to plan for concrete aspects of care (Broadhead, Gehibach, DeGruy, & Kaplan, 1988). The Bereavement Risk Index (BRI) assesses eight areas of bereavement risk and can be used to plan supportive care for family members after a patient has died (Kristjanson, Cousins, Smith, & Lewin, 2005).

Taken together, these resources provide standards, practices, and tools for addressing the social domain of a patient and family in the context of serious illness across a variety of health care settings. Ideally a dynamic and iterative process, care plans change along with the trajectory of illness. Specifically, patient-family needs, goals, and strengths evolve over time, potentially impacted by changes in setting and providers, necessitating reassessment. Figure 5.1 illustrates the social aspects of palliative care and how they may be integrated into a holistic plan of care. The resource list included at the end of this chapter further delineates social needs linking to assessment and interventions, providing a sampling of internet sites useful for learning and care planning.

Active listening, to assess and reflect on the relevant elements of the social lives of patient and family, is a central social work skill. The person-in-environment perspective and attention to the social context of the patient-family system informs a plan to address biopsychosocialspiritual distress. It might be most important for the medical team to understand the meaning to family when a patient is no longer able to work and provide for the family, or they may be most impacted to hear of the anguish of isolation when important social activities or friendships are altered consequent to hospitalization. Appreciating the social layers to the patient-family system can enrich understanding about what matters to patients and families, and how their care can best align with their priorities.

SOCIAL ASSESSMENT

Social assessment focuses on understanding the patient's situation in her environment. This considers micro-level factors such as interpersonal relationships and family systems, environmental and cultural contexts, as well as practical aspects of patients and families' lives related to meso and macro social systems.

While standardized assessment such as SWAT (NHPCO, 2008) can provide a beginning, in situations of serious illness, social aspects cannot be evaluated separately from the physical, cultural, and intersectional contexts.

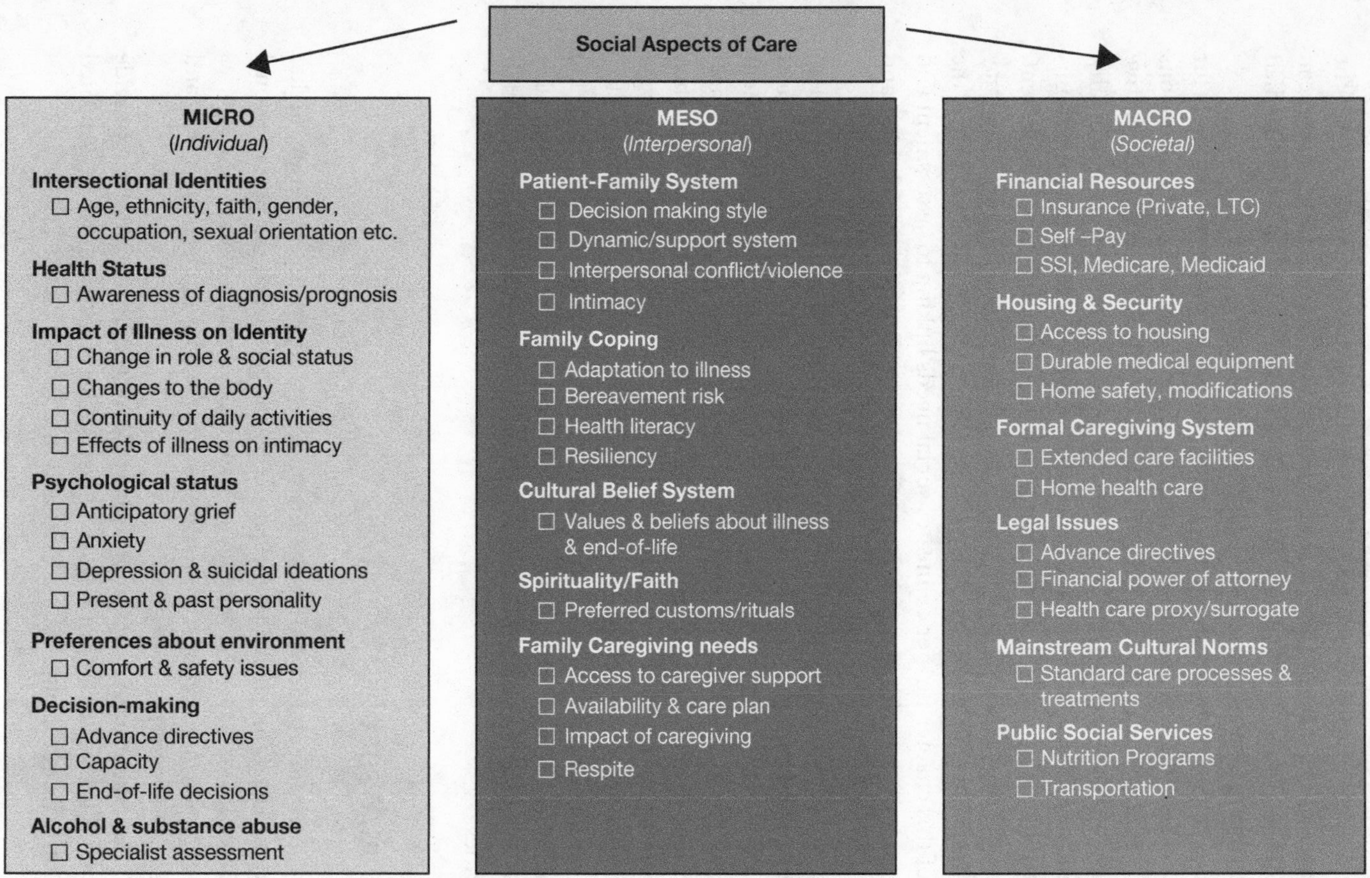

Social Aspects of Care

MICRO
(Individual)

Intersectional Identities
☐ Age, ethnicity, faith, gender, occupation, sexual orientation etc.

Health Status
☐ Awareness of diagnosis/prognosis

Impact of Illness on Identity
☐ Change in role & social status
☐ Changes to the body
☐ Continuity of daily activities
☐ Effects of illness on intimacy

Psychological status
☐ Anticipatory grief
☐ Anxiety
☐ Depression & suicidal ideations
☐ Present & past personality

Preferences about environment
☐ Comfort & safety issues

Decision-making
☐ Advance directives
☐ Capacity
☐ End-of-life decisions

Alcohol & substance abuse
☐ Specialist assessment

MESO
(Interpersonal)

Patient-Family System
☐ Decision making style
☐ Dynamic/support system
☐ Interpersonal conflict/violence
☐ Intimacy

Family Coping
☐ Adaptation to illness
☐ Bereavement risk
☐ Health literacy
☐ Resiliency

Cultural Belief System
☐ Values & beliefs about illness & end-of-life

Spirituality/Faith
☐ Preferred customs/rituals

Family Caregiving needs
☐ Access to caregiver support
☐ Availability & care plan
☐ Impact of caregiving
☐ Respite

MACRO
(Societal)

Financial Resources
☐ Insurance (Private, LTC)
☐ Self -Pay
☐ SSI, Medicare, Medicaid

Housing & Security
☐ Access to housing
☐ Durable medical equipment
☐ Home safety, modifications

Formal Caregiving System
☐ Extended care facilities
☐ Home health care

Legal Issues
☐ Advance directives
☐ Financial power of attorney
☐ Health care proxy/surrogate

Mainstream Cultural Norms
☐ Standard care processes & treatments

Public Social Services
☐ Nutrition Programs
☐ Transportation

Figure 5.1. Ecological model applied: Social aspects of care.

Along with assessment of patient-family understanding of illness comes the opportunity to explore how they are managing that illness and the consequent adaptations. Building relationships to encourage the patient-family system to teach clinicians about their coping styles, strengths, and resiliencies requires listening, observing, and reflecting. Understanding how the social roles and family system have been impacted by illness provides insight into styles of adaption and adjustment, as well as the losses, challenges, and stressors they may be experiencing. These insights bring meaning to evolving professional relationships that have the potential to elevate personhood and to honor unique family narratives. In the present, this can protect against depersonalization, and for the future, can inform how the illness is integrated into family legacy.

CULTURE

In all aspects of social care, cultural beliefs and backgrounds are essential components of assessment and intervention. Generally, medical care in the United States privileges a patient's informed consent. While this reflects the dominant cultural values of individualism and autonomy, informing someone about disease trajectory or imminent death may be contradictory to a patient and family's cultural beliefs and traditions (Samovar, Porter, McDaniel, & Roy, 2012). Determining what a patient and family understand, cognitively and emotionally, in their cultural frame of reference may be quite nuanced and complicated. In some instances, a well-intended offer to provide home care or referral to a skilled nursing facility may be perceived as an implicit criticism in cultures where the family naturally assumes or is expected to provide that care. These variations underscore the importance of starting where the patient and family are, and in providing opportunities, whether brief or extended, to inquire and listen. Attuned clinicians can learn about the patient-family system, their unique family culture, and the larger meso and macro contexts influencing their experience (See Chapter 7; "Cultural Aspects of Care").

Systems of power and privilege create bias, stereotypes, and assumptions, making it possible to misapply general understandings of cultural norms. For example, in Iranian communities, doctors and nurses may help to create and sustain a culture of nondisclosure of cancer diagnoses, a norm for most Iranian patients (Beyraghi, Mottaghipour, Mehraban, Eslamian, & Esfahani, 2011; Valizadeh et al., 2012). However, this is not universally applicable, and the literature demonstrates that some Iranian patients may prefer disclosure from their health care providers (Samimi Ardestani et al., 2015). As such, assumptions relying on general trends or a clinician's past experiences, rather than a unique assessment of the specific patient-family system, though well intentioned, may do harm. Moreover, as the following narrative demonstrates, different members of a given patient-family system may have conflicting inter- and intrapersonal needs, requiring responses that honor multiple and diverging value systems.

Mrs. Farahan

In working with a self-identified Persian family in their home, the social worker was greeted by three adult daughters who immediately asked to speak privately before meeting with their 89-year-old mother with end-stage cancer. The daughters were unanimous in their directive that there would be no disclosure to their mother that she was dying. They explained, in their culture, it would be unacceptable and a violation of their beliefs to share this information, as doing so would be an undue burden on their mother and might hasten their mother's death. They asked for a promise not to mention the words "death" or "dying." The social worker explored possible benefits and opportunities that might be created by a shared dialogue about the end of life; however, they remained firm in their position, which was respected to honor their familial and cultural norms. However, Mrs. Farahan requested to meet privately with the social worker. The daughters acquiesced, with assurances that death or dying would not be mentioned. During this private meeting, Mrs. Farahan explained that she knew she was dying but requested her daughters not be told. She stated this news would be too upsetting and she wanted to protect them, an aspect of her role as a mother that she wished to maintain. The social worker honored the requests from all the members of this patient-family system and respected their micro-culture of mutual pretense. Interventions focused on the sharing of memories, activities, thoughts, and emotions, validating relationship and informing legacy even though the words "death" and "dying" were never spoken.

INTERSECTIONALITY

Identity and positionality, or one's position in relation to others and society at large based on one's identity, comprise an intersection of many factors, including ability, age, class, culture, education, ethnicity, gender identity and expression, immigration status, language, race, religion, and sexual orientation. Patients and families bring intersectional identities—the combination of their lived experiences and positional reality—when they come into contact with providers who bring their own positionality. Exploring a patient and family's culture, as well as their intersectional identity and history, helps contextualize the social assessment and provide quality care tailored to the individual. For example, a patient's past experiences with the health care system, positive and negative, are important, as they may have resulted in feelings ranging from empowered and supported, to marginalized and misunderstood. These experiences may vary within one family system.

For some patients, access to care may have been limited, delayed, or denied; they may not have had any care providers from their own background; they may have experienced knowledge, language, and/or cultural barriers, resulting in confusions, substandard care, late diagnosis, and/or mistrust in health care (Marsiglia & Kulis, 2015). Honoring these experiences is to build the trust needed for effective communication and care delivery (Boucher, Raghavan, Smith, Arnold, & Johnson, 2016; Payne, 2016; Washington, Bickel-Swenson, & Stephens, 2008). Appreciating a patient's history may create space to explore issues of trust, willingness to engage, and receptiveness to recommendations of providers.

Awareness of the multilayered, nuanced experience of patients and families allows for advocacy within a medical system rooted in Western culture, which privileges a scientific approach informed heavily by autonomy. This affects patients and families from the micro to macro levels, as providers may not know how to engage with a style of decision-making that varies from the standard medical model. This cultural sensitivity informs a nuanced social assessment aimed at avoiding unnecessary frictions that may negatively affect clinical relationships, disrupt the equilibrium of a family during crises, or impede decision-making. Providers possessing self-awareness, humility, and curiosity might be better able to learn about patients and families, relying less on assumptions and stereotypes.

IDENTITY CONFLICT

A patient-family system may not be unified or of one point of view. There may be conflict or intergenerational differences, which may be tolerated or which may create internal divides that prevent patients and families from formulating a coherent narrative. Such situations require engaging, with consent, multiple members of the patient's family system differently. For example, among persons along the continuum of sexual identities, there may be a family of origin and community either unaware of, or in fact hostile to, the patient's chosen family system (Rawlings, 2012). An inability to integrate differing perspectives may create pressure to choose between groups of people and metaphorically deny aspects of identity. The following narrative illustrates patient and family subsystems who did not share the same positionality, creating ongoing conflict and choices, causing suffering for all involved.

Pam and Susan

Pam is a 35-year-old lesbian with pancreatic cancer who has been given a prognosis of weeks to months. Pam has been living with her partner Susan, and Susan's eight-year-old daughter, Samantha, for the last two years. Raised in an Evangelical Christian family, Pam was out about her sexuality to her parents, who never accepted what they considered her "lifestyle." Susan and Samantha would leave their home when Pam's parents visited. Pam's parents told her if she did not repent she would go to Hell and they would never be reunited in Heaven. The social worker in the outpatient oncology practice met with Pam, who was torn between the love and allegiances she felt to Susan and Samantha and to her parents. She had not renounced her faith and was fearful and unsure about what would happen in the afterlife. She was simultaneously afraid of further disappointing her parents and feeling profound guilt about the suffering she was causing Susan and Samantha.

Pam's parents were increasingly desperate to "save" their daughter and refused to meet with the social worker, feeling well supported by community clergy. Given the high bereavement risk, a referral was made for counseling services for Susan and Samantha to begin before Pam's death. The social worker met with Susan, who was overcome with complex feelings of longing, grief, guilt and anger with Pam and her parents, and worry about the pressures on her dying partner. Samantha appeared to be getting "lost" within this family system crisis, isolated and coping on her own, occupying her time with a mix of video games and drawing. With Susan's consent, the social worker met individually with Samantha, giving her the space to voice her perspectives, and share her understanding and questions through her drawings. Validating Samantha's expressed confusion supported her in a developmentally appropriate way (NHPCO, 2017). Samantha understood Pam was dying, and she felt left out and rejected. Samantha expressed a strong desire to escape the situation and to "get her mom back." In support of Susan's role as mother, education focused on how to listen and talk with Samantha and how to understand Samantha's possible reactions to separation, loss, illness, and dying. Ultimately the worry about redemption and the immediacy of death created an untenable dilemma for Pam, who came to the end of her life in the care of her parents, while Susan and Samantha were excluded. In the context of intractable family conflict, the social worker intervened to honor the individual and shared suffering and grief of Pam, Susan, and Samantha.

STRENGTHS-BASED ASSET MAPPING, RELATIONSHIPS, AND RESOURCES

Strengths-based asset mapping of relationships and resources, as defined by the patient-family system, provide an opportunity to begin to leverage existing social capital in service of the patient. Not only is this valuable for reducing stress on the social system, it empowers the patient and family to self-determine their care over time with as much integrity as possible. Mapping the family system and their community relationships and resources using an eco-map can be a useful technique, providing a clear depiction of the social assessment in one visual diagram (Hartman & Laird, 1983).

Family, friends, neighbors, religious organizations, clubs, and other community members can be identified as potential sources of support. A decision to access these resources for support may change the nature and balance of a patient's relationships with persons or organizations. Anticipatory guidance involves considering this dynamic and exploring its meaning so that a decision to engage these sources of support is an informed one. In assessing social networks, a patient may identify a friend or neighbor as a significant source of support, while indicating a relative as a source of stress. If a patient has attended a house of worship or community center historically and is no longer able to leave her residence, facilitating transportation and/or visits from this community can help maintain these connections. Identifying how existing relationships can provide emotional and social support, while assessing availability and appropriateness through discussion with patients and families, makes it possible to enlist and organize a schedule of volunteers to arrange visits, rituals, shopping, chores, transportation, and perhaps provide hands-on caregiving. For some, personal care is best provided by a professional rather than a friend or family member, and the iterative assessment of individual needs, values, and preferences is as essential here as in other aspects of care. When clinically appropriate, activating support may be preferable and also may conserve needed financial resources. The support system may not appear traditional; the patient might identify a best friend, a former spouse, a postal carrier, a Meals-on-Wheels delivery person, a doorman, a former coworker, or an apartment manager as persons they might identify as members of their support system.

A patient may have been providing support or direct care to family members, including children, and as illness progresses, these responsibilities may gradually become unsustainable. The patient may find this role of caring for others to be fulfilling, an important aspect of identity, and it can be delicate clinical work to balance the patient's changing abilities with the feasibility and safety of continuing and/or adapting these roles.

Recognizing that grief can often accompany the loss of role and one's own ability for self-care, honoring what is lost and what remains, is clinical work, as is creating a plan to delegate those responsibilities and to adapt the role to one of expert guide. Patients who are sole caregivers for a minor child or a disabled adult may need support and guidance as they consider the emotional and practical work of planning for adoption, guardianship, or conservatorship. At end of life, this issue may become emergent and a metaphor for a legacy reflecting a patient's caring and planning for someone who has become dependent on them.

PSYCHOEDUCATION

Psychoeducation and anticipatory guidance are interventions that focus on many aspects of palliative care, which may include disease-directed topics such as expected trajectory of illness and available treatment options, their benefits and burdens. These interventions range beyond the physical to exploring the needs of children and grandchildren who may be impacted by the illness of a significant person in their lives. At times the patients may choose or may not be well enough to participate in discussions and decision-making, and psychoeducation may be primarily within the family system or with the appointed health care agent. Patients may be able to give consent for meetings to be held with family, friends, or health care agent, with the agreement that there will be a report back with a summary of process and tentative plans. Whether this education is provided over time or in an emergent situation, the intent is to create an opportunity to prepare mentally, emotionally, and practically—modified by the emotional readiness of the patient and family. Being able to anticipate future circumstances can inform decision-making and maximize self-determination.

Asking the patient and family what *they* understand and observe will inform and guide the psycho-educational process. While the patient and family are considered the "unit of care," they are made up of subsystems and individuals, who may have very different understandings, perceptions, hopes, and opinions. The social worker may identify information gaps, stories, assumptions, and generalizations that have significance as providers listen for emotional context and address areas in need of clarification. This honed listening creates opportunities to facilitate shared understanding, validate unique perspectives, prioritize needs, and enhance the potential that care may move forward with consensus.

Making decisions, whether about treatments, finances, or future plans, is enhanced by understanding the medical condition in the context of a unique life. The Institute of Medicine (2004) defines health literacy as "the degree to which individuals have the capacity to obtain, process, and understand basic health information and services needed to make appropriate health decisions" (p. 32). Consequent to the emotional and cognitive challenges presented by an illness experience, translating medical terminology and jargon into clear, familiar language facilitates understanding. Sometimes patients may seem to understand, or may nod affirmatively because they are listening, not necessarily comprehending. This essential process of communication requires time and repetition to integrate cognitively and emotionally the meaning and significance of information provided.

When patients or families are non-English-speaking or bilingual, there is an added imperative to provide documents and information in the primary language. Using a professional medical interpreter has been shown to increase patient satisfaction, improve outcomes, and reduce adverse events (Juckett, 2014). If a patient and family insist on using a layperson as an interpreter for patients with limited English proficiency, it has to be done carefully and with the patient's consent (Ho, 2008). Family dynamics and linguistic skills can set the stage for misunderstanding and misinformation. Family members may not sufficiently understand the medical vocabulary in either language, and they are consenting to act as an interpreter without awareness of the words and content they will be asked to communicate. The clinician has no way of knowing if the information being relayed is correct, potentially creating significant misunderstanding and possibly issues of liability. As a member of the family system, a family interpreter may be afraid or reluctant to speak about specific topics with the patient or others, just as the patient may be reluctant to speak through her family member. Use of a professional interpreter or an interpretation phone service, and documents translated into the first language of the family, can help maintain the integrity of the communication. That said, family and friend interpreters may also be a great source of comfort for the patient, so these needs must be balanced on a case-by-case basis (Ho, 2008). Providing that source of comfort does not preclude having a professional interpreter present who can ensure the accuracy of interpretation. Hospitals, nursing homes, or other medical settings can be disorienting and frightening enough in one's own language or country; in a foreign language or place, it can be even more overwhelming and intimidating (See Chapter 7; "Cultural Aspects of Care").

Psycho-educational resources and materials in multiple languages can be used to assist patients and families as they integrate illness and make emotional and cognitive adaptations. Some members of the patient-family system may find them helpful; for some the suggestion of reading material normalizes their experience, but for others it may increase distress or be overwhelming. These psycho-educational tools can be integrated in a way that is consonant with the patient-family system and individual references.

CARE CONFERENCES

The care conference, sometimes called a family meeting, is a meeting between the patient-family and members of the patient's health care team, which may include multiple providers. A whole-person and family approach, at its best, brings together the key players of the health care team and the patient-family system as partners to plan and deliver care, an ideal that becomes most challenging when there are disagreements—often a point at which a palliative care consult is requested. Social work, through advocacy and mediation, can facilitate discussions where multiple perspectives are heard, working to integrate the personal into the medical. Maximizing patient and family voice may also involve arranging for an interpreter, a faith leader, or any other important participant to be present, reflecting the unique needs and constellation of each patient and family system.

Care conferences can be relatively time-consuming, and thus palliative care is sometimes described as a "high-talk, low-tech" service (Periyakoil & Von Gunten, 2007). The experience of being listened to can be rare in busy medical settings, yet it may be one of the most important interventions in the clinical toolbox. For the patient and family, this is their body, their family or friend, their illness, their crisis, possibly their end of life; the willingness of clinicians to join and be present with this experience is itself an important form of acknowledgment, support, and care. This kind of engagement, through active listening and reflecting, enables clinicians to better understand and respond to hopes and worries, while encouraging their own sense of connection and contribution to the overall well-being of patients and families, potentially increasing provider satisfaction.

A family care conference is a distinctive approach to care planning and positions providers to meet a wider range of patient and family concerns. The care conference provides team members with a more complete exposure to the patient-family system and helps them build rapport, as well as co-create and implement a responsive plan of care (Altilio, Otis-Green, & Dahlin, 2008; Baile et al., 2000; Joshi, 2013). The care conference, whatever the setting, is an opportunity for the patient-family system to be heard and validated by health care providers, to receive and share information, to explore current and future caregiving needs, and to clarify and express what is most important. These conversations may also provide a space for reflection and appreciation from patients and families and providers.

While the outcome of a care conference may be consensus, there are times when the decisions made by patients or family are contrary to patient's preexisting directives or the values and recommendations of the medical team. These decisions may range from treatment choices to truth telling to engagement of children in the illness experience. Iterative social assessment often discovers patient-family history, dynamics, and sociocultural belief systems, which anchor these decisions and consensus builds. Reflecting self-determination and a patient-family definition of quality of life, there may be ethical principles which infuse these difficult processes that complicate and warrant specialist consultation. (See Chapter 10; "Special Issues in Children and Older Adults".)

Conference Process

The process of the family meeting will vary, depending on the setting and other situational factors; however, in general the conferences follow a common approach, such as the six-step SPIKES protocol described in Table 5.4 (Baile et al., 2000).

Explaining the process and purpose of the care conference in advance prepares the patient-family system for what to expect, noting specific questions and concerns to make sure they are addressed. Provider pre-meetings offer an opportunity for clinicians to review unique interpretations of medical history, current condition, treatment options and outcomes and understandings of the patient-family context. Together, providers evolve a message that aims toward coherence across specialties and honors difference in opinions, ensuring that

Table 5.4 SPIKES Protocol

Step 1. Setting	Setting up the meeting in a private space, with significant others, making space to sit together, connect with each other, minimizing interruptions.
Step 2. Perception	Assessing the patient's perception of the situation, asking what she understands about her medical condition.
Step 3. Invitation	Obtaining the patient's invitation to be informed about her medical situation, & how she would like information to be disclosed.
Step 4. Knowledge	Giving knowledge & information to the patient in terms she understands.
Step 5. Emotion	Assessing the patient's emotions with empathic responses by observing behavioral cues & validating her feelings with compassion.
Step 6. Strategy & Summary	Strategy & summary of what the plan of care will be going forward.

SOURCE: Baile et al. (2000).

patients and families are given access to the spectrum of interpretation. During the meeting, social work interventions may include checking at various points with patient-family members to identify emotions, putting words to nonverbal communication, and creating opportunities for further clarification.

Care conferences may be emotional, and the needs of the patient and family, as well as the skill sets of different providers, influence the structure and process of the meeting. Social workers may stay after a meeting has officially ended to assist with pertinent cognitive, emotional, and relational processing and practical concerns. Critical decisions are presented, anticipated and/or made in care conferences, and the experience can be monumental, impacting the present as well as the future psychological well being of family members. Social workers possess the clinical acumen to access patient and family strengths and resources that serve to sustain and support.

In many settings, post-conference debriefing is a learning opportunity and occurs formally or informally. In addition to discussing what went well and what could be done differently in future meetings, providers can address next steps, including necessary follow-up. Debrief may also foster self-reflection and a time to honor feelings related to this particular patient and family.

EMOTIONAL AND SOCIAL SUPPORTS

The provision of emotional and social supports is an overarching aspect of the social care plan that is fundamental, whether the relationship is short or long term, begins at diagnosis, during the course of treatment, at the time of death, or after. Emotional support is at its core a *joining*, fostering a therapeutic relationship by engaging with what is seen and heard. Serious illness can be lonely; patients and families can feel isolated and alienated, an observation that invites inquiry and clinical curiosity. The social worker can mediate the fragmentation often found in health care by acting to promote non-abandonment, bridging gaps between care settings and providers, and honoring meaningful attachments that have evolved over time.

Attending to the social domain positions patients and families in time and developmental stage: Have they just retired, or are they displaced from their work life? Is there an upcoming family reunion, graduation, wedding? Identifying and understanding milestones highlights the meaning attributed to these events beyond illness and treatments. Timing medical interventions to allow for participation, whether in person or through the use of technology such as video call, may be important to the narrative of the family. This is an aspect of social care planning that can make a meaningful difference, informing legacy beyond the life of the patient.

FINANCES AND INSURANCE

For some, identity and self-worth can be closely linked with earning ability, work and career, and the ability to provide for themselves and others. A patient may fear becoming a financial burden on her family; a family may feel resentment in having to support a family member. The practical aspects of a plan of care cannot be separated from the clinical work of engaging the meaning of aspects such as the costs of care, relational impacts, sacrifices, and economic dependency. Exploring the psychosocial implications for members of the patient-family system is essential to maximizing adaptation during times of financial change, uncertainty, or insecurity.

Supporting a family in identifying entitlements, benefits, and resources, including income, disability payments, retirement, Social Security, Medicare, Medicaid, and other forms of insurance, may be one of the determining factors in creating or maintaining a plan of care. Finances have an impact on personal identity and family systems. Social workers can facilitate discussions about the impact of care needs on a patient's sense of self, family system, and fears about the future. Moreover, financial stress, when a family is already experiencing a serious illness, compounds the crisis and can have a lasting impact on well-being over time for all involved. Even with insurance, medical costs can bankrupt a family (Olen, 2017). Therefore, psychoeducation related to financial and legal planning has implications for the present and the future.

MEDICAL AND LEGAL DOCUMENTS

Completing, locating, or updating medical and legal documents, such as advance directives, is both a practical and clinical aspect, bridging domains of palliative care. Similar to finances and insurance, these documents may be laden with symbolic significance and meaning beyond the literal content and existence of the documents themselves. Declaring wishes and surrogates may bring into high relief family conflicts, existential questions, and the reality of possible incapacity and mortality (See Chapter 9; "Legal and Ethical Aspects of Care").

HOUSING

Housing is a primary human need. Illness and disease process may necessitate changes in living environment that can be fraught with emotional as well as practical challenges. Bringing medical equipment into the home—having to sleep in a hospital bed, no longer being able to sleep in one's own bed or with one's partner—can have deep emotional significance. It may disrupt the nature of home. Even when hidden or camouflaged, equipment may represent the loss of independence and change of physical space, as it has been known. Continuity of place, routines, familiar people, personal possessions, art, music, food, aromas, and pets can provide immeasurable comfort. Maximizing the ability of patients to remain in their own familiar surroundings might be a patient and family priority, explored through an assessment of values and wishes, and a valuable service to patient and family. For persons who have to move out of their home into a family member's or a care facility, all of these implications are magnified. Leaving one's home may be the most pivotal and devastating point in the progression of illness, and social support at this time cannot be underestimated. Creating a familiar environment, perhaps by bringing symbolic and treasured items, in a new location is one way to provide comfort at a time of loss and uncertainty.

CONCLUSION

The social domain of care encompasses a broad array of issues and practices that are distinct from, yet overlap and integrate with, the biological, psychological, and spiritual aspects of care. The social worker searches for "the story" that contextualizes and locates the patient in her social environment. Culturally responsive strengths-based advocacy lies at the core of the social assessment, care conferencing, and planning, so the interdisciplinary team, no matter how conceptualized, can provide the highest quality of care to maximize *self-determination, dignity, and worth of the person*. This work is at the heart of health social work no matter the setting or the disease and indispensable to patient-centered family-focused care.

LEARNING EXERCISE

1. Mrs. Kozak is a 79-year-old Polish-speaking, Catholic widow, mother of two sons and grandmother to five children who range in age from 4 to 19 years. She is admitted with failure to thrive, a broken hip, and pain from osteoarthritis. She has a primary care physician who speaks Polish and has cared for Mrs. Kozak for over 10 years. She has agreed to sub-acute rehabilitation and is preparing for transition to an extended care facility. As the social worker assisting with this transition, what aspects of Mrs. Kozak's story need to be incorporated

into the transition plan to enhance continuity and minimize the disruption of a change in setting and caregivers? What social aspects of her life are most important to maximizing her sense of self?

ACKNOWLEDGMENT

The author wishes to thank Vanessa Myrie for her immeasurable assistance.

RESOURCES: SOCIAL ASPECTS OF PALLIATIVE CARE

Organizations, Practice Standards and Guidelines:
CaringInfo: Advance care planning, caregiving, hospice, and palliative care, grief, and loss. www.caringinfo.org

National Hospice and Palliative Care Organization: Education, resources, advocacy about hospice and palliative care. www.nhpco.org/

National Consensus Project (NCP) for Quality Palliative Care: Clinical practice guidelines. www.nationalcoalitionhpc.org/ncp-guidelines-2013/

National Quality Forum: Preferred practices for hospice. www.qualityforum. org/Publications/2006/12/A_National_Framework_and_Preferred_Practices_for_Palliative_and_Hospice_Care_Quality.aspx

National Association of Social Work, Standards of Practice and Practice Guidelines: Practice standards for social work- health and palliative care. www.socialworkers.org/Practice/Practice-Standards-Guidelines

Children's Grief, Loss and Bereavement:
Children's Grief Education Association: www.childgrief.org/documents/HowtoHelp.pdf

Sesame Street in Communities: www.sesamestreetincommunities.org/topics/grief/

National Hospice and Palliative Care Association: www.caringinfo.org/files/public/brochures/child_cope_death.pdf

Tools and Protocols:
SPIKES: Six-step care conference protocol. theoncologist.alphamedpress.org/content/5/4/302.long

Duke-UNC Functional Social Support Questionnaire

(FSSQ): Social support assessment tool. adultmeducation.com/AssessmentTools_4.html

Modified version of the Bereavement Risk Index (BRI) for family or close friend: Bereavement. www.virtualhospice.ca/Assets/Bereavement%20Risk%20Assessment%20Feb%2014%202013_MUHC_20141107131931.pdf

RESOURCES: GUIDELINES FOR SPECIFIC SOCIAL NEEDS

Social Needs	Assessments	Interventions & Resources
Medical, legal, & financial documents	Locate & assess existing medical & legal documents. Evaluate need for legal documents or protections such as guardianship, protection of assets. Assess whether existing documents continue to reflect the patient's wishes.	Educate to enhance awareness of how & when documents are used. Provide access to medical & legal expertise to complete necessary documents. polst.org/programs-in-your-state/ www.agingwithdignity.org/ www.practicalbioethics.org/resources/caring-conversations
Housing & placement	Explore home setting: Is there a need for housing or shelter? Will housing physically accommodate patient's needs, including medical equipment? Explore meaning to patient & family of possible changes in home, need for home care, or transfer to a facility.	Interventions focused on emotional & cognitive responses to change in home, need for personal care, or place of care. www.medicare.gov/nursinghomecompare/Resources/Nursing-Home-Alternatives.html www.alz.org/care/alzheimers-dementia-residential-facilities.asp
Financial resources & insurances: Medicare, Medicaid, private insurances, self-pay	Assess emotional & cognitive responses to sharing financial information & applying for benefits. Evaluate financial resources, income & assets. Evaluate benefits, insurance, & benefit eligibility for financial & medical assistance.	Advocate or teach self-advocacy to secure benefits & needed cooperation from providers who need to complete forms. www.medicare.gov/ www.medicaid.gov/ www.ssa.gov/ www.va.gov/healthbenefits/

Social Needs	Assessments	Interventions & Resources
Safety	Evaluate physical safety of home environment & living situation. Assess for indication of abuse or neglect— physical, emotional, & fiduciary. Assess for substance abuse & medication diversion. Assess patient's emotional responses to questions related to safety.	Collaborate as needed to ensure safety: physical & occupational therapy, psychiatry, protective services, law enforcement. Preserve confidentiality & sustain relationships with patient & family as possible. www.assets.aarp.org/ external_sites/caregiving/ checklists/checklist_ homeSafety.html www.nchh.org/What-We-Do/Health-Hazards--Prevention--and-Solutions/ Injury-Prevention-and-Safety.aspx
Roles, identity, & status	Assess self-report of the meaning of illness in the context of identity, current roles, & status.	Life review, legacy work such as memory books with photos, collages, & stories, recordings, reminiscence, regardless of expected outcome of disease. www.growthhouse.org/ lifereview.html Normalize impacts of specific changes in function & role framing as one part of the patient's intersectional identity; consider what has changed & what has not. Support intersectional identity & personhood beyond illness.
Nature of illness, benefits & burdens of treatment options	Assess understanding of illness, disease trajectory, benefits & burdens of medical treatments. Collaborate with medical team to understand illness, expected trajectory & treatment outcomes.	Support collaboration in order to enhance shared understanding of medical issues & patient's hopes. Psycho-education, including written & Internet resources focused on illness trajectory, benefits & burdens of treatment, & decision making. www.caregiver.org/fact-sheets

Social Needs	Assessments	Interventions & Resources
Continuity of daily life, activities, hobbies, sources of meaning & pleasure.	Identify sources of joy, meaning, & connection such as music, nature, art, friends, family, & spiritual practice. Explore goals, hopes, & wishes.	Develop a plan to continue or modify meaningful activities; consider inviting members of spiritual community to visit patient at home. Plan for activities & events accommodating to abilities & within a context of uncertainty.
Family & social system(s)	Assess family & social systems as identified by patient, family, & social system. Identify existing alliances, discord, & fractured relationship within the social system.	Family meetings to enhance understanding, preparation, & adaptation to changes in family system. Acknowledge discord & alliances to identify opportunities for growth, change, or reconciliation created by illness experience. Support family & social network, respecting their unique & shared history. Use technology to maintain, enhance, or re-establish relationships. www.strongbonds.jss.org.au/workers/cultures/ecomaps.html www.template.net/design-templates/print/ecomap-template

Social Needs	Assessments	Interventions & Resources
Caregiving Activities of daily living (ADLs) Instrumental activities of daily living (IADLs)	Identify current caregiving needs for assistance with ADLs & IADLs. Explore patient's feelings & thoughts about depending on others. Identify needs that cannot be met by family & social network because of lack of availability or because caregiving tasks are emotionally incongruous with the nature of existing relationships. Assess resources for obtaining additional care (private or public insurances, private pay); placement outside of the home. Work with medical team to determine likely trajectory of illness & potential for increasing needs.	Work with patient, family, social network, & community agencies to develop a plan to provide this care for each need identified. Consider a written plan with a time schedule assigning tasks, providing contact information for each caregiver, and back-up or emergency plans. Work with patient and family to locate and learn how to interview nonfamily caregivers. Explore emotional and cognitive response to need for additional caregiving and possible introduction of paid caregivers into the family system. www.caregiver.org/

REFERENCES

Altilio, T., Otis-Green, S., & Dahlin, C. M. (2008). Applying the national quality forum preferred practices for palliative and hospice care: A social work perspective. *Journal of Social Work in End-of-Life & Palliative Care, 4*(1), 3–16.

Baile, W. F., Buckman, R., Lenzi, R., Glober, G., Beale, E. A., & Kudelka, A. P. (2000). SPIKES—A six-step protocol for delivering bad news: Application to the patient with cancer. *Oncologist, 5*(4), 302–311.

Beyraghi, N., Mottaghipour, Y., Mehraban, A., Eslamian, E., & Esfahani, F. (2011). Disclosure of cancer information in Iran: A perspective of patients, family members, and health professionals. *Iranian Journal of Cancer Prevention, 4*(3), 130–134.

Boucher, N. A., Raghavan, M., Smith, A., Arnold, R., & Johnson, K. S. (2016). Palliative care in the African American community #204. *Journal of Palliative Medicine, 19*(2), 228–230.

Broadhead, W. E., Gehibach, S. H., DeGruy, F. V., & Kaplan, B. H. (1988). The Duke-UNC functional social support questionnaire: Measurement of social support in family medicine patients. *Medical Care, 26*, 709–723.

Bronfenbrenner, U. (1979). *The ecology of human development: Experiments by nature and design.* Cambridge, MA: Harvard University Press.

Gitterman, A., & Germain, C. (2008). Ecological framework. In E. L Davis & T. Mazrahi (Eds.), *Encyclopedia of social work* (pp. 97–102). New York: Oxford University Press.

Hanson, L. C., Scheunemann, L. P., Zimmerman, S., Rokoske, F. S., & Schenck, A. P. (2010). The PEACE project review of clinical instruments for hospice and palliative care. *Journal of Palliative Medicine, 13*(10), 1253–1260.

Hartman, A., & Laird, J. (1983). *Family-centered social work practice.* New York: Free Press.

Ho, A. (2008). Using family members as interpreters in the clinical setting. *The Journal of Clinical Ethics, 19*, 223–233.

Institute of Medicine. (2004). *Health literacy: A prescription to end confusion.* Washington, DC: The National Academies Press.

Joshi, R. (2013). Family meetings: An essential component of comprehensive palliative care. *Canadian Family Physician, 59*(6), 637–639.

Juckett, G., & Unger, K. (2014). Appropriate use of medical interpreters. *American Family Physician, 90*(7), 476–480.

Kondrat, M. (2008). Person-in-environment. In E. L Davis & T. Mazrahi (Eds.), *Encyclopedia of social work* (pp. 348–354). New York: Oxford University Press.

Kristjanson L. J., Cousins K., Smith J., & Lewin G. (2005). Evaluation of the Bereavement Risk Index (BRI): A community hospice care protocol. *International Journal of Palliative Nursing, 11*, 610–618.

Marsiglia, F. F., & Kulis, S. (2015). *Diversity, oppression and change: Culturally grounded social work.* Chicago: Lyseum Books.

National Association of Social Workers (NASW). (2004). *Standards for palliative and end of life care* [Brochure]. Washington, DC: NASW Press.

National Association of Social Workers (NASW). (2008). *Code of ethics of the National Association of Social Workers.* Washington, DC: NASW Press.

National Association of Social Workers (NASW). (2016). *Standards for social work practice in health care settings* [Brochure]. Washington, DC: NASW Press.

National Consensus Project for Quality Palliative Care (NCP). (2013). *Clinical practice guidelines for quality palliative care,* 3rd ed. Pittsburgh, PA: NCP.

National Hospice and Palliative Care Organization (NHPCO), Caring Info. (2017). *Helping children cope with death of a loved one.* Alexandria, VA: NHPCO.

National Hospice and Palliative Care Organization (NHPCO), Social Work Outcomes Task Force. (2008). *Social Work Assessment Tool (SWAT): Guidelines for use and completion.* Alexandria, VA: NHPCO.

National Quality Forum (NQF). (2006). *A National framework and preferred practices for palliative and hospice care quality.* Washington, DC: NQF.

Olen, H. (2017). Even with insurance, Americans can't afford their medical bills. *The Atlantic.* Retrieved from www.theatlantic.com/business/archive/2017/06/medical-bills/530679/.

Payne, R. (2016). Racially associated disparities in hospice and palliative care access: Acknowledging the facts while addressing opportunities to improve. *Journal of Palliative Medicine, 19*(2), 131–133.

Periyakoil, V. S., & Von Gunten, C. (2007). Mainstreaming palliative care. *Journal of Palliative Medicine, 10*(1), 40–42.

Rawlings, D. (2012). End-of-life care considerations for gay, lesbian, bisexual, and transgender individuals. *International Journal of Palliative Nursing, 18*(1), 29–34.

Reese, D., Raymer, M., Orloff, S., Gerbino, S., Valade, R., Dawson, S., . . . Huber, R. (2006). The Social Work Assessment Tool (SWAT). *Journal of Social Work in End-of-Life & Palliative Care, 2*(2), 65–95.

Samimi Ardestani, S. M., Faridhosseini, F., Shirk Hani, F., Karamad, A., Farid, L., Fayyazi Bordbar, M. R., & Motlagh, A. (2015). Do cancer patients prefer to know the diagnosis? A descriptive study among Iranian patients. *Iranian Journal of Psychiatry and Behavioral Sciences, 9*(4), e1792:1–7.

Samovar, L. A., Porter, R. E., McDaniel, E. R., & Roy, C. S. (2012). *Communication between cultures*, 8th ed. Boston: Wadsworth/Cengage Learning.

Saunders, C. M. (1978). *The management of terminal malignant disease*. London: Edward Arnold.

Valizadeh, L., Zamanzadeh, V., Rahmani, A., Howard, F., Nikanfar, A. R., & Ferguson, C. (2012). Cancer disclosure: Experiences of Iranian cancer patients. *Nursing & Health Sciences, 14*(2), 250–256.

Washington, K. T., Bickel-Swenson, D., & Stephens, N. (2008). Barriers to hospice use among African Americans: A systematic review. *Health & Social Work, 33*(4), 267–274.

Spiritual, Religious, and Existential Dimensions of Care

**DANA RIBEIRO MILLER, MELISSA STEWART,
AND BRIDGET SUMSER** ■

When people share a memory of some small gesture that healed them, it is always from someone who listened, someone who was present, someone who simply saw them as they were.

—WAYNE MULLER

Meaning can be found in life literally up to the last moment, up to the last breath, in the face of death.

—VIKTOR FRANKL

INTRODUCTION: SPIRITUAL CARE IS ESSENTIAL TO HEALTH CARE

Spirituality may be understood as an individual's belief system, informing how she understands life. Spirituality is a universal human experience that responds to the questions that many people ask themselves at one time or another: "Where do I come from?" "Why am I here?" and "With whom do I belong?" (De Jager Meezenbroek et al., 2012). Belief systems provide the ground, structure, and landscape of each person's reality and relationships, which support necessary adaptations, and inform the purpose of an individual's life. The meaning ascribed to life events, arising from values, beliefs, and assumptions, drives adjustment to new ideas and information throughout life. Spirituality considers an individual's sense of connectedness: with oneself, with others, with nature, and with the transcendent (De Jager Meezenbroek et al., 2012). Conceptualized as the framework through which people view, engage in, and experience their lives, spiritual beliefs are a source of meaning and strength, and are often at the core of healthy coping.

This chapter will discuss spirituality, including religious expression or affiliation, and will explore how social workers can integrate this information in practice, informing whole-person care and family assessment and intervention. By listening for patients' beliefs about health and illness with spiritual attunement, clinicians engage in the work of spiritual care in a meaningful way, while enriching the value, depth, and sustainability of clinical practice. Finally, by exploring how clinicians frame their work with patients, through discussion of personal and professional self-awareness, this chapter aims to honor the experience of the clinician as central to providing optimal patient care that is spiritually sensitive.

SPIRITUALITY: UNIQUE AND EVOLVING

The individual experiences and interpretations of spirituality often evolve over time as a life unfolds. Spirituality in theory and practice manifests itself differently for each unique person. To provide spiritually sensitive care is to delve into the realm of the inner life, for this singular person, at this singular time, with respect, compassion, and intentionality (Nelson-Becker, Nakashima, & Canda, 2006).

When diagnosed with a serious illness, the experience of self and the rules that have guided one's life change. The road forward will likely include periods of instability and a need to recognize and integrate a "new normal" (Tako, 2017). This requires adjustment to an altered body, an evolving sense of self and identity, as well as changing interpersonal roles: socially, professionally, and familially. This evolution can be understood as spiritual, as it is often navigated and expressed through systems of values and beliefs, the ways in which a person makes sense of the world, and her experiences in it.

During serious illness, some of the changes may be obvious and easily recognized, while others may be personal, internal, and harder for others to identify. A person's spiritual beliefs, for example, may be strengthened or challenged by illness. This process may be visible, as evidenced in outward expression, such as participation in religious ritual, or it may be invisible and private, known only to the individual. For example, how one relates to the sacred or divine, whether one believes in a particular God or deity or universal energy, may involve a process of discernment that is private and not shared aloud with others.

Becoming seriously ill may cause a crisis of identity, triggered or accompanied by lost or changed meaning, if a previously held belief system is threatened or no longer makes sense in new circumstances. Illness may also serve as a catalyst to reaffirm beliefs, or encourage psychospiritual evolution and exploration. Either path may involve a continuum of emotions that range from anger to sadness and despair to a place of equanimity, well-being, and joy. Social workers have the opportunity to affirm the essential place of these processes in the illness experience of patients and families.

Clinical social work with patients and families is tailored to the setting of care. The social work role looks different depending on the culture of the organization and often the nature of the setting (i.e., in an ambulatory care center, emergency department, skilled nursing facility, or inpatient hospice). As patients and families negotiate different environments, they interact with clinical staff working with various implicit and explicit expectations about their role regarding spiritual care. While the capacity of any one social worker to respond to spiritual needs varies, basic skills in spiritual assessment and intervention promote person-centered care. Spiritually sensitive care can enhance patient and family well-being and can strengthen and support inherent resilience. Attending to patient's spirituality, belief systems, and values can provide important context for navigating medical decision-making and care planning (Puchalski et al., 2009; Puchalski, 2013).

No matter the setting, the ecological lens helps to provide perspective on the role of spirituality and religion in patient care and experience on the micro, meso, and macro levels. It is often necessary to focus on the most immediate issues such as how a patient understands and adjusts to a new diagnosis. However, it is beneficial to consider how community and systems support and honor this aspect of experience within the health care system as illness proceeds and patients' needs change over time. On an institutional level, are patient's values identified and documented? Is this prioritized? Are there opportunities to practice faith traditions and rituals, such as attending chapel or joining a prayer group? Awareness of multilayered realities within varying health care systems allows social workers to provide care that may transcend single encounters, influencing patient well-being and encouraging spiritual support across community and institutional settings.

Spirituality and religion are often used interchangeably; however, there are important differences between the two concepts, as identified in Box 6.1. As not all patients will identify with being spiritual or religious, it is important to think beyond these categories. Spirituality is a broader concept than religion, which refers to a particular faith tradition and practices that are often expressed in

Box 6.1

UNDERSTANDING SPIRITUALITY AND RELIGION

Spirituality: ". . . the aspect of humanity that refers to the way individuals seek and express meaning and purpose and the way they experience their connectedness to the moment, to self, to others, to nature and to the significant or sacred" (Puchalski et al., 2009).

Religion: "set of texts, practices, and beliefs about the transcendent (divine), shared by a particular community; religion refers to a coherent set of beliefs, practices, knowledge, rituals, etc., for fostering a sense of connection and meaning" (Canda & Furman, 2009).

community. Spirituality, on the other hand, is a personal experience. Spirituality is the way an individual understands her place and purpose in the world and guides how value is attributed to life experiences. Spiritually sensitive social work practice is a strengths-based approach, which includes respect, unconditional positive regard, openness, and empathy. It helps social workers engage patients in discussion about their distinct spiritual perspectives and how they may influence their experience of serious illness (Nelson-Becker et al., 2006). Spirituality can include the philosophical, ethical/moral, and existential underpinnings of one's belief system. For example, a young woman who does not identify as religious was recently diagnosed with cervical cancer. She avoids speaking the word "cancer." She spends time every day imagining herself as healthy and disease-free, believing she can influence the outcome of her treatment and therefore her future through regular visualization exercises. By learning more about how she is making sense of her diagnosis and treatment, the social worker is able to support her intrinsic strength and promote time without interruption for her spiritual practice. The social worker also helps other providers understand why the patient does not speak of cancer in an effort to increase empathetic discussion that provides information in a way she can hear. Religion is an aspect of spirituality, or a specific expression of one's spiritual life that may be formalized and shared with others. Religious practice can connect participants with their understanding of the sacred and the world at large, with their immediate community, and history, traditions, and rituals familiar not only to themselves and their families, but also to "strangers" around the globe who may similarly identify with, and belong to, the same religious group.

Social workers may find it useful to review the 11 spiritual domains proposed by Nelson-Becker, Nakashima, and Canda (2006), and listed in Table 6.1, both

Table 6.1 Domains of Spirituality

1. Spiritual affiliation	1. Group/s
2. Spiritual beliefs	2. Perspectives & ideas
3. Spiritual behavior	3. Practices/actions
4. Emotional qualities of spirituality	4. Positive or negative feelings associated with the preceding
5. Values	5. Guiding moral principles
6. Spiritual experiences	6. Private or shared transcendent experience shaping sacred meanings including both ordinary & altered states of consciousness
7. Spiritual history	7. Developmental trajectory; includes gradual change & pivotal points involving crisis or life-enhancement
8. Therapeutic change factors	8. Unique spiritually focused strengths & environmental resources available for healing, growth, improvement of spiritual well-being
9. Social support	9. Assistance & support from others who promote coping/well-being
10. Spiritual well-being	10. Subjective sense of happiness/ satisfaction related to spirituality
11. Extrinsic/intrinsic spiritual focus	11. Extrinsic spiritual identity tied to group membership/conformity; or intrinsic identity, more flexible & relatively self-determined

SOURCE: Nelson-Becker, Nakashima & Canda (2006).

to understand their own spiritual development and to become familiar with the words and ideas that serve to open rich and meaningful dialogue with patients.

SPIRITUALITY AND SOCIAL WORK

In health care, social workers are in an excellent position to identify and support the values and beliefs that comprise the spiritual fabric of patient and family lives. It is common for patients and families to discuss emotional worries related to serious illness and end of life with the social worker before they are ready to talk with their physicians about prognosis (Stewart, 2014). Similarly, some patients or family members may be more comfortable raising questions about spiritual strengths and/or doubts with someone who is not religiously affiliated (Hodge, 2006). The social worker may provide a neutral sounding board during illness, promoting the integration of their evolving illness and identity in the world (Stewart, 2014).

Following the thread of spirituality often leads to identifying sources of strength and resilience that can be an invaluable resource as one lives with illness. The social worker can help a patient identify, build, and expand a reservoir of coping strategies. This can be both a psychoeducational and a learning opportunity for the patient and family, who have not explored these themes previously, or have used them explicitly to enhance adjustment and coping in other aspects of their lives.

Through spiritual exploration, a patient may highlight the importance of connection, identifying new or old ways to engage with the self, the family, community, pets, nature, or a Higher Power or Divine Source. Conversely, physical aspects of religious engagement, such as attending mass, temple, or daily prayer at a mosque, are often not possible when one is seriously ill, potentially removing one from both a source of spiritual sustenance and social support. The social worker can help identify these spiritual resources and obstacles to patient participation and can work to restore connections by arranging visits from community clergy, supportive spiritual friends, or the health care chaplain.

Spirituality and religion have a symbiotic relationship to culture. These domains are often overlapping, and at times, are impossible to separate. Specifically, organized religion can provide transmission of cultural identity across generations, creating community and fostering connection, therefore shaping relationships and social roles (See Chapter 7; "Cultural Aspects of Care"). These values and spiritual beliefs are translated through everyday activities and routines, choice of dress, food, and styles of communication, relating to others, meaning-making, and decision-making. Learning to articulate, centralize, and integrate belief systems into the setting of care promotes curiosity, humility, and shared human experience, creating relational opportunities for understanding and connection. This can increase patient and family satisfaction, and ensure culturally and spiritually congruent care, while reducing distress and frustration on behalf of providers (National Association of Social Workers, 2015).

ROLE OF SPIRITUALITY AND RELIGION IN INTERSECTIONAL IDENTITY

Spirituality and religion are components of intersectional identity (race, class, ethnicity, education level, gender, gender identity, sexuality, nationality, language) and inform experiences of power, privilege, and oppression. The clinical lens must consider the impact of systems of oppression, power, and dominant culture in order to best support experience over time, and to understand and meet patient needs. Health care providers may make assumptions or underestimate experiences of marginalization central to many patients and families on the micro, meso, and macro levels.

It is not hard to imagine that a cis-gendered, white, Christian woman may have a different experience of the health care system than a same-gender-loving, black, Muslim man. Identifying and supporting the role of identity, while acknowledging the realities and impact of power and privilege, are not aimed at qualifying some experiences as better or worse. These are cues for exploration, with the goal of addressing systemic obstacles, and possible injustice, which may be as evident as not having access to a prayer rug during Ramadan or being provided privacy during prayer or meditation.

Another example is Julia, a 54-year-old primarily Spanish-speaking Latina woman, a Jehovah's Witness, who arrives in the emergency department describing overwhelming fatigue. Recently diagnosed with localized colon cancer, she has not begun any chemotherapy or radiation, as she is currently in discussion with her community's clergy regarding how to best move forward with her treatment plan. After labs are drawn, it is clear she is severely anemic, likely from her cancer. The doctors recommend a blood transfusion. While Jossetti, a Spanish interpreter, is present, providers feel that cultural and spiritual nuances are lost, as long periods of discussion between Julia and Jossetti result in a short summary for providers. The health care team is surprised, and extremely uncomfortable, when Julia refuses the blood transfusion.

From their perspective, it seems like a relatively benign intervention, with low risk and much benefit, and does not rise to the level of the very serious religious struggle it represents for Julia. They wonder about Julia's capacity and request the social worker assess and "help the patient accept the necessary interventions". The social worker's intervention focuses on understanding the religious root of this decision and verifying that Julia fully comprehends the choice, appreciates the consequences, and confirms that this remains her choice. When the team learns that Julia's faith deems blood transfusions unacceptable due to the Jehovah Witness interpretation of religious scripture, they struggle to accept her decision and miss opportunities to think creatively about her care. They expect her health to decline without the support of blood products, feel helpless to intervene, and, consequently, relationships suffer. Julia feels isolated and misunderstood.

To better understand the role of power in regard to Julia's experience, it is important to consider the religious demographics of the United States. Christianity sits at the center of the power structure in the United States, as approximately 70% of the population identifies as Christian, 40% of Christians are Protestant, and .08% of the population identifies as Jehovah's Witness (Pew Research Center, 2015). While it is a sect of Christianity, it is often misunderstood. Consequently, it would be uncommon for health care providers to assume that a patient was Jehovah's Witness and by default they would offer medical interventions from the perspective of the scientific, medical model.

On the micro level, the influence of Julia's spiritual and religious background affects her health care decisions and potential medical outcome. On the meso level, the doctrine of her faith is held and reinforced by her community, and there is no space for flexibility of interpretation within that space. Choosing blood transfusions creates a risk she will be isolated, lose the support of her community, and destabilize the parts of her identity rooted in her religious beliefs. By choosing to receive blood products, she may feel she is threatening her relationship with God. On the macro level, she is receiving care from a health care system that does not generally understand her belief system and as such has little to offer in terms of respectful alternatives. The primary medical ethos assuming a focus on extending life makes it difficult for staff to understand individual beliefs that could threaten safety or result in a choice to limit life expectancy. A commitment to do no harm, correlated with a moral drive to preserve life, sits in tension with Julia's choice to decline an intervention that could extend her life and allow her to pursue treatment for a curable condition. Her refusal to accept blood products potentially challenges a deeply ingrained code of ethics for physicians.

Not every Jehovah's Witness patient would make the same choice as Julia. Social workers who "meet patients where they are" accompany them, assess, and intervene along an evolving continuum of illness and related decision-making. Skillful and spiritually sensitive intervention might influence the outcome and the same story could evolve in many different directions. The social worker's assessment may have discovered that Julia wanted to extend her life by accepting blood products and has done the profound work of reflecting on the potential consequences and exploring alternatives. Her need is for support from the social worker to feel safe to do so, in light of her life and her religious community, and to stand by that choice. In addition, if blood products were indeed not in alignment with Julia's preferences, some hospitals now offer bloodless treatment options for Jehovah's Witnesses. The social worker, aware of such resources, may suggest consideration of a transfer to a hospital better able to care for Julia.

INFLUENCE ON MEDICAL DECISION-MAKING

Understanding spirituality as a layer of culture, it becomes clear that this may directly impact how patients and families approach medical decision-making and identify what is most important to them. Spiritual beliefs are linked with hopes and worries. Spiritual beliefs and themes are shared both explicitly and implicitly in discussions with health care providers. When a decision needs to be made regarding treatment and future care plans, meaning-making intersects directly with the medical model and meso and macro systems influencing care.

Social workers, listening with a sense of spiritual attunement, remind interprofessional providers of the significance of the patient and family's beliefs and, in collaboration with chaplaincy colleagues, can help facilitate a deeper understanding between them. The idiosyncratic and subjective nature of spiritual and/or religious belief may sometimes lead to a rift in understanding due to assumptions about what is clear and obvious to some, such as when families wish to "wait for a sign" (from God, the universe, or their intuition) before allowing the initiation or withdrawal of a medical intervention. Patients and families may need assistance to help them find ways to express themselves in language that their health care providers understand. Similarly, providers sometimes need interpretation of a patient's beliefs, provided by social worker or chaplain, which invites looking beyond the medical parameters and encourages seeing persons and families in their wholeness.

Often, in conversations about goals of care, the social worker may sense that there is an unspoken current affecting the decision-making process. There may be roadblocks that seem to arise out of nowhere that prevent the patient and family from engaging in effective discussion about a proposed medical intervention. For example, medical providers recommend a morphine infusion to help alleviate pain. The social worker notices discomfort in family members and, knowing their commitment to religious observation of prayer and ritual, inquires about hopes and worries as end of life approaches. Some may worry about loss of the ability to participate in prayer and ritual; others may worry about hastening death, and need reassurance and further explanation of the intent of medical interventions and specific medicines.

Being able to notice and explore spiritual cues in conversation may help the medical team reach a better understanding of the patient and family, which will lead to care plans that are congruent with identity and values. Social workers can play a valuable role in helping to navigate these conversations. For example, a doctor who predicts a time frame within which death is expected may be heard as insensitive to beliefs about the power of words and/or may be viewed as attempting to usurp the will of God. Being aware of patients and families' spiritual parameters can help guide interprofessional colleagues to frame a conversation about prognosis in a way that is met with receptivity rather than resistance.

SCREENING AND ASSESSMENT

Many social workers feel unprepared to ask about a patient's spiritual life. The tenets of palliative care and the congruence between social work and comprehensive biopsychosocial assessment, including spirituality, honor patients and families' spiritual health and well-being as central goals in the care of people living with serious illness. Practitioners inform the process of clinical assessment by starting where the patient and family are. Social workers are encouraged to listen with openness and humility and to engage in conversations with patients about what is most meaningful and valuable to them, particularly during times of personal crisis and challenge. A comprehensive assessment process serves to provide a deeper understanding of the emotional, existential, intellectual, and spiritual needs of patients and families.

A spiritual assessment process is iterative as evolving therapeutic relationships mature and may be understood as a supportive and affirming intervention in and of itself. How questions are phrased, and then explored, can convey the social worker's stance of acceptance, respect, and commitment. Initial assessment can include screening for immediate spiritual strengths, resources, and/or distress. Exploring if and how patients, their family and friends experience a spiritual connection can be a fruitful and meaningful place to begin a dialogue about spirituality. How their faith, beliefs, and values help to make meaning of life events is a clinical landscape that provides the content and context for an ongoing therapeutic relationship.

When counseling patients and families, there are spiritual themes that are likely to arise. It is helpful to recognize the significant overlap of spiritual themes with emotional, existential, humanistic, and/or interpersonal ideas. Counseling with a social worker provides a safe space for patients and families to wonder, explore, and share an ever-changing understanding of their life, if they desire. Common spiritual themes to listen for may include, but are not limited to, sources of joy and contentment, hopes and wishes, fears and anxiety, pain and suffering, the hope for miracles, need for control, acceptance and/or spiritual surrender, consideration of one's own mortality, previous experience with death and dying, thoughts of the afterlife, regret, punishment, forgiveness, gratitude, pride, ritual, and prayer (Stewart, 2014).

In addition to words spoken and silences observed, there is much to be learned by looking around the physical space that patients occupy and have claimed as their own within a health care setting, temporarily or permanently. Items present are often chosen with great care and provide an opportunity to explore personal significance. Are there rosary beads and Bibles from home on the nightstand? Have family members brought in pictures of healing deities or revered religious figures to fasten to the pillowcase? Are clergy or members of a religious or spiritual community visiting the patient? Is there a prayer blanket or intention shawl on the bed? Does the patient have tattoos? Do they hold meaning or spiritual significance? These visual clues, in plain sight, may provide invaluable insight into patients' private and historical world, offering an opportunity to recognize and inquire about what is true for them.

Inadvertent misunderstanding, making assumptions about or disrupting patient beliefs, can lead to a breakdown in communication (Bowman, 2016). For example, a patient may identify as Hindu, but may have spiritual beliefs, values, and mores ideologically different from that identity. Or, a patient may be a member of a Catholic church, but also incorporate aspects of Santeria. Further, many patients are in interfaith couples/families where beliefs, traditions, and practices have been blended, eliminated, and/or expanded to accommodate their unique spiritual needs as an evolving family. As with many erroneous assumptions, presuming that a clinician's religious identity is identical to that of a patient or family member may lead to errors and omissions in assessment and intervention. Being able to separate personal beliefs from those of patients/families allows us to listen with an open mind, join across disparate values and beliefs, and provide valuable information to colleagues as a starting place for their engagement.

SCREENING AND ASSESSMENT TOOLS

Screening and assessment tools can be used across settings and serve as useful guides in building a practice integrating spirituality. An assessment is often initiated through the following screening questions to identify relevance and needs:

Are spirituality and religion important in your life?
Are your spiritual/religious needs being supported?
Are you at peace? (Steinhauser, 2006)

Once relevance, need, and/or distress are identified, the following three tools provide a foundation to enhance comfort and confidence when assessing aspects of spirituality. It is important to note that, even if a patient or family does not explicitly identify as spiritual or religious, the tools outlined in Table 6.2, or portions of them, may be useful for all as conversation starters. They point toward basic philosophical and existential concerns related to the human experience.

Table 6.2 SPIRITUAL AND/OR RELIGIOUS ASSESSMENT TOOLS

Tool	Domains	Questions & Clarification
FICA[a]	F: Faith or beliefs	F: What do you believe gives meaning to your life?
	I: Important & influence	I: How important is your faith to you?
	C: Community	C: Are you part of a religious or spiritual community?
	A: Address or application	A: How would you like me to address these issues in your health care?
SPIRIT[b]	S: Spiritual belief system	S: Do you have a spiritual life that is important to you?
	P: Personal spirituality	P: In what ways is your spirituality important to you?
	I: Integration with spiritual community	I: Do you belong to any religious & spiritual groups or communities?
	R: Ritualized practices & restriction	R: What specific practices do you carry out as a part of your religious or spiritual life?
	I: Implications for medical care	I: Would you like to discuss religious or spiritual implications of health care?
	T: Terminal events	T: Are there particular aspects of medical care that you wish to forgo or have withheld because of your religion/spirituality?
HOPE[c]	H: Sources of hope	H: What gives you hope (or comfort, peace, strength)?
	O: Organized religion	O: Are you a part of a religious community? Does it help you? How?
	P: Personal spirituality & practices	P: What aspects of your spirituality do you find most helpful?
	E: Effect on medical care & end-of-life issues	E: How do your beliefs affect the kind of medical care you would like in the coming time?

[a] The George Washington Institute for Spirituality and Health. FICA spiritual history tool. www.gwumc.edu/gwish/clinical/fica.cfm. Accessed July 14, 2018

[b] Maugen, T. A. (1996). The SPIRITual History. *Arch Fam Med, 5*, 11–16.

[c] Anadarajah, G., Hight, E. (2001). Spirituality and medical practice: using the HOPE questions as a practical tool for spiritual assessment. *Am Fam Physician, 63*, 81–89.

INTERVENTION

Screening and assessment provide the foundation for selected social work interventions that aim to support patients' spiritual preferences and needs. The objective of any intervention is, most broadly, to focus on the whole person. As such, interventions that promote and support spiritual concerns reinforce patient and family strengths, enhance their well-being and coping, provide linkage to appropriate community resources, and identify spiritual factors that may contribute to medical decision-making. Furthermore, supporting this dimension of patient experience can influence how the health care team provides information regarding prognosis, introduces new strategies for symptom management that are consistent with patients' beliefs, responds to the individual's understanding and expectations related to suffering, and honors the role of family caregivers.

Supportive and therapeutic counseling is a central social work intervention. Identifying which counseling skills or techniques are utilized, and to what end, will help promote clarity and productivity in the therapeutic relationship. Using precise and active language to describe interventions ensures that other team members, across disciplines, will understand the value and depth of what is commonly documented too simply as "provided support." The following list is provided in order to best name the therapeutic aim of counseling, honoring the depth of skill and thoughtfulness that social workers bring to their work with patients and their loved ones:

- Meaning of diagnosis
- Hopes, values, fears
- Role of belief systems in the experience of suffering, pain, and other symptoms
- Need and desire for ritual
- Effect on interpersonal relationships; relationship with the sacred/divine
- Evolving sense of self; self-esteem; self-worth
- Sense of peace and calm
- Adaptive coping mechanisms
- Loss of control; locus of control; acceptance; surrender
- Personal definition of dignity, quality of life, purpose
- Adjustment to loss and grief
- Themes of guilt, reconciliation/forgiveness.

Table 6.3 highlights spiritual aspects of common social work interventions that further refine the therapeutic aims described above.

Table 6.3 SPIRITUALLY FOCUSED GOALS AND INTERVENTIONS

Goals	Interventions
Effective language	Contextualize spiritual/religious language family uses to describe illness experience Documentation reflecting patient & family perspective
Enhancing medical decision-making	Identify & assist with distress that may evolve from spiritual/religious guidelines for life-sustaining therapies; partner with health care chaplain/clergy as needed Support completion of culturally & religiously appropriate advance directives
Anticipatory guidance	Tailor the manner & content of information regarding disease course, treatment options, prognosis, & advance directives to the context of spiritual identity Invite & support display of spiritual symbols Ensure space for appropriate ritual during dying & post-death Address needs related to ongoing loss, grief, & bereavement
Family meetings/Care conference	Include chaplain or community clergy Acknowledge patients' religious/spiritual values & raise spiritual concerns on behalf of patient & family
Community linkage	Referral to chaplain/spiritual care Connect with clergy from community
Advocacy	Ensure effective symptom management/spiritual care in response to spiritual distress Sign-out/handoff to social workers across settings
Concrete resources	Culturally congruent funeral planning Connection to ongoing support in the community Referral to spiritually sensitive &/or religiously based health care or counseling programs

Prayer is a practice that can be simultaneously personal and communal, spontaneous or prescribed, and is often meaningful and centering for patients and families in health care settings (Stewart, 2014). Prayer can be a vehicle for those who are not religious to express a hope or wish for something. Particularly before diagnostic tests or procedures, during times of physical pain and distress, and at end of life, prayer may be a source of strength and comfort. Social workers may be in the position to encourage, witness, and/or join in prayer with a patient or family. This can be an invitation for respectful observation in silence and/or affirmation by bowing one's head or saying "amen" or an equivalent response. This is also an opportunity to connect with clergy members or chaplains who might lead or engage in prayers with the family in a way that is meaningful and familiar.

John

John Scott is s a 68-year-old white man who self-identifies as gay. He has chronic heart failure, dialysis-dependent end stage renal disease, and stage 4 penile and anal cancers. In the past year, he was hospitalized four times, seeming to always wind up in the same room on the same floor of the hospital, which created familiarity with providers. He was intensely private, and did not appear to outwardly acknowledge his fondness for the staff, although in conversations he often referred to feeling safe and at home. The social worker from the floor built a strong therapeutic relationship with John over time and ensured that transitions back to community were enhanced by collaboration with the dialysis social worker.

John's cancers were inoperable and incurable. He previously received palliative radiation with the intent to extend his life; however, the treatments caused increased symptom burden and further compromised his autonomy. He could no longer use the bathroom independently, as both the cancer and the treatment eroded his genitals. His prognosis of weeks to months was directly related to his ongoing decisions surrounding the continuation of dialysis, which had become a part of the pattern of his life. He had integrated dialysis into his routine and felt it was manageable, although not easy.

John lives independently on the top floor of a rent-stabilized brownstone. He vividly describes a home filled with antiques he lovingly collected after "walking away from everything" and rebuilding his life with Tom, his life partner, who died fifteen years ago. John lived on a fixed social security income and a small pension. His income was enough to provide for day-to-day life but not enough to allow him to supplement care with privately hired aides. He was over-income and therefore ineligible for Medicaid.

John came of age at a time when being gay was not socially accepted in his community and he internalized this, rejecting an essential part of himself. He married a woman, and began a career as a teacher, hoping to live an engaging life that would distract him from his identity. They had two children, Luke and Paula. He talked fondly of when his children were small and how much he enjoyed being their father. When his children were 8 and 10 years old, he met Tom, who he described as his "one true love." John left his family, albeit with a great sense of shame, to pursue a life with Tom. His wife, Marion, enraged at this betrayal, cut off all contact and prevented him from seeing Luke and Paula. After Tom died, John reached out to his children, who were now adults; their relationships were tense and inconsistent. However, after making similar efforts to connect with Marion, they eventually found a sense of peace with one another and developed a friendship reflective of the mutual respect that initially brought them together.

Born a Catholic, John now considered himself more spiritual than religious. John viewed Tom's death from AIDS as his penance for choosing to prioritize his truest desire and self over the life he had built with Marion, Luke, and Paula. He also felt his particular cancers were additional punishment that he deserved for his earlier choices and in a symbolic way linked his disease affecting the genitourinary organs to his betrayal of his family.

Through the last year of his life, the inpatient social worker engaged John in a process of life review, where he explored his decisions, past and present, in a neutral, nonjudgmental space. He was provided a therapeutic frame within which to explore his thoughts and feelings related to his illness course and subsequent hospitalizations. Through these conversations, it became clear that he felt a need to be fully transparent with his family before dying. Although they suspected the reason he left their family, he had never "come out" to them as gay.

Over time, the social worker engaged in therapeutic dialogue related to John's lack of self-acceptance, and his shame and guilt associated with his sexuality and subsequent life choices. John eventually came out to both Marion, and his son, Luke. Role-play with the social worker helped prepare John for these conversations, by practicing various responses and exploring his emotional and cognitive readiness to manage what might happen. John's daughter, Paula, was not interested in an ongoing relationship with her father; however, she visited him in the hospital once, bringing her children to meet their grandfather, something she knew would be important to John.

At his disclosure, and as anticipated, he found that his sexual orientation was in direct conflict with Marion's religious beliefs as a Pentecostal Christian. However, she was able to compartmentalize those beliefs and simultaneously honor their shared hope to maintain their recovered connection. Achieving this balance required her own spiritual exploration of what this commitment to him now required of her as it related to her psycho-spiritual maturity.

Though he was initially angry, after nonpressured time to reflect, Luke understood that his father came of age in a different world, where a gay man raising a family was unthinkable and unacceptable. Luke was able to develop empathy for his father. Luke was then able to forgive John for being absent, and felt a deeper sense of connection that moved them toward reconciliation.

Dialysis, which John had received for years, was becoming less and less effective and it became physically challenging to go for sessions. However, the treatment and the relationships with the dialysis team had become a part of his world and identity. At the same time, he took solace in the increasing suffering and struggle related to dialysis as a continuing source of retribution for the pain he had inflicted on his family.

John eventually grew weary of pursuing treatment and spending so much time in the hospital. He declared that he "wanted to go home to die." However, he was not sure this decision was his to make, as he attributed much spiritual meaning to suffering and wondered whether the extent of his suffering was sufficient for God's forgiveness and redemption. John selected his former wife, Marion, to be his health care agent and his son, Luke, as the alternate agent. He and daughter Paula remained estranged and distant.

Marion's perspective, as a Pentecostal Christian, was to value life at all costs, and her medical decision-making appeared to be in direct conflict with John's desire to die at home. However, John, torn by ambivalent feelings, felt he "owed her control for ruining the family." Alert and oriented, he allowed her to make decisions consistent with her explicitly stated values, not his. Although a referral for chaplaincy was offered and encouraged by the social worker, John repeatedly declined speaking with a chaplain or clergy person. He felt he had been judged and abandoned by religion and religious figures throughout his life and expected they would continue to misunderstand and reject him.

In exploring the intersection of his religious beliefs and their relationship to his illness, John came to recognize that he was intensely angry with and felt abandoned by God. He believed God to be a benevolent force who loves and accepts him unconditionally, and yet this same God created him in a way that caused him great difficulty and pain and then took away his beloved Tom. John's complex relationship to his God informed his fear of what came after death, and it became clear that he deferred decision-making to Marion because her beliefs and choices would delay the prospect of immediate death.

Through ongoing therapeutic counseling and the support of the social worker, John had time and space to reconcile the fracture between his historical religious beliefs and his current sense of his truest self, allowing healing in his relationships with his family, and slowly discovering his own sense of peace. He felt empowered to make his own choices and honor his own wishes and entertained the possibility that his suffering was sufficient for redemption. John came to the end of his life with hospice care at home after deciding to stop dialysis. Marion was a frequent visitor, and his son came to live with him in his last days to help provide care—both providing a comforting presence. Although he spent the last chapter of his life examining the intersection of his spirituality and life choices, when he died, it was unclear if there was resolution with God.

DOCUMENTATION

Documenting spiritual assessment and intervention in the medical record provides an important opportunity to share essential information related to patient and family values, beliefs, and coping strategies. Ideally, notes are written in a succinct and clear way, offering context and insight that inform culturally and spiritually congruent care. Providers are asked to synthesize a rich and dynamic past. Clear documentation allows for previous therapeutic work to travel across medical settings with a patient, building a thread of continuity, and avoiding a potentially frustrating need for repetition. Incorporating what has been learned from spiritual assessment may provide commentary on

- Communication style
- Meaning-making as it relates to treatment choices, wishes, hopes and fears and coping
- Primary lens through which information is interpreted: medical/ scientific or spiritual or dogmatic
- The values and beliefs that inform the experience of "quality" time
- Family and community responsibilities and role
- Community clergyperson contact information, if relevant
- Religious beliefs and ideology related to care
- Ritual and practice needs such as prayer, ceremony, chanting, and anointing
- Specific considerations for care at the end of life and after death including location of death, rituals and funeral preferences

Box 6.2 provides an example of social work documentation from John Scott's care.

Box 6.2

MODEL DOCUMENTATION

Met with Mr. Scott at bedside. Explored thoughts and feelings surrounding his illness course, current changes, and how to best share information with his family. Explored their prior conversations and discussed the impacts of life-limiting illness on family roles and dynamics. Validated self-knowledge and feelings. Discussed ways to talk to son; psychoeducation focused on anticipating possible reaction and ways to respond Reinforced availability to facilitate and/or support this process. John shared his sense that he is "running out of time." Explored hopes and worries related to end-of-life issues, specifically attending to spiritual concerns.

Plan:

Continued emotional support with focus on exploring coping, meaning-making, and impact on family system given progressive nature of disease.

Will explore opportunities for legacy work.

Will continue therapeutic dialogue with patient tomorrow; do not hesitate to page if needs arise.

SPECIAL CONSIDERATIONS AT THE END OF LIFE

Patient and family's needs during the dying process through death, post-mortem care, and bereavement may emanate from spiritual and religious background and beliefs, current affiliation, family traditions, and rituals. At many points along the illness trajectory, spiritual and religious values inform conversations about the role of life-sustaining therapies such as mechanical ventilation, attempts at resuscitation, artificial nutrition, and dialysis, and lead to an understanding of end-of-life preferences.

Some of the language commonly used to describe preferences related to end-of-life care focuses on comfort, quality of life, and dignity (Chochinov et al., 2011). It may be assumed that these standards are best honored by a "peaceful death," a "do not resuscitate" (DNR) order, and forgoing the use of life-sustaining interventions. For some, interpretation of religious mandates to preserve sanctity of life prioritizes and results in a commitment to sustain a life, for example, that may be supported by a ventilator or artificial hydration and nutrition. Some hold the belief that physical signs such as a breath or a heart-beat equal life, and treatments that support these biological functions need to be continued. Often, conversations about "quality" will fall short as the family and sometimes the patient are focused on different values and understanding of the meaning of life and being "alive." The patient may be comatose, unable to interact or participate meaningfully, or perhaps cannot experience subjective existence. Or, as in the case of John Scott, may choose suffering as a path to further redemption and sacrifice. Consulting with a trained health care chaplain or clergy person about these profound aspects of life and death is a valuable way to help one another provide optimal patient/family care and to honor interdisciplinary work.

In some faith traditions, speaking explicitly about anything related to dying and death may not be culturally appropriate and to ask, repeatedly, may be offensive and isolate patients and families from providers. For some, to speak of death is in direct conflict with honoring and respecting the sanctity of life. Understanding the role of religious parameters and dictates will help to inform the clinical approach and perhaps suggest a path to blending the religious needs of patients within the context of the medical system. A practice of cultural humility does not require extensive knowledge about each religious tradition, rather the capacity to ask questions, remain open-minded, think critically, and research the ideology as it is practiced and applies to a specific patient's life. Additionally, this stage of illness and its relationship to spiritual and religious values and beliefs speak to the importance of linking to community clergy who may be able to further explore patient or family spiritual concerns or assist in the interpretation of religious texts. This linkage also serves to affirm connection and bridge to community systems that will support and sustain families through transitions and long after they separate from the health care system. Regardless of spiritual or religious background, if possible and appropriate, exploring specific wishes and ideas regarding the final moments of life allows social workers and the entire health care team to better serve patients and families. The following are exploratory questions that engage preferences and suggest the possibility of creating a unique experience within the universality of dying (See Chapter 8; "Care of Patients and Families at the End of Life"):

- Do you have preferences related to the location of death?
- What do you want the environment to be like while dying or after death, including specific prayers, rituals, practices, music, video, television, company, to be touched or not? What people would you like to be with you? Would you prefer to be alone?
- Do you have preferences to guide how your life is honored? Funeral? Obituary? Viewing? Opened or closed casket? Cremation? Burial? Clothes you would want to be wearing? Have any of these arrangements been made?
- Have you thoughts and feelings about burial of your remains in the country of your birth?

COLLABORATION ACROSS HEALTH CARE TEAMS AND PROVIDERS

It is natural for patients and families to share different aspects of their experience with different health care providers, sometimes with intention and sometimes spontaneously. Appreciating spirituality as a way patients and families make meaning of their experiences, in the context of their unique intersectional identity, means that everyone on the team has the potential to contribute to the holistic understanding and most appropriate interventions for the person and family under their care (Breitbart, 2009). It is important for each member of the team to listen for the spiritual references as health care providers describe their interactions. Health care settings generally prioritize a scientific worldview, which may mean that the language patients and families use to share their experience is missed, as are the signals that may alert the team to a patient's spirituality, such as having a Bible by the bed.

CLINICAL ATTUNEMENT

For some, listening with an intention to identify spiritual themes may come easier than for others. Like any other skill, developing a clinical prowess to listen and hear for spiritual needs can be honed over time. Repeated awareness helps to build comfort and familiarity, training our ears to identify the themes of meaning-making, and incorporating this rich work into our practice wisdom. As the ability *to be with* grows through the sharing of genuine presence, attention, and authenticity, specific assessment tools become more natural, and each clinician builds her own lexicon to discuss spiritual ideas, all of which enhance connection with patients.

This collection of connection-enhancing skills can be described as *attunement*. Listening with attunement seeks to bring into harmony the inner and outer selves one might allude to in conversation. Like music, conversations often have a top note and a bass note. The top notes can be distracting, or the "noise" in a conversation, while the bass note is more closely aligned with what people are communicating. Spirituality comes from a deeply personal space, and finding the markers for these "bass notes" can help social workers tune into the rhythmic drumbeats of a patient's lived experience. John Scott, for example, had conversational top notes focused on the conflict surrounding medical decision-making, but his bass notes revealed the themes of redemption, legacy, shame, and genuine self-expression and authenticity.

Family members may share a spiritual framework through which they navigate their lives individually and interpersonally. This might be revealed through stories that reflect their past experiences, choices, and patterns that may influence their current perceptions, decisions, behaviors, and interactions. This knowledge can help clinicians learn who this patient and family are and contextualize how they engage with care providers. Are they in spiritual distress or crisis? Does this illness or death upend everything they thought they knew and believed in? Are they feeling spiritually unmoored? Are family or friends imposing their beliefs on them? These conversations can create openings in the narrative of the patient–provider relationship that may have seemed closed.

Often, patients provide information regarding their beliefs without making overt references. It is important for clinicians to retain a nonjudgmental stance, to remain curious and open-minded, to avoid jumping to conclusions, and to listen from a place of humility. Inferring meaning or making assumptions can abort or further complicate already complex conversations. Listen for the patient's unique expression of perceived/lived reality, and do not assume that "God" is similarly defined by each person who uses the word to refer to a potentially very complex idea. Each person's sense of the spiritual is subjective and requires individual exploration.

Engaging the patient and family in a conversation means joining with them in the flow and pace of the interview. Some respond well to gentle facilitation and exploration, or others provide cues woven within a more narrative way of storytelling. When engaged with respect and sensitivity, patients may provide a glimpse into their innermost thoughts and experience. By keeping reflective statements open and maintaining a safe space, patients may reveal themselves without the fear of repercussions and/or the judgment many worry about when discussing such intimate and potentially complex topics.

Perhaps, in engagement, the patient has not revealed any specific or symbolic spiritual language or references; however, the social worker can intuit a spiritual undercurrent or theme. Table 6.4 provides both examples of conversational cues that indicate spiritual undercurrents and expansion questions that might help discover meaning.

Table 6.4 Exploring Religious and Spiritual Language

Religious (God) Language	Spiritual Language	Expansion Questions & Therapeutic Messaging
"We are waiting for Him to reveal his plan."	"The universe has a plan." "The universe is conspiring for my good."	How does this illness, crisis, event, etc., impact the plan you feel God or the universe has for you?
"It's in God's hands." "I'm in God's hands."	"I can't talk about such difficult things—it will put negativity in the universe." "I am visualizing that I am healing & will be completely well."	As you wait for God's (the universe's) plan to evolve, what seems important to you? What do you perceive your role is while living with this challenge right now?
"God doesn't give me more than I can handle."	"It's not for me to decide." "Everything happens for a reason."	How has this experience shaped your understanding of yourself?
"I am ready for whatever he/she gives me."	"There is a balance to things, even if I don't understand."	What strengths are you drawing upon during this difficult & uncertain time?
"This is my cross to bear."	"I made my choices. We all have our struggles." "I did something to deserve this." "I caused (this illness) by not expressing my (anger/grief)."	How do you think your past choices are playing a role in what you are experiencing now?

Rarely working in isolation, it is helpful to become sensitive to the language of patients and families as well as the language used by members of the health care team. Listening for "God language" can help illuminate moments where conversations may have been unintentionally influenced by a care provider. For example, a colleague may use the phrase "God forbid" in a family meeting, which to the provider may have been nothing more than a colloquial expression. Yet to a family it could imply alignment with their belief that God is stronger than any medicine, and life-sustaining treatment must be continued until God's plan is revealed. Remembering the broad reaching power of language and the profound meaning that religion and spirituality may have to clinicians, as well as patients and families, can help to mitigate and prevent unintended misunderstanding affecting care (See Chapter 2; "Structure and Processes of Care").

THE SOCIAL WORKER'S USE OF SELF: THE ROLE OF SELF-AWARENESS

Each social worker brings a unique experience to every clinical relationship. Personal histories and beliefs influence clinical availability to patients and their families in both explicit and implicit ways. Commitment to ongoing self-reflection allows for deeper authenticity in practice and sustained professional satisfaction. Intersectionality relates to clinician experience as well. Clinicians need to be clear about their own sense of identity, social location, and perception of their own biopsychosocial and spiritual circumstances.

Whether the social worker identifies as spiritual, religious, or neither, it is central to the human experience to make meaning and sense of our lives. This process is informed by the individual's personal beliefs, values, worldviews, and philosophy. This may be conscious or unconscious. For many, clinical social work requires the development of beliefs, evolving over time, which serve as a buoy in the uncertain territory of being alive. Unrecognized, they can influence how clinicians interpret the experiences of patients and families. One way to protect both patients and clinicians from unintentional bias or influence is to have a deep sense of one's self, as well as incorporating mechanisms for developing ongoing self-awareness.

As practitioners, social workers need an awareness of personal belief systems and behaviors before delving into those of others. Without this nuanced understanding of self, the possibility of unintentional harm arises. One of the most honest questions social workers can ask themselves before engaging with patients and families is, "Am I able to distance myself from my personal beliefs and attitudes in order to sufficiently respect and support the spiritual and/ or religious beliefs and observances of the populations I serve?" It is equally important to recognize when it feels impossible to put personal beliefs and attitudes aside and seek guidance of colleagues and mentors.

Engaging in this deeply sensitive and contemplative work requires that social workers turn the mirror of reflection to themselves. This intensely personal activity of self-exploration, added to the emotional capacity required to do the day-to-day work, is challenging and labor-intensive. It can, at times, cause periods of despair and doubt, if the clinician is not attending to her own need for emotional, physical, and spiritual nourishment and replenishment. As helping professionals working with other helping professionals, being mindful of the familiar tendency to overextend oneself emotionally, at the cost of self-preservation, requires shared vigilance. Social workers engage with great mystery, joy, compassion, evolving faith, and intimate caring. This work also reveals the grim and painful realities of the human experience. Whether patients are known for brief or extended periods of time, go on to live or die, social workers can "learn to be vigilant about recognizing their own cumulative trauma in caring for dying patients and attend to their self-care" (Nelson-Becker et al., 2015, p. 116).

Many spiritual practices hone this awareness, while adding meaning and enhancing resiliency in our work, and can be sources of solace and balance to our professional lives. Irrespective of chosen self-care practice, it is only through caring for ourselves that we can continue to do well the work of caring for others (See Chapter 1; "The Convergence of Social Work Practice"). Harrison and Westwood (2009) have introduced a therapeutic perspective to the discussion of self-care, describing the attributes of clinicians that enhance professional satisfaction while mitigating compassion fatigue. They challenge the notion that being empathetic must lead to emotional depletion, introducing the concept of exquisite empathy, which promotes the clinician's balancing of clear and consistent boundaries, expanded perspective, and highly present, intimate, and compassionate interpersonal connection with patients. They suggest that this intimate connection or "bi-directionality" with patients and the enhanced self-awareness and empathy of the clinician are invigorating rather than depleting (Harrison & Westwood, 2009).

CONCLUSION

Spirituality is a broad term incorporating some of the themes quintessential to human experience: connection, belonging, uncertainty, suffering, mortality, and physical impermanence. This is the domain of values and beliefs providing the structure for living a meaningful life, and is considered a central part of humanity. The story of John Scott highlights how patients at end of life may grapple with spiritual and personal conflicts that have defined a sense of self through key moments in their life. Creating a therapeutic relationship that joins patients in safe exploration, examination, and reflection can provide a North Star in a time of flux.

Health care social workers are in the unique position to assess and support patients and their family members as whole people with important and relevant spiritual lives. Social workers can assure that this aspect of the patient's identity, social experience, and philosophical framework is acknowledged and integrated, as possible, into the experience with the health care system, especially during serious life-threatening illness. This is rich work, rooted in the notion that when people are confronted by an illness, there is an opportunity to identify and strengthen a well of spiritual resources, whether familiar and long held, or newly discovered and embraced, that can be used to build a sense of internal steadiness in the face of uncertainty. Understanding the way patients and families make sense of their illness experience, in the context of a whole life, enhances capacity to provide more spiritually and culturally congruent care and to assure that these essential needs are attended to and respected from diagnosis through bereavement. This is the heart of the work.

LEARNING EXERCISES

1. You have been caring for John Scott as his primary social worker. For a case conference, you must present a succinct summary, in 100 words or less, to share with interprofessional providers identifying the spiritual strengths, concerns, and recommendations for next steps. Write this presentation as if Mr. Scott is in the room and listening to your words.
2. Working in an outpatient cancer center, you meet regularly with Ms. Smith, who asks you to pray with her at the beginning of your time together. She wears an amulet from her grandmother, who had the same type of cancer, believing it confers protection against advancing illness and references its power often. How could you explore these aspects of her faith together?

REFERENCES

Anandarajah, G., & Hight, E. (2001). Spirituality and medical practice: Using the HOPE questions as a practical tool for spiritual assessment. *American Family Physician, 63*(1), 81–89.

Bowman, T. (2016). Spirituality and countertransference: Individual and systemic considerations. *Death Studies, 41*(3), 154–161.

Breitbart, W. (2009). The spiritual domain of palliative care: Who should be "spiritual care professionals?" *Palliative and Supportive Care, 7*(2), 139–141.

Canda, E., & Furman, L. (2009). *Spiritual diversity in social work practice*. Oxford: Oxford University Press.

Chochinov, H. M., Kristjanson, L. J., Breitbart, W., McClement, S., Hack, T. F., Hassard, T., & Harlos, M. (2011). Effect of dignity therapy on distress and end-of-life experience in terminally ill patients: A randomized controlled trial. *The Lancet, 12*(8), 753–762.

De Jager Meezenbroek, E., Garssen, B., Van Den Berg, M., Tuytel, G., Van Dierendonck, D., Visser, A., & Schaufeli, W. B. (2012). Measuring spirituality as a universal human experience: Development of the Spiritual Attitude and Involvement List (SAIL). *Journal of Psychosocial Oncology, 30*(2), 141–141.

Harrison, R. L., & Westwood, M. J. (2009). Preventing vicarious traumatization of mental health therapists: identifying protective practices. *Psychotherapy, 46*(2), 203–219.

Hodge, D. R., & Bushfield, S. (2006). Developing spiritual competence in practice. *Journal of Ethnic and Cultural Diversity in Social Work, 15*(3–4), 101–127.

Maugans, T. (1996). The SPIRITual history. *Family Medicine, 5*(1), 11–16.

National Association of Social Workers. (2015). *The standards and indicators for cultural competence in the social work practice*. Retrieved from www.socialworkers.org/LinkClick.aspx?fileticket=PonPTDEBrn4%3D&portalid=0.

Nelson-Becker, H., Ai, A., Hopp, F., McCormick, T., Schlueter, J., & Camp, J. (2015). Spirituality and religion in end-of-life care ethics: The challenge of interfaith and cross-generational matters. *British Journal of Social Work, 45*(1), 104–119.

Nelson-Becker, H., Nakashima, M., & Canda, E. (2006). Use of spirituality in interventions. In D. Kaplan & B. Berkman (Eds.), *Oxford handbook of social work in health and aging* (pp. 797–807). New York: Oxford University Press.

Pew Research Center. (2015). "Nones" on the rise: Religion and the unaffiliated. Retrieved from www.pewforum.org/2012/10/09/nones-on-the-rise-religion/

Puchalski, C. (2013). Integrating spirituality into patient care: An essential element of person-centered care. *Polish Archives of Internal Medicine, 123*(9), 491–497.

Puchalski, C., & Romer, A. (2000). Taking a spiritual history allows clinicians to understand patients more fully. *Journal of Palliative Medicine, 3*(1), 129–137.

Puchalski, C. M., Ferrell, B., Virani, R., Otis-Green S., Baird P., Bull J., . . . Sulmasy, D. (2009). Improving the quality of spiritual care as a dimension of palliative care: The report of the consensus conference. *Journal of Palliative Medicine, 12*(10), 885–904.

Steinhauser, K. E., Voils, C. I., Clipp, E. C., Bosworth, H. B., Christakis, N. A., & Tulsky, J. A. (2006). "Are You at Peace?" One Item to Probe Spiritual Concerns at the End of Life. *Archives of Internal Medicine, 166*(1), 101–105. doi:10.1001/archinte.166.1.101

Stewart, M. (2014). Spiritual assessment: A patient-centered approach to oncology social work practice. *Social Work in Health Care, 53*(1), 59–73.

Tako, B. (2017). New normal: Life before and after cancer. *Cure*. Retrieved from www.curetoday.com/community/barbara-tako/2017/10/new-normal-life-before-and-after-cancer.

Cultural Aspects of Care

YVETTE COLÓN ∎

Culture is the learned and shared knowledge that specific groups use to generate their behavior and interpret their experience of the world. It comprises beliefs about reality, how people should interact with each other, what they "know" about the world, and how they should respond to the social and material environments in which they find themselves. It is reflected in their religions, morals, customs, technologies, and survival strategies. It affects how they work, parent, love, marry, and understand health, mental health, wellness, illness, disability, and death.

—GILBERT, GOODE, AND DUNNE (2007, p. 13)

INTRODUCTION

Social workers in all settings work with patients whose cultural identities are different from their own. Professional standards for culturally competent practice exist for social workers and other health professions. Social work standards consider the complexities of practice in an elaborate and evolving global society, explore beliefs and attitudes about culture, and identify related issues at micro, meso, and macro levels (National Association of Social Workers, 2015). Bullock (2011) describes cultural competence as a standard of care, yet competence is not an end, rather a beginning framework enriched through respectful inquiry. Serious illness can have profound effects on the psychological, social, and spiritual lives of patients and families, and honing the skills necessary to learn about and respond to the cultural domain honors the unique lens of each patient and their family of choice and origin. Culture is expressed both explicitly and subtly, and in relation to serious illness affects health beliefs and practices, communication about illness and styles of decision-making, relationship to being ill and needing care, and to care providers themselves, both personal and professional.

According to the US Department of Health and Human Services (2001), "Culture defines how health is perceived, how health care information is received, how rights and protections are exercised, what is considered to be a health problem, how symptoms and concerns about a health problem are expressed and interpreted, who should provide treatment and how and what kind of treatment should be given" (p. 4). The United States is increasingly diverse and multicultural, and social workers must enhance their capacity to serve people from all backgrounds. Diversity includes the sociocultural experiences of race and ethnicity, class, religion and spirituality, gender identity or expression, age, marital status, ability, nationality, language, immigration status, sexual orientation, and more. In the context of serious illness, it is possible to imagine the widest sense of diversity, including health status. While the United States is particularly diverse racially and ethnically, paradoxically, the social work profession is highly homogenous, as 86% of all licensed social workers in the United States are white non-Hispanic (National Association of Social Workers, 2006). This means there are bound to be cultural differences between social workers and patient-family systems, reinforcing the importance of culture as a fundamental priority of assessment, understanding, and source of support.

Social workers often work with people who are vulnerable and have experienced marginalization acutely or over time, emphasizing the importance of examining issues of power, privilege, and unconscious bias. This invites humility, self-awareness, and an openness to learning, informing culturally sensitive practice and enhancing the likelihood of patient and family satisfaction and trust.

CULTURAL PERSPECTIVES OF PALLIATIVE CARE

Research confirms that palliative care is relatively unknown among consumers of health care (Center for the Advancement of Palliative Care, 2011). Patients and families may not understand that palliative care provides care for the whole person and seeks to diminish suffering at all levels—body, mind, and spirit. Steinberg (2011) suggests that offering to integrate palliative care into a care plan can be an emotionally charged decision because beliefs and attitudes about this specialty have evolved over time and often been misunderstood. This requires social workers to be particularly attuned to listening for previous experience, misconceptions, beliefs, and values. The ability to listen for and correct misconceptions is a shared responsibility and highlights an opportunity to provide education about what palliative care is while enhancing the receptivity and expectation of receiving patient-centered, family-focused care.

At the same time, the guiding values of palliative care evolved within a Western medical and ethical model, privileging informed consent, autonomous decision-making, and truth-telling, and generally science over religion. There is growing awareness that these values do not cohere with the cultural and spiritual beliefs of many patients and families. This means misunderstanding and conflict might arise. The cultures of providers and health care systems, with their values, beliefs, and pressures, have a momentum that can minimize individuality, while a palliative care focus seeks a return to discovering, understanding, and respecting values and beliefs in support of patient-centered, family-focused care. Exploring relationships to meaning, autonomy, decision-making, information preferences, and advance care planning can be essential processes in negotiating an illness and anticipating end of life.

Patients' and families' relationships to the health care system are central to their coping and meaning-making and are often essential to survival. This process of discovering the degree of coherence with institutional values occurs within systems where power dynamics and relationship to authority are inherent, and often exert unspoken influences within patient–provider relations and the institution at large. It is at this juncture of discovery and influence that the skills of observation and mediation are critical. For example, while values such as informed decision-making and self-determination often drive clinician and institutional behaviors, some patients and families may privilege parentalism or family decision-making as humane, responsible, and supportive of patient and family history and structure. For some, a decision to establish a do not attempt resuscitation (DNAR) order or the sharing of prognosis can be viewed as assaultive, a threat to hope or faith, or a challenge to the will of a Higher Power. Caring for a family member with dementia supported with artificial hydration and nutrition may not be viewed as burdensome, and the life of the patient is understood to have quality and meaning simply by virtue of their breath. Social workers mediate the unique spiritual and cultural backgrounds of patients and families to customize care, maximizing cultural strengths that include personal expression, meaning-making, rituals, and connection to community.

CULTURAL COMPETENCE: A BEGINNING

The Institute for Democratic Renewal and Project Change Anti-Racism Initiative (2001) defines culture as "[a] social system of meaning and custom that is developed by a group of people to assure its adaptation and survival. These groups are distinguished by a set of unspoken rules that shape values, beliefs, habits, patterns of thinking, behaviors and styles of communication" (p. 32). However, the concept of culture expands considerably beyond single groups. As mentioned earlier, culture can be inclusive of, but not limited to, gender, age, sexual orientation, gender identity and expression, religious identity or spirituality, physical and mental abilities, language, nationality, immigration or refugee status, socioeconomic status, and education and literacy—identities that are interconnected and cannot be examined apart from each other. Whether in practice, policy, or research, social workers integrate skills and techniques at the micro, meso, and macro levels to reflect understanding and respect for the importance of culture (National Association of Social Workers, 2015).

Figure 7.1 depicts the multitude of social identities and roles that may exist within one person and family system, informing expressions that can be considered culture. This model applies to all and leads practitioners to look beyond the protective and fragile distinction of qualifying patients and families as the "other," and to consider that the "other" is in fact "us."

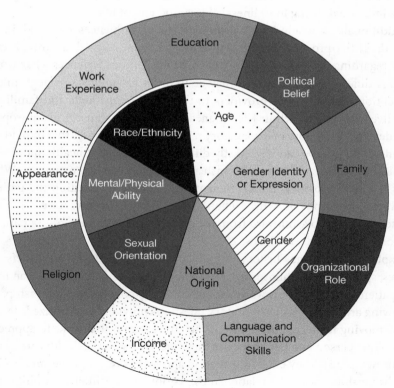

Figure 7.1. Diversity wheel.

On the practice level, it is critical to engage effectively with people through their cultural lens to develop therapeutic alliances, craft interventions, and identify internal sources of strengths and resilience. This inquiry begins the process of the practice of cultural humility (Ortega & Faller, 2011). It seems evident that it is important to know something about the cultures of patients, and yet a generic or stereotypical approach is inappropriate and myopic. It is in-structive to consider acquired knowledge about different cultures as hypotheses to be tested and corrected by an inquiry that individualizes the person and family. An individual cannot represent the totality of her culture, yet she may present nuanced perspectives critical for social workers to understand.

Cultural groups may share strong heritages, but each subgroup of the pop-ulation has distinct cultural beliefs and customs influencing their experiences of the world, including health care. It can sometimes be instructive to have a concrete illustration of the magnitude of diversity among subgroups. Africa is made up of 54 countries, Asia is made up of 48 different countries, and Latin America is made up of 28 different countries and territories. Each possesses a diverse mix of people, cultures, beliefs and values, languages and dialects, histories, and political systems. These elements shape the relationships and ideas individuals bring to wellness, illness, and end of life.

Additionally, considering the wide range of influences explored in the preceding, the process of getting to know someone is guided through curi-osity regarding her expression of values, beliefs, and experiences—her world-view. A different cultural model may be in order to guide assessment, inform perceptions, and sensitize providers to the worlds of patients and families as they live with illness. Arthur Kleinman, a psychiatrist and medical anthropolo-gist, developed a theory of explanatory models which proposes that individuals, families, and groups can have vastly different beliefs about health and disease (1988). Kleinman suggests that instead of simply asking patients, "Where does it hurt?" providers enrich their understanding by eliciting the patient's answers to questions of "why," "when," "how," and "what next" (see Table 7.1). These inquiries move outward from the physical self and often forge a path to a person's culture and worldview.

Exploring language, history, family and kinship, education, beliefs and values, spirituality or philosophy of life, and folk and health practices can move the patient and clinician toward a more culturally congruent relationship. The following are examples of exploratory questions provided to sensitize listening, while moving from superficial inquiry to conversation that seeks to appreciate the unique person and her history as they interface with the health care system (Andrews, 2013). They elicit information about culture, language, and history; family, kinship, and social relationships; worldview; spirituality or philosophy

Table 7.1 ELICITING THE PATIENT'S EXPLANATORY MODEL

Kleinman (1988) suggests the following questions to enhance understanding of how a patient sees her illness: What do you call the problem? What do you think has caused the problem? Why do you think it started when it did? What do you think the sickness does? How does it work? How severe is the sickness? Will it have a long or a short course? What kind of treatment do you think you should receive? What are the chief problems the sickness has caused? What do you fear most about the sickness?

of life; and folk/health practices; they are offered with sensitivity and aware-ness of the vulnerability of many who may be cautious about responding to questions.

- What cultural or ethnic group do you identify with?
- What is your primary language? What language is spoken at home?
- How would you prefer to be addressed while here?
- Would you describe what good care means to you?
- Are there others whom you would like to be involved in your care? How would you like them to be involved?
- Will anyone other than yourself be participating in decisions affecting your care?
- How long have you lived in this country? (if born outside the United States)
- Sometimes when people leave their country of origin, they make very difficult decisions and encounter unpleasant experiences. Is there any experience we should know about that might be important to your care?
- Both men and women work in this service and are typically involved in caring for patients or entering their rooms. Are there any special considerations we should know about related to persons of the opposite gender being involved in your care?
- Please share with me what you believe caused your illness?
- How will this illness/hospitalization affect your life and the life of your family?

- What do you turn to when life is challenging such as prayer, God, nature, or family? Are you able to connect to it and find comfort in it now?
- Where did you most often receive care for regular checkups or when you were feeling ill?
- It is helpful to know about any medications and herbal or vitamin supplements you are taking. Dosage, frequency, and for what reason?
- Is there anything else you would like us to know to help us take the best care of you?

INTERSECTIONALITY

Intersectionality examines forms of discrimination as they manifest through components of diversity. This approach provides a perspective of overlapping social identities and related *systems* of oppression, domination, or discrimination (Crenshaw, 1991) and suggests that various biological, social, and cultural forms of identity interact on multiple and often simultaneous levels. Intersectionality theory holds classical conceptualizations of oppression within society, such as racism, sexism, classism, ableism, homophobia, transphobia, xenophobia, and belief-based bigotry, do not and cannot act independently of each other. It also seeks to examine how power and privilege negatively affect those who are vulnerable and disenfranchised, a state often compounded by serious illness and the consequent need to interface with health care providers and systems. Systems and their structures can also support and empower patient and family experience. The clinical task is to understand how patients and families are positioned in relationship to the dominant culture, in the United States, represented by Western medicine, in order to understand the degree of alignment with systems of power. Discovering this degree of alignment provides some insight into the degree of support, empowerment, marginalization, and isolation experienced in relationship to care. For example, a patient who has explored with family and providers preferences for end-of-life care, and has completed documentation such as POLST or MOLST forms, may experience feelings of validation and control during a time that is often emotional and uncertain. (See Chapter 9; "Legal and Ethical Aspects of Care"). These processes and documents may facilitate smoother transitions of care, enhancing continuity. On a relationship level, providers may feel more at ease knowing how to be most helpful as disease advances and therefore be more comfortable attending to the emotional and psychological needs of patients and families. This represents cultural alignment of both patient-family and institutional values and serves to provide a validating and empowering experience, where patient preferences and style have a degree of congruence with institutional practices.

Social categorizations such as race, class, and gender, as they apply to a given individual or group, capture the interconnected nature of identity. This conceptualization of identity allows for a great deal of complexity and a multidimensional experience in the macro context of power and hierarchy in the United States. Authentic and respectful therapeutic relationships support a multidimensional awareness that may bring social justice issues to the surface. Often in health care, individuals are reduced to their diagnoses, gender, and at times race or ethnicity, and yet there is so much more to "see." Intersectionality links the ecological model within one person; the social worker can see and explore how the micro through macro perspectives inform the clinical relationship.

CULTURAL HUMILITY: A NEW MODEL FOR SOCIAL WORK PRACTICE

> A cultural humility perspective is one that encourages social workers and other service providers to take into account an individual's multiple identities and the ways in which they impact their worldview, particularly as it relates to their expression of their culture.
>
> —ORTEGA AND FALLER (2011, *p. 33*)

In their seminal work developing the model of cultural humility, pediatricians, public health educators, and community activists Tervalon and Murray-Garcia (1998) raised awareness of the cultural differences between patients and service providers, emphasizing that those differences refer to a relationship between two, not just one, perspectives. All providers are encouraged to develop a respectful partnership with each patient, recognizing the patient as expert in her own life and encouraging the patient's empowerment and/or amplifying her voice in health care settings when she cannot speak for herself. The starting point for a culturally humble approach would include an intertwined exploration of the patient's belief system and experience paired with curiosity and consideration of the values, assumptions and beliefs embedded in the understandings and perceptions within the self and other providers. This reflective process includes the values privileged not only by their personal experience in the world, but also by their professional discipline, specialty, and organizational view. Tervalon and Murray-Garcia (1998) view cultural humility as a service provider's recognition of her own cultural differences in interactive relationships with patients and families. This recognition extends not only to those who are marginalized and disempowered, but also to those who are privileged and, by virtue of this privilege, might be different from those providing care. In the United States, when integrating palliative practices across settings and cultures, sensitivity to the privileging of informed consent, decision-making, and self-determination, with an intention to reduce suffering and enhance quality of life, represent specific value systems that may or may not align and resonate with patients and families.

According to Fletcher (2007), the most serious barrier to culturally appropriate care is not a lack of knowledge about any cultural orientation, but providers' failure to develop self-awareness and a respectful attitude toward difference. Identifying each patient's beliefs, values, and goals through a person-in-environment, strengths-based approach and exploring the similarities and differences in each of their cultures contributes toward shifting the power dynamics within relationships. In addition, providers adopt a learning mode, rather than working to maintain control and authority over cultural experiences about which the patient is far more experienced and knowledgeable (Ortega & Faller, 2011).

The field of cultural anthropology studies subjects holistically with the critical intent of understanding, as much as possible, the context in which an individual's life happens. All elements playing a role in the lives of individuals, families, and communities are considered in relationship to each other; no single aspect can be considered in isolation. Yet Peoples and Bailey (2012) caution, "Taken literally, a holistic understanding of a people's customs and beliefs is probably not possible because of the complexity of human societies. But anthropologists have learned that ignoring the interrelationships among language, religion, art, economy, family, and other dimensions of life results in distortions and misunderstandings" (p. 16). Each patient exists at different levels of an interactive ecological system involving personal history and responses, relationships with intimate partners, family, and friends, communities in which social relationships take place (e.g., work, school, neighborhood), connections to country of origin, and social institutions, such as health care agencies and health policies. Social workers can consider these elements in an intersectional way when engaging with patients and families. These are the realms where legacy and story are made, affecting patient care in the present, and family integration, coping, and meaning-making over time, through bereavement periods.

Initially conceived as a way to provide more effective multicultural medical education, Tervalon and Murray-Garcia's (1998) model of cultural humility has been incorporated into different kinds of professional practice. It can be a useful form of reflective practice, providing a foundation to challenge biases. Bias, in this instance, acts as a form of privileging or disadvantaging certain experiences and value systems. This is implicit and explicit in health care settings. For example, the bias in the emergency department may be to save lives, in intensive care units it may be to maximize interventions, and in hospice it may be to help individuals die at home. These biases may be silently acted upon and can conflict with patient and family goals, hopes, and preferences about how they receive care through the course of serious illness. As an antidote to bias, reflective process invites providers to assess and analyze personal attitudes and beliefs in relation to diverse patients across a wide range of professional practice settings. The relational and educational aspects of cultural humility support the importance of this model in providing community-based care, advocacy, and institutional consistency. Cultural humility extends to identifying, supporting, and enhancing the inherent strengths in all peoples and communities, with heightened sensitivity to vulnerabilities and disenfranchisement. Tervalon and Murray-Garcia (1998) additionally called for organizational efforts in cultural humility to ensure diversity in staff and programs, and to exemplify the importance of holding themselves accountable to the community in which they are situated.

Having system-wide, organizational commitment to the ethos of culturally competent care improves the quality of care delivered (Allen & Spitzer, 2016). Committed organizations assess their policies and practices regularly, with ongoing education to expand cultural knowledge and resources, and importantly support diversity initiatives in hiring, developing, and retaining staff. Commitment to diversity manifests throughout the entire organization, from its clients to its board of directors. Allen and Spitzer provide a structured checklist to assess an organization's own cultural diversity and cultural competence that includes communication styles, values and attitudes, physical environment, materials, and resources (2016, pp. 431–434).

The Importance of Language and Interpretation

Language difference is a common barrier in accessing and using health care (Lyke & Colón, 2004). Working with patients with limited English proficiency and limited health literacy can be challenging (National Academies of Science, Engineering, and Medicine, 2017); providers might be concerned about content, meaning of information, as well as nuance and intention, being lost during communication and interpretation. There might also be practical challenges of time and coordination with interpreters. According to the US Department of Health and Human Services (2001), Title VI of the Civil Rights Act mandates that interpreter services be provided for patients with limited English proficiency who need this service, in any health care organization receiving federal financial assistance. This often requires preparation and planning, adding further challenges for providers. While professional interpreters are most effective, often this responsibility is assumed or expected of family, friends, or untrained staff. Untrained interpreters are more likely to make errors, violate

confidentiality, or withhold distressing information. The use of a trained interpreter is a right and a protection for patients and families to guard against the
potentially distressing experience of a family member or friend being asked to
share information that might be sensitive or emotionally difficult. Even when
an appropriate interpreter is involved, complete accuracy when communicating
through a third person is difficult (Searight & Gafford, 2005). Consequently,
information provided with clear and precise language, with minimal jargon,
not only minimizes the power differential in medical communication, but also
contributes to the possibility of enhanced comprehension (See Chapter 8; "Care
of Patients and Families at the End of Life").

Enhancing Conversations across Cultures

Culturally attuned conversations occurring in health care settings explore
patient and family preferences regarding such topics as communication, autonomy, truth-telling, informed consent, advance directives, decision-making,
code status, and more in a manner that invites expression of difference. These
communications occur in settings where space and/or time are often not coherent with the desire to create a protected setting where the pace of conversation is determined by patient and family, rather than institutional demand or
limitation. They sometimes occur with clinicians receiving pages, texts or with
laptops open for documentation, appearing to distract. Providers who attend
to maximizing setting and meeting the pace of the family are messaging the respect accorded the profound nature of both the work, the patients and families,
and the providers themselves.

The patient and/or family can be asked about their cultural, psychological,
or spiritual beliefs that create the context for receiving treatments and care.
Spending the time to explore these preferences and styles in the setting of illness and health care in itself is a sign of support and interest in the perceptions
and values of patients and families. Social workers can support patients and
families as they share what is most important to them and make space for cultural expression and ritual within Western health care settings.

Providing end-of-life care when working with diverse patients and
populations creates abundant opportunity to explore differences with sensitivity, attunement, and openness. Searight and Gafford (2005) note that
African-American, Latino, and Asian patients complete advance directives at
much lower rates than white patients, highlighting an opportunity to understand the meaning attributed to these conversations and documents by different
individuals and cultures. Some may view acknowledgment of illness and death
as disrespectful or a threat to sustaining the patient's hope. Some believe that
open discussion could create or exacerbate depression or anxiety in the patient.

Others are eager for direct communication, valuing the empowerment that comes with information and some sense of the future. The following questions, while setting and circumstance specific, provide additional context to aspects of care that may be impacted by patient preferences grounded in cultural values.

"Do you prefer to make medical decisions about future tests or treatments for yourself, or would you prefer that someone else make them with you or for you?"

"Will you please let me know if there is anything about your background that would be helpful . . .to know in working with you or your (mother, father, sister, brother)?" (Searight & Gafford, 2005, p. 519)

These questions intend to center cultural identity and preferences, helping to strengthen rapport between the patient and care team, and assisting the team to communicate in a respectful and accessible way. The following question places a lens on an aspect of care that is often not acknowledged, yet quietly or loudly informs the quality of communication and relationship.

"Sometimes people are uncomfortable discussing these issues with [someone] who is of a different race or cultural background. Are you comfortable with me [providing care for] you?"

Discomfort brought to light does not mean there is a change in provider. Rather, it becomes a catalyst for further inquiry into worries and fears and perhaps a prelude to further authentic sharing.

Araceli

A social worker, Elsa, worked at a nonprofit community mental health center that often receives referrals to help individuals and families adjust to illness. Araceli, a 60-year-old woman born and raised in Puerto Rico, was referred for support in caring for her adult son who had advanced colorectal cancer. Anticipating that his care would create a challenging emotional process and logistical concerns, she expressed a need for psychosocial support.

Alejandro, 40, had lived in the United States for 20 years when he was diagnosed with advanced colorectal cancer. He left Puerto Rico to pursue work in the theater; moving to New York City, he became fully bilingual and found success as a stage manager and set designer. He loved his work and the artistic community where he felt he belonged. He had been married briefly, and he and his wife did not have children; he was unpartnered at the time of his diagnosis. His community was supportive, providing help with meals and companionship. As his illness advanced and his needs became more complex, he realized he needed to complement their contributions with professional help. He agreed to have visiting nurse services and asked his mother to come to New York to help.

Alejandro understood traditional Western views of health and illness, supporting the belief that illnesses were caused by bacteria, viruses, defects, or dysfunction. He followed his treatment plan as recommended by his care team. Initially given medication for pain, he preferred complementary approaches, especially hypnotherapy and guided imagery. Prayer was important to him, providing comfort and solace. He believed in prevention and wellness practices; his diagnosis felt particularly devastating as he had always taken good care of his health, maintaining an assumptive belief that these efforts might protect him. He had vague symptoms and was so involved in his work that he did not see his primary care doctor until he began experiencing pain. He had surgery, followed by radiation therapy and chemotherapy. He thought he was doing well enough after treatment, only to find out the cancer had metastasized to his lungs and brain. He tried to function on his own, but his symptoms, including confusion, memory loss, blurred vision, shortness of breath, and extreme fatigue, made it necessary to ask his mother for help, a difficult dynamic for mother and son to navigate. Latino sons and their mothers can be close and mutually dependent, and older Puerto Rican women often assume an active role in caring for an ill family member (McGoldrick, Giordano, & García-Preto, 2005). The ill person is expected to assume a passive role; this contradicted the Western beliefs about illness and self-care Alejandro had adopted and he refused to take on this traditional sick role.

While Alejandro had traditional Western beliefs about health care, his mother had a personalistic belief system. Although she often used Western health care at home, she also attributed illness to supernatural powers or a human being with special powers targeting individuals in retaliation for spiritual or moral failings. Her view of health care included prayers and supplications to gain favor with supernatural forces. She believed in the "evil eye"—tragedy or ill health that could be caused by an evil person's look, envy, or hatred. She grew up believing this culture-bound syndrome was a normal experience of life. Although she had never met Alejandro's former wife, she did not believe in divorce and blamed him for not preserving his marriage. Her support of Alejandro's standard cancer treatment coexisted with her view that spirits were punishing him for his transgression. Both were grounded in their own belief systems, and the differences in their beliefs was a cause of tension in their relationship. She struggled with believing his illness was retribution for moral failures while wholeheartedly supporting her son, a tremendous conflict she was trying to work through with Elsa.

Araceli was not interested in knowing the details of Alejandro's illness, treatment, and prognosis. Alejandro was very open about his illness and prognosis with his friends and chosen family, while Araceli wanted to keep this information private. After a lengthy discussion with his social worker, Alejandro had signed a do not attempt resuscitation (DNAR) order in consultation with his doctors, a decision which felt unacceptable to Araceli it seemed like to her that he was giving up hope. If they had remained in Puerto Rico, she's not sure she would have agreed to have the doctor tell Alejandro so much about his illness, believing this information would cause additional suffering and affect his will to live.

Alejandro was open about his advancing illness and prognosis, though he wanted to protect Araceli and did not talk about this with her. Alejandro's social worker provided a space for him to hold his need to protect his mother and his simultaneous wish for open communication. Araceli was afraid of illness and even more afraid to talk about death, believing that open discussion would anger malevolent spirits. She wore religious amulets for good luck and didn't see a contradiction in wearing both traditional religious and personalistic amulets.

Elsa was significantly younger than Araceli and, although bilingual, had been born and raised in the United States and was more comfortable speaking English. She made assumptions about Araceli based on their shared Puerto Rican heritage and asked many questions to explore their similarities and differences. Through a process of reflection, Elsa was able to acknowledge what were assumptions and what was true for Araceli. This allowed Elsa to build a more authentic rapport with Araceli, which better facilitated communication and strengthened their relationship. Elsa took an affirmative approach and validated Araceli's beliefs and experiences as important and meaningful to her. She acknowledged the importance of *respeto* (respect), formal and appropriate behavior toward others based on age, gender, social and economic position and authority, and of *personalismo* (personalism), the importance of personal rather than institutional relationships. Both were significant values in Latino culture. She helped Araceli separate the distress she felt about her son's divorce from the distress she felt about his serious illness and limited life expectancy, so she could focus on a mutually supportive relationship with Alejandro. With psychoeducation and medical information about Alejandro's illness, treatment, side effects, and care preferences, expressed through advance directives, Araceli was able to put aside the disagreements about her son's decisions. They grew closer in the last months of Alejandro's life and they were profoundly grateful for the love and support they were able to share with each other.

CONCLUSION

Integrating an awareness of personal values and cultural expression with a humble curiosity about the experience of others is a beginning. Starting here might lead to ease in joining with patients and families in the complex navigation of health care where shared understanding and respect are often discussed, yet remain aspirational. Cultural background, informed through many facets of identity, provides a rich foundation of strength and resilience in the face of serious illness. Seeking to centralize cultural strengths is a primary skill of social workers. These processes and skills invite introspection and investment as part of a social worker's ongoing professional development.

Many cultures collide in health care—those of patients, families, providers, and institutions themselves. Reflecting on and cultivating an awareness as to how these dynamics come together to inform care is creative and adventurous work. There are myriad opportunities—whether in supervision, with peers, or within teams—to make observations and ask questions to invite shared inquiry that explores stereotypes, biases, assumptions, and cultural paradigms privileging dominant power structures. Without intentional vigilance, social workers may inadvertently participate in discrimination and oppression, intended or unintended, that flows from the customs, practices, hierarchy, and power differences inherent in a service setting (Sue, Arredondo, & McDavis, 1992). Social workers, by virtue of their training, are often in a place of participant-observer, a part of the group process while at the same time aware of dynamics that may go unnoticed by others. This highlights a unique responsibility to raise awareness of what might be subtle undertones or implicit judgments. Grounded in curiousity, raising questions creates dialogue, encouraging thoughtfulness and reflection about the patient and family's cultural values, expression, and traditions. The capacity to really care for the whole person asks providers to constantly question what is assumed and what is overlooked. It also supports a depth of exploration and connection in clinical relationships that can be deeply rewarding. Seeking to understand and honor the unique experience of personhood for patients, families, and self allows providers to meet patients and families where they are, from an authentic place in oneself. This promotes therapeutic relationships and clinical interventions that can influence how care is provided and perceived, contributing to meaningful experiences for all along the continuum of illness through bereavement.

LEARNING EXERCISE

1. Select one aspect of health care, such as family caregiving or decision-making; select a culture most represented in your setting, and research how cultural beliefs and practices might inform these topics. Please consider how variables such as gender, age, generation, and ties to

country of origin might modify beliefs, values, and behaviors within a family and in relation to health care systems.

2. As a social worker in a dialysis center, you frequently have contact with patients and their families. You feel closely aligned and identified with a patient and her large family who accompany her to dialysis three times a week; an alignment based on what you perceive to be many cultural similarities. During an interaction, it becomes clear that the family is offended by your comments which evolve from your assumptions of shared experiences. What do you do next?

REFERENCES

Allen, K. M., & Spitzer, W. J. (2016). *Social work practice in healthcare: Advanced approaches and emerging trends.* Thousand Oaks, CA: Sage.

Andrews, J. D. (2013). *Cultural, ethnic and religious reference manual for healthcare providers* (4th ed.). Kernersville, NC: JAMARDA Resources.

Bullock, K. (2011). The influence of culture on end-of-life decision making. *Journal of Social Work in End-of-Life & Palliative Care, 7*(1), 83–98.

Center to Advance Palliative Care. (2011). *2011 public opinion research on palliative care: A report based on research by public opinion strategies.* Retrieved from media. capc.org/filer_public/3c/96/3c96a114-0c15-42da-a07f-11893cca7bf7/2011-public-opinion-research-on-palliative-care_237.pdf.

Crenshaw, K. (1991). Mapping the margins: Intersectionality, identity politics, and violence against women of color. *Stanford Law Review, 43*(6), 1241–1299.

Fletcher, K. (2007). *Are you practicing cultural humility? The key to success in cultural competence.* Retrieved from cahealthadvocates.org/are-you-practicing-cultural-humility-the-key-to-success-in-cultural-competence/.

Gilbert, J., Goode, T. D., & Dunne, C. (2007). *Curricula enhancement module: Cultural awareness.* Washington, DC: National Center for Cultural Competence.

Institute for Democratic Renewal and Project Change Anti-Racism Initiative. (2001). *A community builder's tool kit.* Retrieved from www.racialequitytools.org/resourcefiles/idr.pdf.

Kleinman, A. (1988). *The illness narratives: Suffering, healing, and the human condition.* New York: Basic Books.

Lyke, J., & Colón, M. (2004). Practical recommendations for ethnically and racially sensitive hospice services. *American Journal of Hospice and Palliative Medicine, 21*(2), 131–133.

McGoldrick, M., Giordano, J., & García-Preto, L. (2005). *Ethnicity and family therapy* (3rd ed.). New York: Guilford Press.

National Academies of Science, Engineering, and Medicine. (2017). *Facilitating health communication with immigrant, refugee, and migrant populations through the use of health literacy and community engagement strategies: Proceedings of a workshop.* Washington, DC: National Academies Press.

National Association of Social Workers. (2006). *Assuring the sufficiency of a frontline workforce: A national study of licensed social workers.* Retrieved from www.socialworkers.org/News/Research-Data/Workforce.aspx.

National Association of Social Workers. (2015). *Standards and indicators for cultural competence in social work practice.* Washington, DC: NASW Press.

Ortega, R. M., & Faller, K. C. (2011). Training child welfare workers from an intersectional cultural humility perspective: A paradigm shift. *Child Welfare, 90*(5), 27–49.

Peoples, J., & Bailey, G. (2012). *Humanity: An introduction to cultural anthropology,* (9th ed.). Belmont, CA: Wadsworth/Cengage Learning.

Searight, H., & Gafford, J. (2005). Cultural diversity at the end of life: Issues and guidelines for family physicians. *American Family Physicians, 71*(3), 515–522.

Steinberg, S. M. (2011). Cultural and religious aspects of palliative care. *International Journal of Critical Illness and Injury Science, 1*(2), 154–156.

Sue, D., Arredondo, P., & McDavis, R. (1992). Multicultural counseling competencies and standards: A call to the profession. *Journal of Counseling and Development, 70*(4), 477–486.

Tervalon, M., & Murray-Garcia, J. (1998). Cultural humility versus cultural competence: A critical distinction in defining physician training outcomes in multicultural education. *Journal of Health Care for the Poor and Underserved, 9*(2), 117–125.

US Department of Health and Human Services. (2001). *National standards for culturally and linguistically appropriate services in health care: Final report.* Washington, DC: Office of Minority Health. Retrieved from minorityhealth.hhs.gov/assets/pdf/checked/finalreport.pdf.

Care of Patients and Families
at the End of Life

SUSAN CONCEICAO AND GINNY SWENSON ■

When the human dimension of dying is nurtured, for many, the transition from life can become as profound, intimate, and precious as the moment of birth.

—Ira Byock

INTRODUCTION

The social meanings of death have changed throughout history (Aries, 1977). In the nineteenth century, death was viewed as a "desirable and long-awaited refuge"; the idea of death was combined with ideas of "eternity and fraternal reunion" (Aries, 1977, p. 409). Prior to World War I, the occurrence of a death affected the social group and community. Yet when writing of a transition in the concept of death later in the twentieth century, Phillippe Aries notes that society has "banished death," describing the onset of "dissimulation" and "medicalization" (Aries, 1977). Just as death can be viewed in a historical framework, it also can be viewed from the perspective of developmental stages or through the lens of life course theory. Erik Erikson (1959) identified the final stage of development, the eighth stage, as one in which the individual may experience conflict between integrity and despair. He viewed this period as a time for introspection and life review, when an individual may look back to discover meaning and worth or despair at a lack of meaning in a life not fully lived.

Accompanied by an unconscious fear of death, Erikson has included the interplay of individual and social factors, described as "intricately woven, dynami-
cally interrelated and in continual exchange" (Erikson, 1959, p. 115). Similarly,
Life-Course Theory considers the temporal and socio-historic aspects of experience as playing an important role, and views human development and aging
as lifelong processes and death as a biological, psychological, and social process
(Elder, Kirkpatrick, & Crosnoe, 2003; Sigelman & Rider, 2015). Whether at the
level of the individual, family or society, end of life creates opportunity to join
another in an exploration that is both unique and universal.

In addition to the temporal context of both patient and family's present and
past experiences, many factors impact the dying process, on the micro, meso,
and macro levels. At the micro level, patients and families present with unique
backgrounds, needs, understandings, and experiences of illness, and range in
ability to navigate a fractured and confusing health care system. Additionally,
the setting of care, patient illness, expected trajectory and prognosis, as well
as relationship to spirituality and culture inform experience on the most intimate level. At the meso level, staff in many settings are frequently managing large numbers of patients and are not afforded the time, nor have they
honed the skills necessary to support in-depth conversations regarding patient
hopes and worries. This impedes both understanding the values that guide
decision-making and providing psychoeducation when death is approaching.
At the macro level, issues such as reimbursement structures for end-of-life
care, pressures to reduce length of hospital stays, eligibility criteria for hospice,
and availability of resources to support caregivers will influence care plans and
thus personal experience. While dying is a universal process, the experience is
highly subjective given the micro, meso and macro dynamics and influences.

RECONCEPTUALIZING A GOOD DEATH

Hospice and palliative care providers have long faced the challenge of understanding a "good death," a concept central to the conversation of many clinicians.
"A good death is generally defined as one that is comfortable, peaceful, and one
in which the patient is cared for in the setting of choice, surrounded by friends
or family" (Vena, Kuebler, & Schrader, 2005, p. 360). At times, this setting of
choice is home, and for others it is an intensive care unit because the medical
condition, values, and preferences lead to a focus on interventions that prioritize life-extending measures (Patrick, Engleberg, & Curtis, 2001). Patients and
families have identified the following domains as important when facing end of
life: effective communication and shared decision-making; expert, respectful,
and compassionate care; and an environment that minimizes burden (Virdun,

Luckett, Davidson, & Phillips, 2015). In practice, directly and indirectly, discovering the meaning of death for each patient and family system evolves from a comprehensive understanding of the values and preferences that emerge from personal history, family systems, and the reality of current circumstances. Often this therapeutic process of discovery leads to decisions and outcomes beneficial to one family yet totally incongruent in another. Social workers who value process can assist colleagues across disciplines to develop respect for process and tolerate the unease that comes when individual outcomes are not what clinicians might have hoped.

DISEASE TRAJECTORIES

Every illness progresses differently, and as medical providers better understand a specific disease trajectory, clinicians are positioned to provide anticipatory guidance for patients and families, responding to emotions, questions and concerns. Four types of trajectories have been described (Figure 8.1). In the first, there may be a fairly long period of relative stability, with a short period of evident decline, as in many cancers. The second pertains to illnesses such as heart failure and chronic obstructive pulmonary disease (COPD), where the patient experiences steady decline over time, with intermittent serious episodes. The third represents sudden decline from acute illness and traumatic death. The fourth is seen in old age and forms of dementia, where the trajectory is one of decline, extending over time, including periods of stability. Sometimes a decline is seen following an acute event, such as a hip fracture or pneumonia (Murray, Kendall, & Boyd, 2005).

In serious illnesses such as heart failure, COPD, and dementia, the trajectories are more difficult to predict. Consequently, clinicians miss opportunities to elicit values and preferences related to evolving illness and end of life. In the case of dementia, the course is frequently long, often lacking a clear demarcation as to when dementia becomes a terminal as opposed to a chronic condition (Sachs, Shega, & Cox-Hayley, 2004). Caregivers and family members are consistently adapting to the subtle changes in the patient's cognitive and physical functioning. The family may have been experiencing ambiguous loss, accompanied by a deep sense of psychological loss, in response to the changes over a period of years. The individual identity of the patient and the psychological essence changes over time, resulting in the family experiencing the death of the person that the patient had been, even though the patient is physically alive—a death of autobiography, yet not a biological death (Doka, 2004). In the instance of sudden death, clinical work begins in the setting of acute grief and shock.

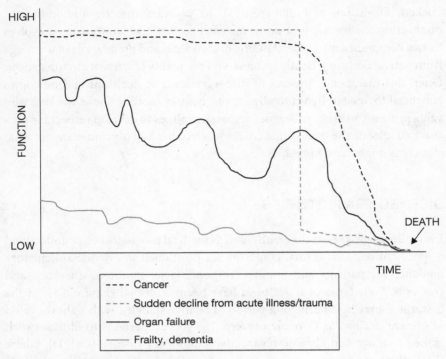

Figure 8.1. The trajectory of decline.

PROGNOSTICATION

One of the challenges to helping patients and families prepare for end of life is the difficulty in predicting prognosis, approximating how long a person might live and the likely course of a disease (Warm, 2015). Research has shown that physicians struggle with prognostication, as evidenced by a study in which 343 physicians were asked to estimate life expectancy for 468 patients. Only 20% were correct, with most physicians overestimating the length of survival (Christakis, 2000). Several researchers have identified the uncertainty in predicting life expectancy until the patient is in the last few days of life (Kennedy et al., 2014; Sullivan et al., 2007).

There is evidence that the longer a relationship between a patient and her physician, the less accurate the predicted prognosis, perhaps a consequence of lost objectivity as relationships develop over time (Christakis, 2000). In some instances, the physician has developed a close relationship with the patient and family and may have difficulty dealing with their own feelings of loss and anticipatory grief. When cure or prolongation of life has been the shared goal, and this is no longer possible, the physician may worry that she has disappointed the patient and family.

Assessing how much patients and families want to know about expected illness course and prognosis provides a starting place. Every patient and family are different and their desire for information reflects the cultural, psychological, spiritual, and religious context of a patient's life. If a patient and family are interested in prognostic information, there is a clear opportunity for anticipatory guidance and, potentially, advance care planning. As accurate prediction is challenging, providers may describe prognosis in ranges from hours to days, days to weeks, weeks to months, and months to years (Christakis, 1998). Sharing prognosis can be the setting to explore previous conversations about end-of-life care and preferences, including code status, location of care, and spiritual and religious needs. In addition to exploring past conversations, these meetings create an environment where patients and families can consider activities that honor legacy. Preparing scrapbooks or video recordings can be introduced and have been found to further enhance family communication and to impact caregiver stress (Allen, 2008). These and related conversations are an opportune time to support patient and family coping in the face of uncertainty.

There is at times an incongruence between the information clinicians feel they have provided and what a patient and/or family have heard and integrated. Some family members may report that they did not know the patient was dying, and had they known, would have made different choices. This occurs even when staff members attest that family was informed about a patient's trajectory. There are a number of reasons why it might be difficult to hear and integrate medical information. Advanced illness and end of life are often high-stress times, and stress reduces the cognitive ability to make sense of new information (MacKenzie, Smith, Hasher, Leach, & Behl, 2006). The language of medicine can be confusing and complex, making it challenging for clinicians to communicate in a clear, direct way and simultaneously tend to the emotional nature of the discussion (See Chapter 2; "Structure and Processes of Care").

Social workers are well positioned to frame patient and family understanding in relationship to hope, psychosocial stressors, and cultural context for other members of the health care team, adapting communication strategies to the uniqueness of each situation. Sharing prognosis begins a process that evolves over time, requiring ongoing attention across settings. Health social workers may intersect with patients and families at many different places of understanding, providing opportunities to revisit prognosis in collaboration with other team members while addressing the psychosocial needs from the practical to the existential.

ENHANCING TRANSITIONS

Patients and families commonly navigate transitions in care and setting as illness evolves. Discharge planning, coordination, and case management are important clinical skills, taking into account the multidimensional impact of changes in the care plan. Social work assessment and intervention can play a central role in supporting patients and families through transitions which often involve changes that have psychosocial meaning. Patients and family members have often experienced multiple care transitions, some anticipated and some unanticipated, due to fluctuations in a patient's medical status or functioning. The transition from a chronic illness state to an expectation that the end of life is approaching may represent another crisis. Regardless of the nature of the transition, patients and families can experience complex feelings as they separate from systems and clinicians they have come to know and are asked to trust new systems of care. This is an invitation for social workers to acknowledge ambivalent feelings, provide appropriate reassurance, and bridge transitions by preemptive contact with the receiving clinicians.

Changes in the focus of care provide the opportunity to explore how patients and families are responding to the demand for adaptation and identify where transitions may represent loss. For example, the presence of professional caregivers in the home might be a source of relief, support, and practical assistance to family and friends caring for a patient. Conversely, it might feel like an invasion of privacy or a negative judgment of a family's ability to provide appropriate care. When a patient transitions to a facility such as a nursing home, there are important practical considerations, including cost, and time spent traveling when minutes shared with a patient become precious in the setting of an anticipated death. The financial life of patients and families is affected by such things as changes in income and benefits, such as Supplemental Security Income and the need to spend resources that may have been symbolic of a legacy. A new environment requires rapid adjustment and adaptation. The utilization of a strengths-based approach, exploring the ways patients and families are coping and managing stress, can be helpful in developing awareness of and the ability to support and maximize their strengths (Turner, 2011) (see Table 8.1).

Studies have shown that when people are asked where they want to die, the majority state they want to die at home (Steinhauser et al., 2000). In one study, 90% of 180 terminally ill patients with cancer stated they wanted to die at home and rated this as "highly important." In a study looking at 71 patient/caregiver dyads, preferences for death at home were met in only 38% of cases (Agar, Currow, Shelby, Plummer, & Sanderson, 2008). Discussions about preferences for place of death provide opportunity for social workers to explore the wishes and values of patients. A wish to die at home could reflect desires to be in a

Table 8.1 THEORETICAL APPROACHES TO SUPPORT STRENGTHS

Theory	Goal	Possible Questions
Strengths-based practice	Identify, develop awareness, & help clients act on their strengths	What helps you cope & manage the stress of illness, caregiving?
Narrative	Understand, broaden, & change the stories clients have organized their lives around	Can you imagine thinking of your situation in a different way; with a different outcome?
Cognitive	Modify thoughts or cognitions that are distortions or problematic for the client	The thought that loosing weight is the result of not eating enough is true in some circumstances; in this circumstance, it is a result of the disease or dying process.
Ego psychology	Restore, maintain, & enhance client's ego functions & coping capacities	Have you thought of what your life might be like after the death?

SOURCE: Turner, Francis. (2011). *Social work treatment: Interlocking theoretical approaches*. New York: Oxford University Press.

comfortable, familiar, and loving environment, surrounded by known people. Alternatively, a wish to be home may reflect a fear of the unknown at a time when one is increasingly dependent and vulnerable. It may become clear, closer to death, that being home is no longer possible or prioritized (Srivastava, 2017). The values reflected in the desire to die at home might be achievable in other settings, with mindfulness and intention on the part of staff by personalizing the space, extending visiting hours, and encouraging time spent sharing food, music, quiet or ritual. Sensitive, culturally congruent, and meaningful care can be provided at the end of life in any setting, and social workers are essential to supporting this vision.

Social workers can play a primary role in exploring the values and needs of patient and family. Psychoeducation regarding hospice, including focus of care, eligibility criteria, and services offered creates an informed discussion of options for end of life. In other situations, patients may decline rapidly, or be highly symptomatic and dying in an acute care setting. The social work role includes assessment of immediate needs, which may range from the presence of spiritual support, guidance as to who might need to be called and advocacy for intensive symptom management, information or a protected space, in a shared effort to honor the singular experience for this person and family.

HOSPICE CARE

Hospice eligibility is determined by an understanding of both stage of disease
and goals related to future interventions and modalities of care. For comprehensive disease-specific criteria, please refer to a review of hospice eligibility
criteria (National Hospice and Palliative Care Organization, 2015). Historically,
hospice care was most appropriate for patients and families who were not interested in pursuing disease-modifying or life-extending interventions. This
was most clear in the case of cancer care and the discontinuation of chemotherapy and/or radiation. Over time, this distinguisher becomes increasingly
complicated, as disease-modifying therapies are often necessary for symptom
management and comfort, as in the role of diuresis in the setting of congestive heart failure. There are variations across hospice agencies regarding what
interventions can or cannot be provided under the umbrella of the benefit.
Hospice liaisons and admission staff are generally available to discuss cases and
to bring questions regarding an individual care plan to their medical director.
This can be a helpful resource in determining what a hospice care plan would
consist of for a specific patient. Regardless of what interventions will be provided, a primary value to listen for when considering the appropriateness of
hospice is a general desire to stay out of the hospital.

Hospice care provides an interdisciplinary approach focused on symptom
management and quality of life. At home, the hospice team supports primary
caregivers, including family members, friends, and professional aides paid for
both privately and otherwise. For some, the experience of caregiving can be
financially, physically, and emotionally stressful. For many caregivers, the experience is a positive one and may be a way of giving back or contributing
to a dynamic caregiving relationship. Caregiving can be accompanied by a
sense of accomplishment and pride in meeting the challenges of providing
care consistent with a family's values. In the skilled nursing facility setting, the
hospice team supports the care provided by facility staff, and can act as a resource for patients, families, and staff. Of particular value to families of patients
approaching end of life is 24-hour access to clinicians available for guidance,
information, and reassurance. Additionally, hospice programs are required to
provide bereavement services for one year following death (Medicare, 2015).
This benefit can relieve patient distress, knowing their families will have access
to services beyond their death. Facilitating a referral to hospice and mitigating
the distress of transition to hospice care is an important social work role.

Enrolling in hospice or a referral to palliative care does not change one's
identity, yet clinical language choice often confuses personhood with an aspect
of health care. It is common to hear practitioner shorthand descriptors such

as "she's hospice," "he's a DNR" or "she's on palliative." While well-intended, abbreviating complex choices and plans of care can lead to assumptions that often are not valid and conflate a human being with a philosophy and service (Altilio, 2011). This can serve to devalue the meaning of important transitions in an individual's life, reducing the complexity of the process and aborting the critical thinking needed in the care of persons coming to the end of life (See Chapter 2; "Structure and Processes of Care").

ASSESSMENT

Assessment is rooted in the ethos of humility and curiosity, aiming to build rapport, to increase understanding of the patient and family's unique circumstances and needs, and to create opportunities for meaningful experiences within the health care system. The focus and pace of assessment are situation specific. For example, the aspects of assessment prioritized in an emergency room in the setting of cardiac arrest may be quite different from those prioritized during hospice intake or an initial interview upon admission to an extended care facility. Assessment is an intervention. The questions asked and the responses chosen are a function of empathetic response and critical thinking evolving organically as rapport builds. This process is ongoing, guides plans of care in the immediate, and often sets the stage for future clinical work. Patients and families can feel heard and simultaneously enabled to enlist the observing ego, an awareness of self and our place in the world which supports their ability to interpret, verbalize, and synthesize information (Blanck & Blanck, 1974).

The domains of assessment in the following list, while presented as discrete topics, are interrelated. For example, discussion about prognosis is often intimately related to cultural and spiritual beliefs. Those who believe the future belongs in the dominion of a Higher Power, rather than the realm of the physician, require accommodation of the language of prognostication, lest clinicians be viewed as presumptuous and lose credibility. The following domains are a guide to sensitize listening and inform inquiry.

The patient and family

- Observations and understanding of the patient's status and prognosis: What have the doctors told you? What are you seeing, or what have you observed over time?

- Coherence, confusion, or discord related to the current approach to care
- Cultural beliefs and traditions (See Chapter 7; "Cultural Aspects of Care"); spiritual and religious concerns and rituals (See Chapter 6; "Spiritual, Religious, and Existential Dimensions of Care").
- Primary language
- Supports; persons and community networks

History

- Prior losses
- Complex family dynamics
- Preexisting psychosocialspiritual stressors
- Health problems, including emotional/psychiatric or substance abuse, trauma, depression, suicide, or requests for hastening death.
- Experiences of marginalization within community and health care systems

Family systems

- Family composition: Who is here? Who is missing and might need to be here? Participation of children and grandchildren
- Impact of illness and expected death on family equilibrium and structure
- Concerns or worries relating to prior decisions or current plan of care, medications, or treatments provided and those withheld
- Communication patterns within family
  - Whose voice is missing?
  - Who is the spokesperson?
  - What are the emotional and cognitive demands of that role?
  - How will large families communicate with each other and the care team?
- Decision-making person and process; advance directives to guide decisions; comfort or stress related to decision-making role and process.

Preparation for death of a patient

- Patient and family unique preferences to receive, or not, prognostic information
- Preferences related to location of death

- Feasibility of death at home
  - Is dying at home a preference?
  - Who lives in the home?
  - Availability of caregivers
  - Cultural, emotional, and financial aspects of considering a home death
  - Symptom burden and ability to manage at home
- Status of final arrangements, if appropriate
- Bereavement needs, risk, and protective factors.

INTERSECTIONAL EXPERIENCE

The social work role has been described as one of "context interpreter" as questions, language, and listening link the worlds of patients and families to the world of medicine (Bern-Klug, Gessert, & Forbes, 2001). Social workers, in consult with other providers, can interpret information for families to enhance understanding and inform decisions about a care plan. Social workers are unique among other disciplines, as their training supports an ability to provide information in a manner that respects culture and empowers and responds to the feelings evoked (Cagle & Kovacs, 2009). Yet providing culturally congruent care moves beyond communication to an understanding of social identity and life course. The psychological, social, and spiritual needs of each patient and family are directly related to their experience of the world and are shaped by race, class, gender, sexuality, nationality, culture, language, immigration status, and education. Each person is unique and no two people are in the world in the same way, even when their social signifiers are the same (See Chapter 7; "Cultural Aspects of Care").

For example, a 40-year-old transgender man, Timothy, is trained as a critical care nurse. Dying of metastatic lung cancer, his pain increases and he receives medications prescribed by a palliative care physician. While his team has a plan to respond quickly when symptoms change, Timothy makes autonomous decisions to increase medications. He repeatedly asserts that "he is the expert on his body" and will know how to keep himself safe. The team understands his response as a reflection of both his training as a nurse and his desire to assert the comfort and self-awareness he has achieved with his body. These assumptions, while potentially valid, miss an essential variable. As a woman, Timothy struggled with endometriosis and associated pain. He brings to this illness a history of having been delegitimized as a woman with pain and thus any inquiry about his pain or effort to influence his use of medications in the present revives the complex feelings associated with the earlier pain experience. Viewing Timothy's experience through an intersectional lens leads to understanding at the micro level of relationship with his body, meso level of relationship with clinicians, past and present, and the macro level where transgender experience is marginalized and the safety of patients, as well as prescribers of controlled substances, influence clinical responses (See Chapter 3; "Physical Aspects of Care").

PSYCHOLOGICAL AND SPIRITUAL TASKS

The psychological and spiritual aspects of living with serious illness and anticipating death are often interrelated. For example, a search for meaning may encompass spiritual or religious values related to death and the hereafter, or may relate to a need to discover meaning in the life lived or to make little meaning of death, but rather to view it as a universal experience. As with assessment, the setting and circumstances in which social workers meet patients and families often determine priorities. Consider a person brought into the emergency department with untreated HIV, cachectic and short of breath, expressing both a psychological and spiritual need quickly provides direction to a social work assessment when she asks for a priest. Whether driven by an expectation of death, a need to seek forgiveness, or some guarantee of an afterlife, the request quickly prioritizes interventions.

With honed listening, some common psychological themes that may emerge include the following:

- Efforts to come to terms with an unavoidable and often foreshortened future
- Fluctuating awareness or acknowledgment of the possibility of death
- Challenges to sense of control and agency
- A need to voice hidden fears, such as abandonment, uncontrolled symptoms, dependence
- Questions about legacy and the integrity of the life lived
- A desire to be treated and feel like a normal person and be part of life
- Hopes and wishes, often including a desire to be comfortable and with caring persons.

Spiritual themes can signal contentment and comfort or turmoil and may include the following:

- Facing a place with God and
- Clinging onto life and that which is loved and familiar and/or anticipating a place with God and reunion with those who have passed before

- Feelings of alienation, loneliness, despair, or fear
- Connection and belonging
- Forgiveness, reconciliation
- Gratitude.

Identifying themes and subsequent interventions happens along the continuum of serious illness and may become more intense and immediate when death is more imminent. Short sentences and simple language are effective. The answers to questions such as "Are you worried?" or "Is there anything you want to say?" or "Anyone you want to see?" link assessment to opportunities for intervention. Cicely Saunders, in her pioneering work with hospice patients, often asked, "How are you within?" Exploratory questions can elicit hopes and joys, feelings of satisfaction and acceptance. They also have the potential to identify psychological or spiritual distress as it relates to meaning, relatedness, hopelessness, and forgiveness (Groves & Klauser, 2005).

Beyond the asking of questions, assessment also is based in observation. There may be signs of cultural identity, religious objects on the bedside table, or religious themes in tattoos, cards, or books in the room or on the wall. Acknowledging and exploring the significance of these symbols may lead to interventions, such as the integration of ritual or clergy. The social worker can play an important role in both providing presence and creating space to discover and honor cultural and spiritual aspects of patient-family experience. As patients approach the end of their life and active dying, there may be opportunity to identify and note preferences relating to spiritual and religious practices, cultural values, and ritual.

BEREAVEMENT

Bereavement is affected throughout the course of illness, from diagnosis through death. Families are creating the story of their person's illness over time, which will affect their thoughts and feelings as they process death. As such, health care providers at every intersection have opportunities to tend to grief, impact legacy and the narrative of the death within the family. Identifying both risk factors and protective factors, sources of strength and resiliency, informs support and clinical interventions in the moment. It is a process that may go on over time, or that may be concentrated in situations of acute end-of-life experiences, as in the emergency department or intensive care unit.

Bereavement is a unique experience that varies in time and tone. Providers can be alert to factors influencing high-risk bereavement in order to mitigate distress. It is important to assess family and friends for likelihood of complicated grief when normal grief reactions do not lessen in intensity with passage of time. Risk factors include sudden loss and death of a child (Brophy McCale, 2005), a perceived lack of support, multiple losses, conflictual or ambivalent relationship with the dying person, and presence of a concurrent life crisis (Worden, 2009). Other complicating factors are history of trauma, mental illness, or addiction. By identifying stressors and risk factors, the social worker can provide anticipatory guidance, alert families to signs of complicated grief, and provide family members with resources for crisis intervention, grief counseling, and other modalities of support. For example, 34-year-old Elise is the daughter of Cynthia, who was dying after a rapid decline from her liver disease. Elise readily talked about her experience with the loss of a 10-day-old baby, Catherine, two years earlier. She shared how no one had told her Catherine was going to die and she still felt shocked. This history magnifies the importance of anticipatory guidance, informing the sharing of prognosis over time, possibly repeatedly, as Cynthia gets closer to death. The therapeutic rapport enabled Elise to share the death of her child, noting trauma and unresolved loss, informing a care plan to include ongoing, daily support from both providers and her community in the present and ongoing assessment of bereavement risk.

Additionally, identifying prior losses or family relationships perceived as difficult or conflictual provides an opportunity to recognize complexity and empathize with unique challenges and history that may complicate the feelings and reactions in the present. There may be comfort and validation in this recognition, a process of normalization that may invite further discussion and enhance healing. A narrative approach, aiming to help the individual to broaden and consider alternate interpretations of her story (Turner, 2011), might allow for the reconsideration of earlier experiences and relationships. Reframing, reflection, and inquiry are techniques to invite a reconceptualization or rewriting of a story.

An exploration of the family's prior experience with death and dying can be instructive. Families may have had no prior experience, but if asked about their worries or concerns, will frequently express fear the patient will suffer or linger. It is not uncommon to hear a family member recount troubling memories, recalling a situation in which a patient was in pain, agitated, or distressed. The awareness of this history and these fears informs the care plan and allows the team to provide psychoeducation, normalize the range of emotions, and reassure that every effort will be focused on expert assessment and maintaining comfort. At other times, families come away from prior deaths with perceptions that clinicians have hastened the death of their family member. While the interventions include transparent expert assessment and psychoeducation, re-assurance often comes from a shared assessment with family as to the level of patient distress and discussion of the intent and anticipated outcome of providing medication to mitigate symptoms and not hasten death. In some instances, the story recalled is a positive experience in which family members were present, supportive and the patient was comfortable. Recalling this type of experience can be helpful in providing a model and goals for the current plan of care by exploring the factors that contributed to a positive outcome for patient and family. For example, was there open communication prior to the death? How did the professionals impact that experience? What helped the family to cope with the impending loss?

ACTIVE DYING

The period of active dying has been defined as "the hours or days preceding imminent death during which the patient's physiologic functions wane" (Hui et al., 2014). End-of-life care may include a change of setting, medications, treatments, and monitoring, representing a shift in focus. Medications are stopped and started in response to the observed needs of the patient in an ef- fort to manage symptoms. These changes often have symbolic significance for families and may be a focus of social work intervention. For example, families might need time and space to adjust to the discontinuation of a medication taken for blood pressure or diabetes, previously important for a patients' health or functioning.

The social worker plays an important role in educating the family about physical and functional changes throughout the dying process. Some of these changes may be clearly observable. Acknowledging and exploring meaning associated with physical changes can normalize and reassure family members and caregivers and create space for processing the dying experience. As the patient gets closer to death, they may sleep more, eat and drink less, and communicate and relate inconsistently. Ankles, legs, and hands sometimes become swollen. Extremities may become cooler and mottled (change in color), and changes in blood pressure occur. Body temperature may fluctuate. Breathing patterns may change, including both rapid and/or slow and inconsistent respirations. The sound of breathing can become more prominent, sometimes referred to as the "death rattle." Changes in mental status may represent delirium, often referred to as terminal delirium, which can be caused by polypharmacy, met-abolic changes, infection, or central nervous system pathology (Ellershaw & Ward, 2003, Weissman & Rosielle, 2014). During the period of active dying, treatment of the multifactorial causes may be incongruous with goals, imprac-tical or impossible, or inconsistent with the goals of care.

Yet for many, a clear mind and ability to connect remain very important, and reporting changes in mental status to a medical colleague moves beyond assumptions to a shared assessment. Understanding the etiology of mental status changes can lead to interventions that include psychoeducation and an assessment for reversible causes. Patients may experience hallucinations, and at times refer to seeing someone who has died (Kuebler, Davis, & Moore, 2005). The family can be assured that this frequently occurs and supported to engage with the patient's experience, rather than distancing out of fear.

When the patient is still able to speak, and death is likely within days or weeks, she may utilize symbolic communication, often culturally influenced, and talk about "going home", "traveling" or "journeys." (Cairns, 2003). When the patient is no longer responsive, families may take comfort from the belief that the patient may still hear (Berry & Griffie, 2006; Callahan, 2008).

Families often express concerns that the patient is in pain; if the patient is no longer communicative, how will the team recognize and treat her pain? Psychoeducation can focus on how pain is assessed in nonverbal patients, through grimacing or moaning and changes in body language or facial expressions (Herr et al., 2006). As patients eat and drink less, families may worry they are "starving to death" (Weissman, 2014). Food and liquid intake can be explored, addressing personal relationships to food and issues of hunger in the context of a specific disease trajectory. This provides an opportunity to join with a family in identifying symbolic meaning and cultural and familial values related to feeding, which is often a primary mode of caregiving. As food is social and represents nourishment, exploring alternative ways of caring and "feeding" may benefit families. Care that focuses on keeping skin, mouth, and lips moistened and, when possible, pleasure feedings are adaptations responsive to the needs of dying persons.

It can be useful to offer ideas about how a family can be with the dying person as they interact less over time. This might involve touch, music, telling meaningful stories, sharing humor and laughter, reading out loud, praying, or sitting at the bedside. Being with dying people often requires a comfort with silence and an awareness of what is happening with oneself. It is important that family and friends be encouraged to care for self, including respite, meeting basic needs such as showering, eating, and drinking water, and other coping strategies that they may bring to this experience.

The dying process is different for everyone. This may be a period of sadness, reflection, contention, rage, peace, celebration, acceptance, and so on. Social work intervention may focus almost entirely on family coping and meaning making. The following questions may provide access to caregiver/family experience and promote reflection.

- What is important about this time for you?
- How are you feeling emotionally? Physically?
- Is there anyone you are concerned about? Anyone who needs more support?
- How are you dealing with what is happening?
- What is helping? What are sources of strength?
- Are there others who want to say good-bye?
- Have you said everything you want to say?
- Have you begun to think about final arrangements?
- Are there rituals that are important to you? Can we contact a priest or clergy?
- Are there traditions or customs that are important at this time? Is there anything we should know about caring for the patient's body?
- Regarding children, adolescents: What is their understanding? What have they been told? What are they asking?

By observing and listening attentively, social workers can respond to indications that the family member may want to talk about her grief and can encourage sharing and reminiscence, promoting connection and relational support. The use of an ego-supportive approach with the goal to maintain, restore, and enhance the individual's ego functions and ability to cope can be helpful (Turner, 2011). For example, if the patient's spouse seems anxious about the future, utilize an exploratory approach: How do you imagine the future might look? How have you managed change or loss in the past? Who else is in your life? to further uncover and explore worries, strengths, and resources. Table 8.1 links strengths-based, narrative, cognitive, and ego psychology theory to a sampling of questions designed to focus interventions to recover or enhance self-efficacy in the setting of an anticipated death.

FINAL ARRANGEMENTS

The period after death marks yet another and more final transition. What happens now? Depending on the setting, family may want or need direction as to what happens to the body. Sometimes religious and cultural beliefs require coordination to accommodate post-death rituals that have profound meaning. Understanding morgue policies can be useful, as every institution is different.

For example, does every person who dies in the hospital and extended care facility go through the morgue, or is it possible to have a funeral director come straight to the room? How long can a body stay in the room? What happens if a family wants to view the body in the coming days? How long can a body stay in a private home? Is home burial allowed in this region? Are there "green cemeteries" that support natural burials?

Helping patients and families with mortuary and final arrangements is supported by concrete knowledge of resources that are culturally attuned, language concordant, or offer financial assistance. Cost related to planning can provoke distress at a time when emotional and financial resources are in demand. Options for financial assistance vary by state, related to Medicaid stipulations and local resources. Many people who are actively dying have not chosen a mortuary or discussed preferences with family. It is helpful to reassure families that it is not necessary to complete arrangements prior to death. This is often a relief to family members, who may find it very difficult and upsetting to plan when the patient is alive. This sensitive topic can be addressed, utilizing language with therapeutic intent. For example, the following questions demonstrate a way to partialize the process so it may be more manageable and acceptable to the family member.

- Have you had discussions with the patient regarding her wishes/ choices (burial/cremation)?
- Have you begun to think about final arrangements?
- Is there any way I can be of assistance?
- Are there any cultural or religious values or rituals that play a part in your choices or that we need to know about to provide care at time of death and after?

Special Consideration: Alzheimer's and Other Forms of Dementia

Alzheimer's disease is a degenerative brain disease and the most common cause of dementia. It is characterized by a decline in memory, language, problem-solving, and other cognitive skills, affecting a person's relationships and her ability to perform everyday activities. Severe dementia frequently leads to immobility, swallowing disorders, and malnutrition, which can increase the risk of other serious conditions such as pneumonia.

Caregivers of individuals with Alzheimer's report higher levels of stress, compared with caregivers of individuals with other illnesses. Twice as many caregivers report financial, emotional, and physical difficulties, and approximately 40% suffer from depression. Depression increased with the severity of the patient's cognitive impairment. In early onset dementia, caregivers may experience high levels of physical and emotional strain and stress. This is related to the disruption of current functions and active roles such as employment, and the disruption of the future one might have imagined (Van Vliet, De Vugt, Bakker, Koopmans, & Verhey, 2010; Werner, Stein-Shvachman, & Korczyn, 2009).

Dementia is often under-recognized as a terminal illness, and this is one of the challenges to providing good end-of-life care. Frequently, the trajectory is one of a slow decline, ranging from four to nine years, with other problems emerging, such as pneumonia, febrile episodes, or swallowing problems, which may not be acknowledged as indicative of an end-stage and therefore a limited prognosis (Mitchell et al., 2009). Thus, families have difficulty recognizing emotionally and cognitively that their family member is dying. Mitchell and others note the importance of preparing family and decision-makers for the trajectory of advanced dementia. The changes that occur are often subtle and gradual, informing a process of ambiguous loss, in which the person is physically present, yet psychologically or emotionally altered in some way (Doka & Aber, 2002). Full understanding of prognosis may reframe decisions related to interventions such as artificial nutrition and repeat hospitalizations (Mitchell et al., 2009).

Eugenia Harris

Mrs. Eugenia Harris is 92 years old. Her medical history included dementia, diagnosed eight years earlier, breast cancer for which she underwent a mastectomy 20 years ago, hypertension, and diabetes. Mrs. Harris was admitted to the hospital from a skilled nursing facility for unmanaged delirium. At the time of admission her Fast score was 7D denoting very severe dementia (Tsai & Arnold, 2015). Lethargic and confused, she was only able to verbalize single words and was noted to have significant skin breakdown.

An African American, born in Alabama, Mrs. Harris had been married for 43 years until she was widowed in 1989. She is a Seventh Day Adventist, the mother of two children, daughter Pamela and son Lucien, both of whom live locally. Pamela, Mrs. Harris's medical power of attorney and primary decision-maker, was recently diagnosed with breast cancer.

During the course of hospitalization, it was decided to transition her to the inpatient hospice unit. Pamela and Lucien did not want their mother to return to the skilled nursing facility and had understood that the goal of transfer to the inpatient unit was to manage her confusion. Her delirium began to improve within two days, and the hospice physician informed family that Mrs. Harris might not continue to meet the general in-patient (GIP) criteria. She explained that GIP level of care is for patients who require pain and symptom management that cannot be managed in residential (routine) settings (Taylor, Bhasvar, Harker, & Kassner, 2015). The change from GIP to routine level of care would require a discharge plan. The family experienced the physician as disrespectful and felt misled by the clinicians who had proposed transfer to the unit. The inpatient hospice social worker worked with the family, explained the guidelines, and validated their concerns and distress. Throughout, the social worker was able to bridge the incongruence between the evolving care plan and the family's expectation, providing education regarding hospice, the role of the inpatient unit, and services provided across settings. She validated their hope for improvement while reviewing the trajectory and stages of dementia, highlighting the potential that regardless of setting, Mrs. Harris may continue to decline.

The social worker also provided resources and psychoeducation on the enhanced care Mrs. Harris would receive in a skilled nursing facility with hospice services. The transition occurred two days later with focused attention on family concerns and a plan for the hospice nurse and social worker to meet Pamela, Lucien, and Mrs. Harris upon arrival. During this initial visit, family shared their perceptions that racial discrimination at both the previous nursing home and in the hospital had influenced the quality of care for their mother which resulted in bedsores and dehydration. The social worker witnessed the range of feelings and the experiences that informed their current vigilance and advocacy as Lucien and Pamela sought to insure the best care for their mother.

Over the coming days, Mrs. Harris's medical status evolved quickly. During a family meeting, the hospice nurse identified the observable signs and symptoms of agitation and pain, behaviors that might have been a response to the transfer but appeared, as per family report, to be more intense and intractable. It seemed possible that Mrs. Harris's distress was not a response to the change in environment, but rather that she was actively dying. The family was tearful and confirmed their desire for their mother to be comfortable. Focusing on patient and family needs and priorities, medication was scheduled to address increasing agitation. Small amounts of liquids for taste and pleasure were offered, unless Mrs. Harris was unresponsive. Setting a clear expectation for what comfort means and looks like allowed the family and hospice team to join in her care and in shared observation.

Following the meeting, the skilled nursing facility social worker assumed the clinical work with Pamela and Lucien. Exploring past losses, they shared that they had not experienced a death of someone close in more than 25 years. The anticipated death of their mother was particularly difficult, as they felt "unready." Interventions included life review, exploring their unique and shared grief attributed to the ambiguous losses related to Mrs. Harris's extended course of illness, and education regarding the signs and symptoms of active dying.

Over the next week, Mrs. Harris continued to decline, becoming less responsive while appearing comfortable. The staff encouraged Pamela and Lucien to bring pictures, share stories and memories, and engage the grandchildren to visit with the clinical goals of creating legacy, and honoring their relationships and connection. Together, with provider support, the family had effected a transition from hopefulness that Mrs. Harris would improve to hopefulness that she would remain comfortable and die surrounded by her family.

Both Pamela and Lucien attended a family support group, led by social work staff, held daily at the facility. As Pamela was expressing her sadness and worries, Lucien abruptly walked out. His sister's grief was distressing, as she was "like his mother"—the "rock" of the family. His apprehension about his mother's death was intensified as he recalled the experience of his father's death, which "hit him hard" and was followed by a period of substance abuse. Counseling focused on identifying the ways his life was different now, noting increased stability and support from his partner. Ultimately, he identified that what was most important to him at this time was supporting his daughter.

Prior to Mrs. Harris's death, Lucien brought his 10-year-old daughter, Daisy, to the nursing home. As she was occupied in the play room, Lucien talked with the social worker about a "difference of opinion" among the family members, some of whom thought Daisy should not see her grandmother dying. The social worker encouraged Lucien to ask Daisy what she wanted; how she might choose to participate. Daisy shared her wish to see her grandmother to say good-bye, but not stay in the room. This plan was acceptable to other family members. By exploring Daisy's thoughts, feelings, and hopes, Lucien brought Daisy into the conversation, modeling open communication and validating Daisy's knowing of her own needs and capacity.

Mrs. Harris remained at the facility until her death, one week after admission. Extended family was present when she died, expressing grief with loud crying. After the family shared their immediate grief together, they were receptive to talking with the social worker. She inquired about relationships and history, which led to further sharing of memories and stories about Mrs. Harris, the matriarch of the family.

The hospice social worker made a bereavement call to Pamela and Lucien one week after the death. Pamela felt she was coping adequately; however, she was troubled by recurrent thoughts of the moment of death. While Pamela had wanted to go home, she felt she had to stay for Lucien. She wished she had left.

The social worker normalized her thoughts and feelings, acknowledging that the meaning and story of her mother's death may change with time, as it might also for her brother. Pamela agreed to have a bereavement counselor reach out to her. Talking with Lucien, he described his sadness. While he missed his mother, he noted that this experience, his current life situation, and the strength he felt in managing his mother's death were notably different from his response to his father's dying. He shared that now his focus was supporting Daisy as she adjusted to the loss of her grandmother.

DISCUSSION

Multiple factors impacted the experience of Mrs. Harris, Pamela, and Lucien. On a macro level, available services and regulatory issues governing reimbursement required care transitions. Multiple transitions in care setting can be extremely stressful for both the patient and the family, necessitating a retelling of their story, renegotiation of goals of care, and developing new relationships with care providers (Burge et al., 2005). Yet transitions can also be a time of building—on work well done, as well as on the missteps and mishaps. Conscious and attuned listening to Pamela and Lucien linked social workers across settings, engaged hopes and expectations and concerns ranging from racial discrimination to assisting Daisy to participate, on her terms, in the dying of her grandmother. Each social worker joined in the present with an awareness of the past and skills that enabled relationships to both support strengths and intervene to enrich the unique and shared experience of family members through Mrs. Harris's dying and beyond. The following are descriptions of social work roles that both enhanced transitions and built care plans to acknowledge and integrate the past and supported the family moving forward.

- Assessing understanding; ongoing support and education
- Providing presence and empathic listening to create a setting for family to express their concerns
- Psychoeducation regarding hospice care and criteria, changes at end of life and symptom management
- Advocacy and reframing of family experience to alter staff's perceptions of family as "difficult"
- Anticipatory guidance and psychoeducation relating to grandchild's needs and ability to participate
- Exploring aspects of grief and loss, bereavement follow-up
- Coordination of care and goals through transitions and between facility social worker and hospice team

CONCLUSION

The experience of the patient and family at the end of life is multifaceted and singularly unique. It is framed within a landscape of the developmental stage of the patient and family, as well as their social, historical, spiritual, and cultural contexts. The social worker plays a unique role, utilizing assessment skills across settings, to gain an appreciation of the complexity of the patient, family, and caregiver's experiences, past and present. Sensitive yet direct exploration about what matters most can inform collaboration, communication, and care planning with clinicians, shaping the experience prior to, at the time of the patient's death, and through the bereavement period.

Working with individuals and families as they are approaching end of life provides the social worker the chance to fully utilize oneself, and a myriad of skills and abilities to accompany the patient and family on their journey. By approaching each situation with respect and compassion, a sacred space is created for the patient and family to negotiate this journey. Social workers are positioned to experience a deep inner knowing that clinical skill, respect, and caring will lead the family to a sense of having been seen, validated, and accepted. The opportunity exists to bear witness to the present, past, and future struggles. The social worker integrates many voices and skills—the educative, the reflective, and the advocate—providing gentle education and information to connect and develop a trusting relationship that will have profound implications for the patient and family's experience of the death, and will carry over into the future. In the blending of the use of self with knowledge and skills, there is the potential to make a difference—often being unsure of the outcome, without a formula to "fix" and with a comfort with things we might not understand.

Social workers in health care frequently enter the realm of mystery; it is often unknown how the story will emerge and how the pieces will, if ever, come together. There is an opportunity to practice in the present informed by the past and affecting the future. Providers impact and sometimes change a patient/family's experience and in the process, may themselves be changed.

LEARNING EXERCISE

1. An elderly resident in a skilled nursing facility receiving hospice services is approaching the end of her life and has essentially stopped eating. Her adult children are sad but accepting of this as a sign of illness progression. However, her siblings, also older adults, are deeply distressed and insist she be fed. Exploring their strong feelings, you learn they endured prolonged periods of food insecurity as children.

How would you prepare for a care conference with family and providers to discuss feeding in light of this information?

ONLINE RESOURCES

Alzheimers disease facts and figures. (2016). www.alz.org/facts/

American Cancer Society. (2017). Helping children when a family member has cancer. www.cancer.org/treatment/children-and-cancer/when-a-family-member-has-cancer.html

Family Caregiver Alliance National Center on Caregiving. www.caregiver.org

Federal regulation on hospice. www.ecfr.gov/cgi-bin/text-idx?rgn=div5;node=42%3A3 .0.1.1.5#se42.3.418_120

Healing Center, Seattle: A grief support community for adults, children and families. www.healingcenterseattle.org/children/books-websites/

Hospice: Talking to children about death. www.hospicenet.org/html/talking.html

National Hospice and Palliative Care Organization (NHPCO), www.nhpco.org/nchpp-sections/social-worker

What's your grief? www.whatsyourgrief.com/childrens-books-about-death

REFERENCES

Agar, M., Currow, D., Shelby, T., Plummer, J., & Sanderson C. (2008). Preference for place of care and place of death in palliative care: Are these different questions? *Palliative Medicine, 22*(7), 787–795.

Allen, R. (2008). Legacy activities as interventions approaching the end of life. *Journal of Palliative Medicine, 11*(7), 1029–1038.

Altilio, T. (2011) The Power and potential of language. In T. Altilio & S. Otis-Green (Eds.), *Oxford textbook of palliative social work* (pp. 689–694). New York: Oxford University Press.

Aries, P. (1977). *The hour of our death: The classic history of Western attitudes toward death over the last one thousand years.* New York: Vintage Books.

Bern-Klug, M., Gessert, C., & Forbes, S. (2001). The need to revise assumptions about the end of life: Implications for social work practice. *Health and Social Work, 26*(1), 38–48.

Berry, P., & Griffie J. (2006). Planning for the actual death. In B. Ferrell & N. Coyle (Eds.), *Textbook of palliative nursing* (2nd ed., pp. 561–577). New York: Oxford University Press.

Blanck, G., & Blanck, R. (1974). *Ego psychology: Theory and practice.* New York: Columbia University Press.

Brophy McCale, H. (2005). Grief and bereavement. In K. Keubler, K. Davis, & C. Dea Moore (Eds.), *Palliative practices: An interdisciplinary approach* (pp. 379–396). St. Louis, MO: Elsevier Mosby.

Burge, F., Lawson, B., Critchley P., & Maxwell D. (2005). Transitions in care during the end of life: Changes experienced following a comprehensive palliative care program. *BMC Palliative Care, 4*(3), 1–7.

Byock, I. (1997). *Dying well: The prospect for growth at end of life.* New York: Penguin Putnam.

Cagle, J. G., & Kovacs, P. J. (2009). Education: A complex social work intervention at the end of life. *Health and Social Work, 34*(1), 17–27.

Cairns, M., & Thompson, W. (2003). *Transitions in dying and bereavement: A psychosocial guide for hospice and palliative care.* Baltimore, MD: Health Professions Press.

Callahan, M. (2008). *Final journey: A practical guide for bringing comfort at the end of life.* New York: Bantam Dell.

Christakis, N. A., & Iwashyna, T. J. (1998). Attitude and self-reported practice regarding prognostication in a national sample of internists. *Archives of Internal Medicine, 158*(21), 2389–2395.

Christakis, N. A., & Lamont, E. B. (2000). Extent and determinants of error in doctors' prognoses in terminally ill patients: Prospective cohort study. *British Medical Journal, 320*(7233), 469–472.

Doka, K. (2004). Grief and dementia. In K. Doka (Ed.), *Living with grief: Alzheimer's disease* (pp. 139–153). Washington, DC: Hospice Foundation of America.

Doka, K., & Aber, R. (2002). Psychological loss and grief. In K. Doka (Ed.), *Disenfranchised grief: New directions, challenges and strategies for practice* (pp. 187–198). Champaign, IL: Research Press.

Elder, G. H., Jr., Kirkpatrick, J. M., & Crosnoe R. (2003). The emergence and development of life course theory. In J. T. Mortimer & M. J. Shanahan (Eds.), *Handbook of the life course* (pp. 3–19). New York: Kluwer Academic/Plenum.

Ellershaw, J., & Ward, C. (2003). Care of the dying patient: The last hours or days of life. *British Medical Journal, 326*(7379), 30–34.

Erikson, E. (1959). *Identity and the life cycle.* New York: W. W. Norton.

Groves, R., & Klauser, H. (2005). *The American book of dying: Lessons in spiritual pain.* Berkeley, CA: Celestial Arts.

Herr, K., Coyne, P., Key, T., Manworren, R., McCaffery, M., Merkel S., . . . Wild, L. (2006). Pain assessment in the nonverbal patient: Position statement with clinical practice recommendations. *Pain Management Nursing, 7*(2), 44–52.

Hui, D., Nooruddin, Z., Didwaniya, N., Dev, R., De La Cruz, M., Kim, S., . . . Bruera, E. (2014). Concepts and definitions for "actively dying," "end of Life" "terminally ill," "terminal care, and "transition of care": A systematic review. *Journal of Pain and Symptom Management, 47*(1), 77–89.

Kennedy, C., Brooks-Young, P., Brunton-Gray, C., Larkin, P., Conolly, M., Wilde-Larsson, B., . . . Chater, S. (2014). Diagnosing dying: An integrative literature review. *British Medicine Journal Supportive Palliative Care, 4*(3), 263–270.

Kuebler, K., Davis, M., & Moore, C. (2005). *Palliative priorities: An interdisciplinary approach.* St. Louis, MO: Elsevier Mosby.

Mackenzie, C. S., Smith, M. C., Hasher, L., Leach, L., & Behl, P. (2006). Cognitive functioning under stress: Evidence for informal caregivers of palliative patients. *Journal of Palliative Medicine, 10*(3), 749–758.

Medicare Benefit Policy Manual. (2015). Coverage of hospice services under hospital insurance. Retrieved from www.cms/gov/Regulations-and-guidance/guidancemanuals/downloads.bp102c09.pdf.

Mitchell, S., Teno, J., Kiely, D., Shaffer, M., Jones, R., Priguson, H., . . . Hamel, M. (2009). The clinical course of advanced dementia. *New England Journal of Medicine, 36*(16), 1529–1538.

Murray, S., Kendall, M., Boyd, K., & Sheikh, A. (2005). Illness trajectories and palliative care. *British Medicine Journal, 330*(30), 1007–1011.

National Association for Home Care and Hospice. (2015). CMS launches concurrent care demonstration. Retrieved from www.nahc.org/NAHCReport/nr/40318_2.

National Hospice and Palliative Care Organization. (2015). NHPCO facts and figures. Hospice care in America. Retrieved from www.nhpco.org/sites/default/files/public/statistics.research/2015_facts_figures.pdf.

Patrick, D., Engleberg, R., & Curtis, J. (2001). Evaluating the quality of dying and death. *Journal of Pain and Symptom Management, 22*(3), 717–726.

Sachs, G., Shega, J., & Cox-Hayley, D. (2004). Barriers to excellent end of life care for patients with dementia. *Journal of General Internal Medicine, 19*(10), 1057–1063.

Sigelman, C., & Rider, E. (2015). *Life span human development.* Stamford, CT: Cengage Learning.

Srivastava, R. (2017). Dying at home might sound preferable but I've seen the reality. Retrieved from www.theguardian.com//commentsfree/2017/may01/dying-at-home-terminally-ill-hospital.

Steinhauser, K., Clipp, E., McNeilly, M., Christakis, N., McIntyre, L., & Tulsky, J. (2000). In search of a good death: Observations of patients, families and providers. *Annals of Internal Medicine, 132*(10), 825–832.

Sullivan, A., Lakoma, M., Matsuyama, R., Rosenblatt, L., Arnold, R., & Block, S. (2007). Diagnosing and discussing imminent death in the hospital: A secondary analysis of physicians interviews. *Journal of Palliative Medicine, 10*(4), 882–893.

Taylor, D., Bhasvar, N., Harker, M., & Kassner, C. (2015). Evaluating a new era in Medicare Hospice and end of life policy. Retrieved from Healthaffairs.org/blog/2015/12/22/evaluating-a-new-era-in-medicare-hospice-and-end-of-life-policy/.

Tsai, S., & Arnold, R. (2015). Prognostication in dementia. Retrieved from mypcnow.org.

Turner, F. (2011). *Social work treatment: Interlocking theoretical approaches.* New York: Oxford University Press.

US Department of Health and Human Resources. (2013). Medicare hospice: Use of general inpatient care. Retrieved from oig.hhs.gov/oei/reports/oei-2-10-00490.pdf.

Van Vliet, D., De Vugt, M., Bakker, C., Koopmans, E., & Verhey, F. R. (2010). Impact of early onset dementia: A caregivers' review. *International Journal of Geriatric Psychiatry, 25*(11), 1091–1100.

Vena, C., Kuebler, K., & Schrader, S. (2005). The dying process. In K. Keubler, M. Davies, & C. Moore (Eds.), *Palliative practices: An interdisciplinary approach* (pp. 335–377). St. Louis, MO: Elsevier Mosby.

Virdun, C., Luckett, T., Davidson, P., & Phillips J. (2015). Dying in the hospital: A systematic review of quantitative studies identifying the elements of end of life care that patients and their families rank as being most important. *Palliative Medicine, 29*(9), 774–796.

Warm, E. (2015). Prognostication. Retrieved from www.eperc.mcw.edu/fastfact/ff030. htm.

Weissman, D. (2014). Syndrome of imminent death. Retrieved from www.eperc.mcw. edu/fastfact/ff030.htm.

Weissman, D., & Rosielle, D. (2014). Diagnosis and treatment of terminal delirium. Retrieved from www.nypcnow.org.

Werner, P., Stein-Shvachman, I., & Korczyn, A. (2009). Early onset dementia: Clinical and social aspects. *International Psychogeriatrics, 21*(4), 631–636.

Worden, J. (2009). *Grief counseling and grief therapy: A handbook for the mental health practitioner* (4th ed.). New York: Springer.

Legal and Ethical Aspects
of Care

KATHRYN M. SMOLINSKI ■

In most ethics consultations, 8 times out of 10, the main issue is one of
communication and not ethics.
—A LONG-TIME HOSPITAL ETHICS COMMITTEE MEMBER

INTRODUCTION

Numerous legal and ethical issues converge in health care settings, especially when the focus of care is patients living with serious illness (Cheon,
Coyle, Wiegand, & Welsh, 2015; Csikai & Chaitin, 2006; Ko, Perez-Cruz,
& Blinderman, 2011; McCabe & Coyle 2014). At the micro level, the individual patient faces multiple decision points throughout the care continuum
requiring consent, mental capacity, knowledge of one's disease trajectory,
and appreciation of personal cultural beliefs and values. On meso and macro
levels, the patient, family, health care providers, and entire patient support
system are influenced by laws, policies, and social norms, impacting the illness experience, including the decision-making process. Social workers can
untangle the legal and ethical components through a range of interventions
as patients and teams make decisions in the setting of serious illness and at
the end of life. When these treatment decisions involve discontinuing or continuing certain therapies, initiating or not initiating others, deciding about
the role of ongoing diagnostic tests and procedures, and ensuring vigilant

symptom management, the decision-making process consistently balances multiple competing interests. Such interests include the patient's autonomy, the values and beliefs of patients, families, caregivers, and clinicians, as well as the health care team's approach to care, culture and practices of the institution, and the community's social norms and laws. Making and communicating a thoughtful, informed, deliberate decision becomes the crux of effective patient-centered health care, especially in the setting of serious illness. Table 9.1 describes a model for assessing capacity, with specific questions to assist in determining a person's ability to guide her care.

Social workers using an ecological lens can intervene by eliciting, documenting, and promoting a patient's values, concerns, and treatment preferences, facilitating family conferences, providing psychoeducation about illness, advocating for community resources to support caregivers, and optimizing a patient and family's decision-making capacity (Snow, Warner, & Zilberfein, 2008; Fineberg, 2010). Patients and families may bring varied social vulnerabilities to illness and the settings where they receive care, which can be exacerbated by the pressures on staff and demands of systems. Social workers aim to uncover and support strengths and can discover aspects of resilience perhaps unrecognized by patients and families and the clinicians who care for them. A social worker may also mitigate providers' distress by involving organizational resources such as ethics and palliative care consultations to join in deliberations or to support difficult treatment decisions. Finally, on a larger scale, social workers can educate the community on how to exercise their rights to vocalize their health care treatment preferences, to complete advance directives, and advocate for more laws and policy to support individuals and their caregivers as they live with serious illness (Figure 9.1).

COMPETING VALUES AND PRINCIPLES

Patients make treatment decisions within the context of their lives. A patient might consider her own spiritual views, cultural values, economic resources, perceived prognosis, family resources and needs, and overall quality of life. As health status changes, and especially when transitions in care and settings are anticipated, there is constant reassessment of what is most important. Therefore, conversations about goals, hopes, and wishes are ongoing and dynamic. Social workers assess patients' strengths, support systems, psychosocialspiritual well-being, and financial concerns, among other aspects of the patient-family experience. The assessment is an intervention as it invites the patient to begin to identify who, why, and what treatment choices make sense over the course of illness. In diseases such as dementia, the trajectory may be protracted, and

Table 9.1 ASSESSING FOR DECISION-MAKING CAPACITY

Model Questions for Assessing Capacity

Ability to choose
1. Have you made a decision about the treatment options we discussed?

Ability to understand relevant information
2. Please tell me in your own words what I've told you about
   - the nature of your condition
   - the treatment or diagnostic test recommended
   - the possible benefits from the treatment/diagnostic test
   - the possible risks (or discomforts) of the treatment/diagnostic test
   - any other possible treatments that could be used, & their benefits & risks
   - the possible benefits & risks of no treatment at all
3. We've talked about the chance that x might happen with this treatment. In your own words, can you tell me how likely do you think it is that x will happen?
4. What do you think will happen if you decide not to have treatment?

Ability to appreciate the situation and its consequences
5. What do you believe is wrong with your health now?
6. Do you believe it's possible that this treatment/diagnostic test could benefit you?
7. Do you believe it's possible that this treatment/diagnostic test could harm you?
8. We talked about other possible treatments for you—can you tell me, in your own words, what they are?
9. What do you believe would happen to you if you decided you didn't want to have this treatment/diagnostic test?

Ability to reason
10. Tell me how you reached your decision to have [not have] the treatment/diagnostic test.
11. What things were important to you in making the decision you did?
12. How would you balance those things?

NOTES: Decision-making capacity is a clinical assessment. Many times it is confused with "competency," which is a ruling in a court of law that determines an individual's ability to make decisions (Ganzini, Volicer, Nelson, Fox, & Derse, 2004). While similar, they are not the same. Capacity is readily assumed in the medical setting and is usually challenged when patients go against medical advice. The clinician who is asking the questions should be doing so in relation to a treatment option, a decision that has to be made, or a plan of care, as capacity is relative. A patient may have the capacity to consent to a blood draw but may lack the cognitive reasoning and factual manipulation to agree to open-heart surgery or lifelong dialysis. It is recommended that primary clinicians assess capacity, as they are most familiar with the patient, have established a relationship over time, and can best address the risks and benefits of the proposed treatment (Ganzini, Volicer, Nelson, Fox, & Derse, 2004). However, any clinician involved in care should be able to assess capacity.

SOURCE: Appelbaum, P. S., & Grisso, T. (2005) (unpublished), as displayed in Ganzini, L., Volicer, L., Nelson, W. A., Fox, E., & Derse, A. R. (2005). Ten myths about decision-making capacity. *Journal of the American Medical Directors Association, 5*(4), 263–267.

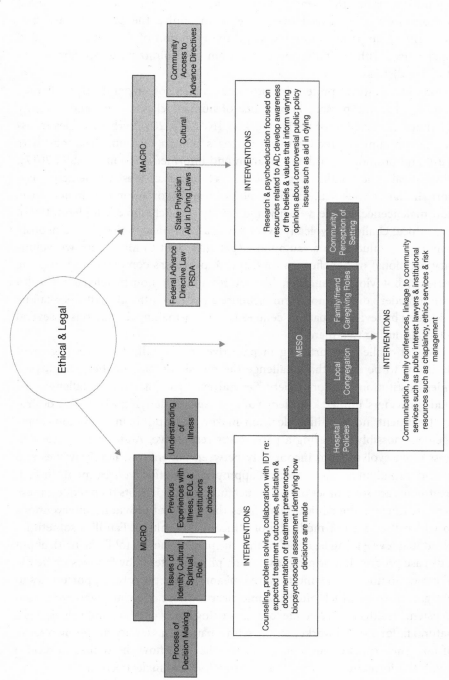

Figure 9.1. Ecological model applied: Ethical and legal.

cognitive capacity threatened. As a result, these often emotionally charged conversations are engaged over time to maximize the patient's participation. They help patients to understand the evolution of their experience and perspectives with the hope and expectation of minimizing future family and clinician distress.

The social work profession promotes values of social justice, dignity, and worth of the person, importance of human relationships, and integrity (National Association of Social Workers [NASW], 2017). These values translate into a clinical practice that prioritizes human relationships, engenders trust, and promotes self-determination and informed consent (NASW, 2017). Biomedical ethics, outlined in Table 9.2, as the basis of Western medicine support similar themes with the principles of respect for autonomy, beneficence, non-maleficence, justice, veracity, and fidelity (Beauchamp & Childress, 1994). The ethical challenge typically exists when a treatment choice simultaneously honors one value, such as autonomy (patient's right to make her own voluntary decisions) or beneficence (health care provider's compassion to help the patient), but violates another, like truth-telling or non-maleficence (health care provider's duty to not harm or injure a patient). Ethical challenges can be mitigated by revisiting patient-centered decision-making discussions at several intervals during treatment.

Ethical challenges surfacing in palliative care usually focus on treatment decisions to be made that challenge the moral compass of the patient, provider, institution, and/or society. Several examples of ethical challenges include providers' limited knowledge of a patient's underlying wishes and desires for treatment, no identified decision-maker, and optimizing symptom management possibly rendering a patient less responsive. Additional ethical distress often evolves from incongruity between patient and family wishes and provider's judgment about what is appropriate or effective treatment. In fact, treatments are sometimes offered reluctantly. When patients then request these very treatments, the clinical team faces the reality of providing interventions to which they are not medically or ethically committed. Families sometimes plead that "everything be done" or that the patient "not be told" the truth about a disease progression or prognosis. Such phrases uttered by families invite exploration to uncover the multilayered meanings and potential opportunities to mitigate distress, which often become clear to those clinicians who are skilled to listen. Health care is a venue for intersecting codes of ethics and values; it is a natural fit for a social worker to join with a patient in identifying her own sense of how she expresses autonomy, and whether and how she wishes to receive medical information, process that information, and make decisions.

Table 9.2 COMMON BIOMEDICAL ETHICAL PRINCIPLES OF WESTERN MEDICINE

Ethical Principal & Definition	Social Work Interventions	Potential Opportunities for Social Work
Respect for Autonomy Respect for the individual patient's own sense of values, beliefs, decision-making rubric, & sources of authority.	• Assess patient decision-making process—who they rely on to help them make decisions & how they make decisions • Discuss with family members the fears that may underlie a request to have information kept from the patient • Assess the family & caregivers for their own beliefs about treatment options that may conflict with the patient's beliefs & values	• Assist providers to understand if patients choose, while conscious, to delegate decisions to family members (e.g., cultural beliefs) this is a form of autonomy & may not violate informed consent but, instead support an individual's decision-making rubric
Beneficence The health provider's inherent obligation to provide care & treatment that benefits the patient.	• Assess patient values, beliefs, support system & treatment preferences to be able to support such during illness trajectory	• Assist providers in understanding the underlying values & beliefs of the patient so they can be supported as much as possible
Non-maleficence The health provider's duty to not intentionally harm the patient in the provision of care.	• Minimize the negative impact or unwanted side-effects of a treatment or healthcare intervention on patient's overall quality of life • Challenge providers to consider when they are only offering an intervention to quell the caregivers' fears, grief or need for more testing or medical treatment or assuage the provider's own fear of litigation	• Provide opportunity for discussion between providers & family members regarding the side effects of treatments. Some side-effects may seem unacceptable to family members, yet necessary to obtain the primary benefit of the treatment.

(continued)

Table 9.2 Continued

Ethical Principal & Definition	Social Work Interventions	Potential Opportunities for Social Work
Justice Care & provision of services are provided in an equitable manner	• Participate in the drafting of policy & procedures & implementation such as on quality review boards, admission & ethics committees & clinical care rounds to promote equitable & fair use of resources.	• Assist leadership in addressing the inadequacies in health access & affordability in the healthcare setting • Become knowledgeable of & utilize resources that can help to equalize the provision of services to all patients & families
Fidelity, Veracity & Confidentiality Information about a patient is protected & only shared when necessary in the provision of care; accurate information is provided to enable a patient to make informed decisions about her care	• Assist other providers in understanding how health information may be perceived by patients • Consider where patient care conversations are held, avoiding public places in the healthcare setting. • Determine who needs to know what information about the patient. Just because family members are present, does not indicate the patient wants them to hear health information. • Utilize the medical record to document relevant information *pertinent to the care of the patient*, not necessarily everything about the patient's life realizing patients & family members, acting as health care agents, for example, may sometime read the words written about them	• The cultural norms for the patient might not embrace full disclosure of diagnosis or prognosis. • Other providers, such as the primary physician or surgeon, will feel the need to disclose, especially for informed consent reasons. • Conversely, a surgeon or physician may withhold prognostication so patients & families will not "lose hope" Social workers can help providers address their own concerns or fears of providing "serious news"

SOURCE: Beauchamp & Childress (1994).

ADVANCE CARE PLANNING

Advance care planning is a process through which the health care team elicits and documents the patient's desires for treatment (Brinkman-Stoppelenburg, Rietjens, & Van Der Heide, 2014). While some health care providers erroneously define this process as the completion of an advance directive document, effective advance care planning views a completed document as only one component (Brinkman-Stoppelenburg et al., 2014; Sudore et al., 2017). The most effective advance care planning involves a series of treatment discussions between the health care team, patient, and caregivers, over time, which are adaptable to change and are patient-centered (Sudore et al., 2017). No matter the setting, the decision-making process for the patient and her caregivers requires active participation of the health care team to provide accurate diagnoses, available treatment options, predicted outcomes and obstacles, and prognoses. There are opportunities for social workers to join with patients and families to do this important work in many non-acute health care settings where they might have the benefit of relationships over time, such as outpatient health centers, skilled nursing facilities, and dialysis centers. Beginning to explore a patient's treatment preferences, values, desires, support system and decision-making norms enhance the possibility of engaging the patient's voice should she not be able to participate in decision making in the future. When the agency of the patient is lost, it is too late to engage the patient in treatment choices, and individuals and systems must fill the void to inform future care.

Social workers, with their knowledge of family systems, engage patients in a shared process of exploring history and considering the present and future impact of decisions on individual family members and the family as a unit, including the legacy of the patient and the family's roles in her care. This anticipatory guidance creates the opportunity for all to hear the patient's voice, hopes, and preferences to mitigate unintended distress. Careful listening and thoughtful questioning can lead to respectful dialogue about the roles that culture, religion, and spirituality might play in the patient's process of advance care planning. Exploration of the effect of cultural constructs, such as the value of truth telling or future versus present orientation, can help inform how, when, and with whom a patient wishes to make medical decisions. For example, a patient may value a faith tradition where prognostication is considered presumptuous or an affront to the authority of a Higher Power. Consequently, she might be reluctant to engage not only in a discussion about illness trajectory, but also in decisions she or family members might make in the future about her care (See Chapter 7; "Cultural Aspects of Care").

Advance care planning involves taking the time to be with the patient, eliciting her values, explaining the care plan, the anticipated benefits and burdens, listening and answering questions, and adjusting the course as necessary. This can look different across health care settings. For example, a social worker in a dialysis center has regular opportunity to talk with patients and her support system about the physical, practical, and emotional impacts of weekly dialysis sessions over time. More important, clinicians engaged in effective advance care planning must consider their own personal biases, values, professional ethics and standards as they operate at the intersection of patient, family, and team and institutional culture, living within community norms and laws.

Advance care planning, by its very nature, fits well into the rubric of skills that social workers bring to patients and families with serious illness or at end of life. A thorough biopsychosocial assessment begins the process by which the patient identifies who she is and what constitutes her culture, values, decision-making norms, and support system. Subsequent appointments with the patient in the outpatient setting or when she is hospitalized for emergent medical care or for scheduled treatments facilitates continued advance care planning. The team documents an individuals' treatment preferences, goals for care, and desires regarding life-sustaining therapies in an effort to honor them when the individual is unable to voice them and to serve as guideposts to clinicians for her care. Patient preferences should be documented even when they are not possible or feasible. For example, symptom management needs or imminent death may be a barrier to discharge home, a preference that a patient may have expressed over time. Respecting the dynamic and uncertain course of illness means there may be times when well-intended and committed family and clinicians are unable to accommodate hopes and wishes or promises made with good intention. During these processes of altering plans, it is possible to build consensus and identify opportunities to make meaning in the setting of a changing plan of care.

The documents routinely used in a hospital setting to capture a patient's wishes are generally classified as advance directives. The term *advance directive* actually encompasses a variety of forms conveying to the team what a patient may want in the future when she cannot voice her preferences (LexisNexis, 2014). Examples of advance directives are living wills, powers of attorney, do not resuscitate orders (DNR), do not attempt resuscitation orders (DNAR), and documents such as POLST (physician orders for life-sustaining treatment) orders. The latter three are signed medical orders for various treatments. While POLST documents are gaining momentum, they are not readily available in most settings, and often these documents do not transition with patients as they move from setting to setting (National Polst Paradigm, 2017). However, all 50 states do recognize either a living will, a durable power of attorney, or both. A patient outlines what types of medical treatment and care she wants to receive in a living will, as well as those she might not want to receive. By appointing a decision-maker, called an "agent" in a power of attorney (health care agent, DPOA, patient advocate designation), this individual is empowered to speak on her behalf when she lacks decision-making capacity. While there remains skepticism regarding the utility of advance directives, studies have demonstrated that individuals who complete them receive care in line with their expressed preferences (Perkins, 2007; Silveira, Kim, & Langa, 2010). Under the law, all hospitals must ask a patient if she has an advance directive (Patient Self Determination Act [PSDA], Omnibus Budget Reconciliation Act of 1990). Although many hospitals provide the form, under the law, they cannot require that it be completed (PSDA, 1990). If a patient declines to appoint a health care agent, she needs information about the process for decision-making that will be followed if she becomes incapacitated. Table 9.3 describes the various types of advance planning documents, linking both to clinical indications and their utility across settings.

Ideally, advance directives travel through systems of care from hospitals to other settings. For the patient living in a skilled nursing facility who might be hospitalized, perhaps frequently, there is an important opportunity to honor the work of others, outlining and respecting that patient's wishes. Consider, for example, the skilled nursing facility resident who is unable to communicate for herself and does not have a decision-maker designated, or the decision-maker who lives out of state and is not easily accessible. Diligence on the part of the facility social worker to ensure that written and expressed advance directives travel with the patient and are acknowledged by the hospital may protect autonomy and provide essential guidance to the treating medical team, including the hospital social worker. Advance directives completed in a hospital setting are an integral part of the hand-off to the receiving health care setting, such as a rehabilitation facility, skilled nursing facility, dialysis center, or a hospice home. If this critical information is lost in transition, it jeopardizes care and negates the efforts of teams to honor the patient's wishes.

The idea of advance directives can be framed as an exercise of choice and control when much is or may feel out of control. In some families, advance care planning can be understood as a process through which a patient expresses concern for family by relieving them of future decisions, which are often emotionally and cognitively distressing, while ensuring that her wishes are known, documented, and honored. Social workers need to be mindful, as patients frequently do not complete advance directives for a variety of practical, religious, cultural, and psychological reasons (Lovell & Yates, 2014; Schickedanz et al., 2009; Van Scoy, Howrylak, Nguyen, Chen, & Sherman, 2014). Patients sometimes have no one to appoint, or believe they are tempting fate or challenging faith by anticipating and documenting a future that has yet to happen. Through education and support, a social worker facilitates discussion of hopes, values and fears with regard to treatment outcomes, and then by conveying these to

Table 9.3 Types of Advance Planning Documents Commonly Used
in Health Care

Document Name	Description	Clinical Indication
Durable medical power of attorney (DPOA) (alternate names: patient advocate designation, advance directive, health care agent, health care proxy)	A legal instrument that allows a patient to appoint a person & grant the authority to make medical decisions in the event the patient is unable to express a treatment decision. This document is invoked when patients have lost decision-making capacity. Usually must be signed by the patient, dated, & witnessed. "Durable" designates that while the patient must sign it when she has capacity, the appointment survives the patient's incapacity. While it is preferred, it may, or may not, provide specific medical instructions for the agent to follow.	• Arguably the most helpful document to providers, as it directs them to an individual with whom they can discuss treatment options regarding the patient. • Its intent is that patients have discussed wishes with their agent & the providers do not have to solely rely on the expressed desires of the patient. • Providers can engage in a dialogue with the power of attorney as the patient's expressed wishes may not have addressed the current treatment or situation.
Living will	A legal instrument that provides instructions or medical treatment preferences that patients want followed, especially under special circumstances such as a terminal illness, persistent vegetative state, or traumatic injury. It does not routinely contain an appointment of decision-maker in the event of incapacity. Usually must be signed by the patient, dated, witnessed, or notarized.	• Health care providers & surrogate decision-makers (proxy, power of attorney, & health care agents) should consult this document to ascertain the patients' expressed treatment preferences. • It may be the only record of a patients' wishes. • As it does not routinely include designating a decision-maker, it is recommended that it be completed in conjunction with a DPOA.

Table 9.3 CONTINUED

Document Name	Description	Clinical Indication
Court appointment of guardian	A legal document that names a court-appointed individual to make decisions on behalf of a legally incapacitated adult. The scope of duty is defined in the appointment & is limited to certain responsibilities.[a] Requires a formal court petition & hearing; usually costs are involved. DPOAs usually render pursuing a guardianship moot.	• Important to note that state laws usually have medical power of attorneys (designated health care agents, patient advocates) supersede court-appointed guardians on medical issues. • It is imperative that providers know with whom to discuss care decisions when both a health care agent (DPOA) & guardian exist.
Do not resuscitate order (DNR); Do not attempt resuscitation order (DNAR)	". . . a medical order written by a doctor. It instructs health care providers not to attempt cardiopulmonary resuscitation (CPR) if a patient's breathing stops or if the patient's heart stops beating."[b]	• Sometimes family members & caregivers express concern that a DNR order will mean that providers will "do nothing." It is helpful to stress that while a particular intervention may not be provided, comfort & care will never cease.
Allow natural death order (AND)	"[A medical] order . . . meant to ensure that only comfort measures are provided . . . [whereby] physicians & other medical professionals would be acknowledging that the person is dying & that everything that is being done for the patient . . . will allow the dying process to occur as comfortably as possible. . . ."[c]	• Seen to support a process that focuses on providing care & comfort versus a DNR order that focuses on limiting treatment. Linguistically, it may be easier for families & caregivers in decision-making roles, as it emphasizes allowing a natural process.[d]

(*continued*)

Table 9.3 CONTINUED

Document Name	Description	Clinical Indication
Physician orders for life-sustaining treatment (POLST, alt. MOST, MOLST, etc.)	"a medical order signed by a physician, after consultation with the patient or . . . legal surrogate . . . [that] specifically addresses medical decisions & options that are likely to arise in the near future . . . [&] provides explicit guidance to health professionals under predictable future circumstances (such as development of pneumonia in a patient with advanced dementia)." [e]	• Meant to be portable so that it moves with the patient from care setting to care setting[f] • Not a federal mandate, but a state-driven initiative; varies by state, so it is important to be familiar with your state's form & procedure, if your state participates • Designed for individuals with an advanced chronic illness & a prognosis of one to two years.[g]
Durable financial & legal power of attorney	A legal instrument allowing a patient to appoint an "agent" to perform financial & other duties, such as manage finances, apply for benefits, and so on, on behalf of the patient. "Durable" designates that while the patient must sign it when she has capacity, the appointment in the document survives the patient's incapacity. Such a document can work in partnership with a medical POA so an individual can support a patient with all of her decision-making needs.	• Can help the family manage state & federal benefits & as other responsibilities if the patient is unable to do so. • May especially assist providers such as social workers & facilities admission staff with understanding of who will ensure proper payment of medical services & treatments. • Can be helpful to utilize if the health insurance provider needs to be contacted & will only speak to the patient or her designee.

NOTES: There are several different legal instruments that can be used to document patients' treatment preferences, especially under certain circumstances such as a persistent vegetative state, terminal illness, or traumatic injury. While some type of advance directive is legal in every state, not all types are legal in all states. Often, lawyers will draft them as part of estate planning. However, usually an attorney is not required to draft or execute some of these documents. Many times a standard form is provided within the law itself. The state bar or medical society may have versions available at no cost to individuals within the state. Providers must be aware of both the utility and limits of these documents.

the team, helps the patient feel heard, supported, and understood as she makes her treatment decisions. It is important and meaningful to document the exploration of patient values, even if explicit discussion of treatment preferences and advance care planning is not possible. There are many online resources available to assist patients, families, and providers to begin conversations that explore values, hopes, and wishes influencing decision-making. Advance directive forms and related information are also available (National Hospice and Palliative Care Association, 2017).

SURROGATE DECISION-MAKING

Many times, the opportunity for advance care planning with the individual patient is lost or limited due to a variety of issues, which may be patient, family, or clinician driven, reflecting time constraints or institutional priorities. If a patient has not appointed a proxy decision-maker and is now incapacitated, the team will rely on a surrogate decision-maker to assume this role. Legally, most states identify who can make a treatment decision when no health care agent has been previously chosen (American Bar Association, 2017). If the state law is silent on this matter, institutions will fill the void with internal policies and procedures. The patient's values and/or treatment preferences may or may not have been previously recorded in a living will document or in the medical record. If they have, it allows guidance for the surrogate to work with the health care team in making treatment decisions aligning with the patient's expressed values or preferences. There are times when a patient appears to have no identified family or friends. The medical setting has an obligation to diligently attempt to find any friends or relatives who may be able to assist with decisions. Beyond the decision-making interests, searching for family and/or

[a] Legal Information Institute (n.d.).
[b] US National Library of Medicine (2016).
[c] Meyer (n.d.).
[d] Schlairet & Cohen (2013).
[e] Meier & Beresford (2009, p. 291).
[f] National POLST Paradigm (2017).
[g] National POLST Paradigm (2017).

SOURCES: Leiter (2015); American Bar Association (2017), *Living wills, health care proxies, and advance health care directives.*

friends recognizes a patient's connections in the world outside the medical setting. Information about how and where someone is, knowing whether they are alive or seriously ill, is often important even within complex relationships that have been fractured or lost over time. In rare cases, hospitals will petition for guardianship to be able to continue providing care when family or friends are not identified.

Decision-making in the setting of serious illness can be stressful, and potentially exacerbated if no previously expressed preferences exist. Social workers can advocate for family conferences, open discussion around treatment options, raise the imagined voice and values of the patient, and support the surrogate in her role to mitigate the emotional and psychological effects of making such decisions. While there is no difference ethically or legally between cessation of life-sustaining treatment and not choosing to initiate such treatment in the first place, there is a difference in the emotional and psychological impact on the family between those choices. Participating with the health care providers in the removal of life support when consenting as the power of attorney, surrogate decision-maker, or designated family member on behalf of the patient can be traumatizing for those making these decisions (Melhado & Fowler Byers, 2011). They may have doubts or regrets, feel as if they are giving up on the patient, or actively hastening a death. In agreeing to not initiate a therapy, a decision-maker may avoid some of these concerns. There might still be feelings of uncertainty about what the outcomes of a therapy might have been, enhancing feelings of guilt and thoughts of "what if?" Providing anticipatory guidance to explore and anticipate the emotions and thoughts that may attach to either decision and the potential outcome is an essential social work role (Buckley & Abell, 2010). The complexity of feelings and beliefs surrounding these kind of decisions are reflected in the numbers of legal cases that have shaped public policy. Table 9.4 describes landmark cases, the impact of the decisions, and their implications for social work practice.

COMMUNICATION

Communication with the team can be impacted if the family members or surrogate decision-makers have difficulty understanding the medical terms or processes. The social worker can support the health literacy of the surrogate by clarifying medical terms and their meanings and ensuring that information is presented in an acceptable and accessible manner. Language barriers exist when the providers speak a different language than the patient. Routinely, health care providers will allow family members or friends to provide language interpretation in these situations as it is convenient and timely. However, allowing family

Table 9.4 SELECTED LANDMARK CASES & POLICY THAT SHAPED DECISION-MAKING & AUTONOMY IN HEALTH CARE IN THE UNITED STATES

Case or Statute Synopsis	Ruling of Effect of Statute	Implications for Practice

1976: New Jersey Supreme court case regarding Karen Ann Quinlan,[1] age 21	The state court issued two major rulings:
	1. The US Constitution's right to privacy clause includes the right to make medical treatment decisions encompassing the right to decline or cease treatment.
	2. The right to decide whether to begin or continue treatment survives incompetency & may be exercised by a surrogate decision-maker.
		• The right to refuse or withdraw life-sustaining medical treatment is a fundamental right under the constitution & can be exercised on the patient's behalf by someone else
		  The following organizations are described in the resource list and link to helpful educational materials:
		  The American Bar Association. Site for related laws.
		  The Conversation Project.
		  National Hospice and Palliative Care Organization
		  The Joint Commission. Has compiled laws that affect language access for patients when making decisions.

1990: US Supreme Court case regarding Nancy Cruzan,[2] age 25	The court held that 1. the state's compelling interest in preserving life may require "clear & convincing evidence" of a formerly competent patient's wishes, expressed while competent, to refuse life-sustaining treatment or to have such treatment withdrawn.	• While the court ruled that a state "may" require clear & convincing evidence, it is up to each state whether to adopt this standard • Know the laws in your state & the policies in your institutional or clinical setting that address what standard of review is necessary

(*continued*)

Table 9.4 CONTINUED

Case or Statute Synopsis	Ruling of Effect of Statute	Implications for Practice
1990 Patient Self-Determination Act (Federal Law)[3] & Federal Policy governing Advance Directives[4]	This law & subsequent regulations require all Medicare (MC) or Medicaid (MA) institutional providers & MC/MA managed care plans to • provide written information to patients, upon admission, of their rights under state law to make medical decisions, including accepting or refusing treatments • inform patients that they can complete an advance directive if they so choose, but it is not a condition of care • document the existence of an advance directive prominently in the medical record • provide staff & community education regarding advance directives	• Providing information becomes meaningful in the setting of medical & clinical guidance to inform decisions & choices. • CMS suggests the following resources: • "A Physician's Guide to Talking about End-of-Life Care": NCBI.NLM.NIH.gov/ PMC/Articles/ PMC1495357 • "Advance Care Planning: An Introduction for Public Health & Aging Services Professionals" (free course offering continuing education credit): CDC.gov/Aging/ AdvanceCarePlanning/Care-Planning-Course.htm • National Hospice & Palliative Care Organization Download Your State's Advance Directives: CaringInfo.org/ i4a/pages/index cfm?pageid=3289 • National Institute on Aging, Advance Care Planning: NIA. NIH.gov/Health/Publication/ Advance-Care-Planning • Since January 1, 2016, Advance Care Planning (ACP) is paid under the Medicare Physician Fee Schedule and Hospital Outpatient Prospective Payment Systems. The new CMS ACP Fact Sheet provides details on how to code & bill for ACP services, provider & beneficiary eligibility information, examples of ACP in practice, etc. www.cms.gov/Outreach-and-Education/Medicare-Learning-Network-MLN/ MLNProducts/Downloads/ AdvanceCarePlanning.pdf

Table 9.4 CONTINUED

Case or Statute Synopsis	Ruling of Effect of Statute	Implications for Practice
1996—HIPAA (Federal law)[5] HIPAA is a long & complex federal law primarily enacted to keep health information private.	• HIPAA has a Privacy Rule (federal law) that sets limits & rules on how protected health information (PHI) can be transmitted & viewed. • HIPAA has a Security Rule (federal law) that sets the requirements for electronic PHI. • In transmitting PHI, providers can use electronic communication, such as email, but they must apply "reasonable safeguards" when doing so.[6]	• HIPAA authorization forms may need to be signed or included as part of ACP so surrogate decision-makers can be as fully informed as possible when discussing treatment options with primary providers on behalf of patients. • The federal government has information on HIPAA for individuals & professionals: www.hhs.gov/hipaa/index.html
1994–2017 State Laws (or court ruling) Permitting Physician Aid in Dying (PAD): California, Colorado, Oregon, Montana, Vermont, & D.C.[7]	• State law addresses whether PAD is allowed or prohibited. • It is currently legal in six states. • There is no federal ruling on physician aid in dying. • Euthanasia is prohibited in the United States.	• General information on the laws permitting PAD can be accessed at: www.euthanasia.procon.org/view.resource.php?resourceID=000132 • The Hastings Center frames the issue, discusses arguments, provides a glossary & resources: www.thehastingscenter.org/briefingbook/physician-assisted-death/

NOTES:

[1] In re Quinlan. 70 N.J. 10, 355 A.2d 647 (1976).
[2] *Cruzan v. Director, Missouri Department of Health*, 497 US 261 (1990).
[3] 42 USC 1395cc(f) and 1396a(w).
[4] 42 Code of Federal Regulations, Part 489, Subpart I.
[5] Pub L No 104-191, 110 Stat 1936 (1996)
[6] 45 C.F.R. § 164.530(c).
[7] ProCon.org. (2017).

SOURCE: Ganzini, L., Volicer, L., Nelson, W.A., Fox, E., & Derse, A.R. (2004).

members to interpret often creates emotional distress as family members offer and agree to do so without truly knowing what information they will be asked to interpret. Family members will have their own emotional response and bias and unbeknown to the clinicians could alter the language and meaning of the information the health care providers are trying to convey. Patients and families may not understand information about diagnosis and prognosis during goals of care conversations when professional interpreters are not used (Silva, 2016). Additionally, patients may receive less adequate symptom management at end of life, including treatments for pain and anxiety, when "ad hoc" (family and friend) interpreters provided the interpretation (Silva, 2016).

Allowing adult children to interpret for their parents (the patients) is fraught with ethical issues. While the patients may agree to have their children provide the interpretation, it unfairly burdens the children with the practical and emotional weight of delivering sensitive, serious, or "bad news" to their parents. Several federal and state laws, policies, and governing organizations, such as the Joint Commission, mandate that professional interpreters be used (The Joint Commission, 2008). Most health care settings will have internal policies to address the procedures for how to access services. Social workers familiar with the laws, policies, and resources can educate their fellow providers on the critical need for and responsibility of providing professional interpreters when there is a language difference. Social workers can also think creatively about their unique institutions and advocate for ways to improve practices to help ensure the use of interpreters when needed (See Chapter 7; "Cultural Aspects of Care").

Lynette

Lynette is a 44-year-old African-American single mother of two teenagers, Lana, age 18 and Lenora, age 14. She was diagnosed with ovarian cancer approximately one and a half years ago. Over the course of her illness, Lynette has undergone surgery, several rounds of chemotherapy, and radiation treatments. She receives all her care at the city's hospital, only a few blocks from her home in Detroit. Lynette was born and raised in Detroit and it is the only home she has ever known. While she never went to college, she is determined that both of her teenage daughters receive a college degree and has been planning financially for this goal. Lynette worked for almost 25 years "on the line" at the local automotive factory inside the city limits, where both of her parents worked. She only left her job because of her treatment regimen and currently receives Social Security Disability. She misses the social rewards and financial security from her job, as her reduced income is placing a strain on her household. Her husband, Bobby, died from injuries sustained in a car accident soon after their second daughter was born. Lynette felt he was the "love of her life" and was devastated by his death. Bobby had been a local minister, and Lynette and he were vibrant in their faith community.

Because of the accident, Bobby had multiple injuries and was placed in the intensive care unit after several hours of life-saving surgery. After three days, Bobby's condition was not showing any signs of improvement. With the strong recommendations of the critical care team, Lynette decided to have the life-sustaining therapies discontinued, and Bobby died immediately. She was sad he never saw their home again. She had made similar decisions for both of her parents, only a year earlier, when they died within months of each other from chronic diabetes. Her church did not support her decision regarding Bobby, as they felt she had "given up" on him and succumbed to pressure from the hospital. Lynette has never remarried, and she remains part of her congregation.

Lynette's parents provided a loving home for Lynette and her two older brothers. Her oldest brother, Desmond, battled addiction his entire life, which has been a source of suffering and sorrow for their family. He is currently incarcerated for possession of heroin and is not expected to be released for at least 10 years. Lynette and Desmond were very close growing up, and Lynette is deeply sad she is unable to see or speak with her brother on any consistent basis now that she is sick. Lynette, after observing the effects of heroin on her brother's life, speaks regularly in her community about the "evils" of addiction. Her other brother Thomas became a pastor at the local Baptist church. Thomas and Lynette never saw "eye to eye" on a lot of issues after Bobby's accident, but Thomas accompanies Lynette to some of her doctor's appointments, procedures, and chemotherapy treatments whenever his schedule allows. Lynette's longtime friend, Phyllis, attends every appointment and is a significant source of emotional support. They have a deep and meaningful friendship, having known each other since grade school, and now attend church together every Sunday.

Lynette's most recent scan indicates that chemotherapy has been ineffective in shrinking her tumor or preventing its spread to nearby organs. Lynette had advocated for every treatment possible to cure her cancer and extend her life, as she could not imagine her daughters living without any parents. Now, however, her treating physicians have no additional therapies to change the course of her cancer. The primary focus of care shifts from efforts to cure her cancer to maximizing quality of life and minimizing symptoms and their impact on her life and her role as mother. Given the expected course of her disease, Lynette's doctors anticipate bowel obstructions to occur soon, as well as increased pain. They are also concerned that her cancer will begin to progress quickly at some future point, and they want to be aware of her treatment preferences, especially for life-sustaining therapies such as artificial hydration and nutrition, ventilator support, and intravenous antibiotics.

This moment in her illness trajectory provides an opportunity for a social worker to work with physicians to help Lynette discover and document her future treatment preferences. These discussions can elucidate Lynette's individual values and goals, while also appreciating the context and life history in which she is making such choices. In discussing expectations for her medical care and desired outcomes, the social worker can assess how Lynette makes decisions. As Lynette identifies significant roles in her life, such as wife, daughter, mother, sister, friend, and congregant, the social worker discerns how she incorporates these roles into decision-making regarding her own health care. She has made decisions in the past regarding others' health outcomes, most notably both of her parents and her husband. Did they leave instructions for her to follow? Was she left to decide in their "best interest?" How did she make choices at those times? What did she observe that she wants to be sure does or does not happen in her own care and at her death, especially important given that she, as opposed to her husband, has time to prepare her daughters? Did she feel the medical team supported her and provided access to clear information if she chose to receive it? Were there people in her life who were sources of support in decision-making? How does she feel now about hospitals? Does she feel knowledgeable about her own illness and treatments available as her disease progresses and symptoms develop? Does she trust that her providers will follow her wishes? Given her faith, were clergy available to help her when making decisions?

Before Lynette chooses a health care agent, it is critical that the team understand what decisions she would want her agent to make. Exploring with Lynette her life's goals and how those can (or cannot) be achieved as she moves along this illness continuum is critical. She has mentioned plans for her daughters to go to college. Given that Lenora is still a minor, Lynette may need anticipatory guidance related to a decision such as appointing a financial power of attorney (an individual who tends to specific financial needs such as paying bills, collecting benefits, etc.) to help her manage her daily life as she becomes too ill to do so herself. She may also want to consider appointing a guardian for Lenora who can assume care of her after Lynette's death. This decision can bring peace to Lynette as she'll know her wishes will be recognized by the state even after her death. As Lynette has worked her entire life, she may want to weigh the benefits of establishing a financial trust with her savings and retirement accounts for her two daughters that will provide for them over their lifetime. Worrying about these types of legal problems impacts the mental health of cancer patients (Retkin, Brandfield, & Bacich, 2007; Zevon, Schwabish, Donnelly, & Rodabaugh, 2007). The social worker can facilitate having legal services come to the home, clinic, or hospital to assist in preparing these documents. This intervention alone can support Lynette in her care for her daughters by getting "her affairs in order." Lynette can then refocus on her health, treatment course, and attention to preparing her daughters for an expected death in a manner which, while fraught with emotion and uncertainty, is different from the unanticipated death of their father.

Lynette's current biological family consists of her two teenage daughters and her two brothers. As the social worker helps Lynette clarify what she hopes to achieve or avoid through treatment, preference for a decision-maker becomes increasingly important. Lynette personally knows the responsibility, as she held the role herself when her parents and husband were hospitalized. Most states, if a decision-maker has not been appointed by the patient, have set a preference for who should be designated (American Bar Association, 2017). Commonly, the laws outline the order of preference to begin with spouse (some states recognize "domestic partner"), then adult children, parents, and siblings. Many states require a "consensus" among members in any decision-making group. Lynette's role as mother and her worry about the well-being of her daughters can be clearly linked to the task of assigning a health care agent as Lana, who is 18 years old, could become an automatic surrogate decision-maker if Lynette has not appointed someone else. Exploring whether this option is acceptable to Lynette is vital, as she has known the responsibilities as decision-maker for her parents and her husband and may choose to protect Lana from the distress emanating from this role.

The appointed health care agent does not need to be related to the patient by blood. Consequently, alternative health care agents can be explored, including Phyllis, as well as Thomas and Desmond. This process addresses issues such as their willingness and confidence in acting as her health care agent. The social worker could also suggest a family conference where all could participate, in person and via technology, and bear witness to Lynette explaining her choice. While Desmond may not be practical, as he might be difficult to reach in a timely manner, his inclusion is a tribute to their valued relationship, the meaning of the expected death, and the influence he might have over the health care agent Lynette chooses. The health care agent needs to be available to the health care team, to participate in discussions, and to express the wishes of the patient. As the social worker is mindful of Phyllis and Lynette's strong bond, she wants to explore their shared and unique relationships to their faith and religious community. Phyllis and Lynette attend the same church, yet some of the parishioners have not always supported Lynette. How may the congregation support Phyllis in her role? Could any pressure from the congregation prevent Phyllis from representing Lynette's wishes? Does Lynette herself have any spiritual concerns about deciding against life-sustaining therapies?

A well-developed family conference may serve several functions, such as exploring fears, enhancing understanding of the medical situation, building trust, providing unified team communication, identifying family strengths, and demonstrating empathy (Fineberg, 2010). It is helpful to have the team pre-meet to discuss the expected issues that may arise in the conference, and then recap the next steps for everyone involved after the conference has occurred. The team elicits all involved to share information in a respectful manner, thus creating a safe environment where family members can speak freely to express their views as the clinicians work to clarify misconceptions and misinformation. The team also needs to end with a plan for the next steps and specify how follow-up is going to be conveyed to the patient and her support network.

If Lynette does decide to appoint an agent, the social worker can facilitate that process. In many states, preprinted forms are available online and do not require a lawyer (National Hospice & Palliative Care Organization, 2016). However, to validate the documents, usually witnesses or a notary's service is required. Some states do not allow members of the health care system or potential heirs to witness such documents; that is why familiarity with the state's requirements is important. It can be detrimental for a patient to have agonized over completing a document and appointing an agent, only to discover that her wishes cannot be carried out because there are no witnesses available or the document is improperly completed and thus invalid because family or staff misunderstood the process or intent. Finally, the social worker will want to review all documents, be sure the entire team is aware of who is the designated health care agent, have the completed form placed in the medical record, and inform the team that it is present.

PHYSICIAN AID IN DYING

Physician aid in dying has emerged as a legally protected medical intervention in those cases where rational adults with a life expectancy of less than six months have decided to request a prescription for lethal doses of medications from their physician, which the patients ingest voluntarily on their own accord (Chamberlain, 2009; Emanuel, Onwuteaka-Philipsen, Urwin, & Cohen, 2016; Karsoho, 2016). While the Supreme Court has heard cases regarding physician aid in dying, it has not ruled that it is a protected constitutional right (*Washington v. Glucksberg*, 1997). Therefore, state law determines whether this is a legally acceptable and viable option for adult patients at the end of life. Currently, physician aid in dying is legal in six states and the District of Columbia, is not addressed in four states, and is prohibited in 40 states (Procon.

org, 2017). It is important to note that physician aid in dying in the United States does not include "euthanasia," a medical practice legal in a small number of countries, where the physician actually causes the death by administering the lethal dose to the patient. Euthanasia is not legal anywhere in the United States. It is imperative that practicing social workers know the law in their state, especially where physician aid in dying is legal. Each state law varies but has similar components, such as requiring both an oral and written request to the physician, a waiting period between request and the prescription being filled, two physicians to examine the patient, and education about other end-of-life treatment options, such as palliative care and hospice (ProCon.org, 2017).

At times, patients may directly or indirectly express a wish to hasten their death. This can cause anxiety for team members who may have moral and ethical concerns and do not know how to respond. During these times, a social worker's expertise may be especially useful to help the team clarify the meaning attached to requests for hastened death and perhaps, concurrently, to invite sharing of individual beliefs and values regarding this important topic. The social worker can assess for hopes, fears, spiritual needs, psychological stress, financial worries, and family dynamics that may be affecting a patient's request.

As these requests can be extremely stressful, it is recommended that a team approach be used to ensure that all facets of care have been addressed (Deschepper, Distelmans, & Bilsen, 2014). The social worker can place an ecological lens over such a request, helping the patient to clarify what is a persistent, thoughtful, reflective request versus a temporal response to bad news, a pain crisis, a family encounter, or a change in financial circumstance. This process may take time and shared expertise.

Whether or not physician aid in dying is legal, social workers can create opportunities for members of the health care team to share thoughts and feelings and consider how to respond. The team may feel despair or disappointment that they are not adequately addressing distressing symptoms for the patient, or may feel helpless in the face of such a serious and permanent wish. It may be valuable to the team to have risk management, palliative care consultation, or the ethics committee provide guidance to quell reactive decisions and to ease anxiety.

ETHICS COMMITTEES, PALLIATIVE CARE CONSULT TEAMS, AND RISK MANAGEMENT SERVICES

Institutional resources such as ethics committees, risk management departments, and palliative care consult teams exist to assist patients, families, and providers when making difficult decisions or facing ethical challenges. While they may not be available across all health care settings, they are commonly found in hospitals and larger health care systems. Social workers frequently serve on ethics committees and palliative care teams, providing insight into family dynamics, facilitating open dialogue, and eliciting underlying values, fears, and concerns to support discussions to fully integrate multiple perspectives into the decision-making process.

Federal law including PSDA and regulatory bodies such as the Joint Commission influenced the requirement that hospitals provide an ethics committee to help resolve patient care issues (Aulisio, 2016). Many ethics committees also draft policy and procedures regarding withdrawal of life-sustaining therapies, advance directives, and decision-making as part of their service. Composed of providers across disciplines, ethics committees may convene case conferences with families or treating clinicians to address care concerns that arise, such as disagreements in treatment plans between providers, patient, and family, dissension among family members, and challenges in identifying appropriate decision-makers. Social workers can request an ethics consult to help providers and families better hear each other's voices, concerns, and ideas through a structured framework to reveal all ethically permissible outcomes. Many times, ethics teams illuminate care options as they are able to assist providers and families to openly discuss their views and misconceptions. Serving on ethics committees, social workers can lend their expertise on a meso level, influencing practices and policies in their health care settings.

Palliative care teams, sometimes known as supportive care services, provide specialized knowledge in symptom management and may bring a new perspective to complex medical decision-making while supporting patients and families and the primary providers who are distressed by ethical dilemmas.

Risk management departments and staff exist to minimize risk to the health care entity, its patients, and providers. Such departments offer a unique opportunity for providers to review care situations with them, prior to implementing treatment plans, to understand what risk such plans may have for all involved. Risk management staff can augment ethics consults by presenting the legal ramifications and liabilities inherent in certain care decision situations. They can be a valuable resource to help the providers understand their legal obligations and limitations when considering or providing a treatment option. Unlike the ethics services, which can hold a consult at the request of a patient or family member, most risk management departments serve only the providers of the health care setting where they are employed. Social workers can suggest risk management staff to colleagues to help quell unfounded litigation fears among providers that may be constraining their desire to implement a particular treatment.

Lynette Continued

Lynette's symptoms have worsened significantly in the past week. She was admitted to the hospital for severe pain and a bowel obstruction. After several days she begins to feel some relief from constant nausea and vomiting. Lynette directed in her living will that no artificial hydration or nutrition be provided and her pain be controlled "as I don't want to needlessly suffer." In accordance with these wishes, the team updates Phyllis, her appointed health care agent, on their continuing efforts to actively address her pain. Lynette is somnolent—a multifactorial consequence of progressing disease, organ failure, and medications. Phyllis comments on how difficult it is to watch Lynette "waste" away, feeling she is hungry but cannot eat because of sleepiness and the bowel obstruction. Phyllis intimates to the social worker that she wishes the doctor could take Lynette "out of her misery," as Lynette would never want her daughters to remember her this way. Thomas grapples with feelings of deep sadness as he watches his sister slip away, knowing he cannot protect his nieces, who hold vigil at her bedside. He reflects thoughtfully about the multiple losses his family has experienced, including his brother's incarceration and absence from another critical family transition. At a loss for how to support Lynette and his family, Thomas requests a feeding tube be placed so his sister "at least, not starve to death." He is aware that this request is incongruous with her guidance. His distress focuses on the hospital system, which he accuses of using medications to hasten her death so they can "free up her bed." At the height of his sense of helplessness, he wonders aloud about obtaining guardianship of Lynette through the probate court so he can make decisions, as he, after all, is her "flesh and blood" and should be "calling the shots." The primary providers begin to feel uneasy being in Lynette's room because of these tensions amidst a slow protracted dying. They realize it is only a matter of days before she will die, and the escalating family discord informs their private and unspoken hopes that death will come as soon and as peacefully as possible.

On the meso level, several variables, often unrecognized, come into play at this juncture in Lynette's illness. The hospital, with its own culture to promote cure, decrease cost and length of stay, and minimize risk, challenges providers to protect the process surrounding Lynette's dying while responding to institutional pressures. Thomas, in his efforts to align with her own faith congregation, desires to ensure that in the eyes of the church, the same mistake is "not made twice" as he reflects on the decisions made during Bobby's hospitalization. On the community level, as the local suburban health care system assumed control of the city hospital, there is suspicion that "outsiders" may prioritize profit margins over caring for the city's own residents. This worry, combined with the history in the African-American community of lack of access and fair treatment in the medical setting, especially at large urban hospitals, creates unspoken fears and assumptions best brought from the shadows to the light. Past egregious activity, such as not informing African-American men of their diagnosed syphilis and withholding the recommended treatment in the Tuskegee Syphilis Study, and using cancer cells from Henrietta Lacks, an African-American woman, without her consent, have been identified as reasons for some of this mistrust (Skloot, 2010). Now, in his sister's hospital room, Thomas may be feeling powerless, re-experiencing the pain of losses of other family members and reflecting on a future without his sister.

Several different interventions are relevant to supporting Lynette, her daughter, caregivers, and her primary providers. To begin, Phyllis may be hinting at some method of hastening Lynette's death as a reflection of the despair, hopelessness, and helplessness she experiences consequent to her role as health care agent. Knowing Phyllis is part of Lynette's congregation, the social worker may want to reach out, with Phyllis's permission, to see if an older adult from her church may be able to support Phyllis during this time. An older congregant may help to subtly influence those members of the congregation who ostracized Lynette in the past due to her health care decisions regarding Bobby, though both Lynette and Phyllis remained in the church. The social worker may be able to find support for Phyllis to help her remain faithful to Lynette's expressed desires for treatment. Additionally, scheduling routine family conferences with a focus on updating Phyllis, Thomas, and Lynette's daughters on the management of her current symptoms and the signs and symptoms of the dying process may provide a forum for each to share feelings and thoughts, and to have their questions and concerns addressed directly by staff (See Chapter 5; "Social Aspects of Care"). By collaborating with nursing and physicians, everyone has an opportunity to share their observations and perspectives on how best to respond to the family's concerns. By anticipating questions regarding Lynette's pain and worry about "starvation," the providers can conduct family conferences that are compassionate and medically informative, and that recognize converging pressures of family history, community, and church (See Chapter 8; "Care of Patients and Families at the End of Life"). In pre-meetings, deciding which clinician is best positioned to facilitate can support coherence and clarity. Each discipline listens from the perspective of their training, and social workers often assist medical providers to explain treatments and side effects in language acceptable to all, listen for unasked or unanswered questions, and encourage the creation of space for emotional expression. Social workers are natural leaders for family conferences, but lead best when they can identify the primary provider whom the family and patient will most likely trust in this circumstance.

The threat of Thomas to obtain guardianship over Lynette, thereby complicating and perhaps protracting her inevitable death, invites inclusion of other hospital resources to provide expert guidance and support the family caregivers, the team, and ultimately, Lynette. Both palliative care and ethics services may provide a level of objectivity and an "audience effect" that allows perceptions, grievances, and concerns to be aired and heard, thereby providing a service in empathy to both the family and the primary providers. Inviting risk management to help the team assess what liabilities are present in their current plan of care may ease the worry of providers who are swayed by any threatened legal action. The ethics service, who routinely meet with the team and may meet with the family, can review advance directives and clarify which treatments support the goals and wishes of the patient. Meeting with families may further help to clarify the relationship between treatment decisions and Lynette's prior expressed guidance and treatment goals and to verify with the team whether a treatment is ethically permissible or not.

Figure 9.1 illustrates the various interventions that social workers across settings may employ when working on cases with ethical and legal challenges.

CONCLUSION

Ethical situations in health care demand timely decision-making when various courses of treatment could be pursued but one must be decided. Sometimes, no matter what the setting, the decision-making voice of the patient is compromised, and the health care team must rely on previously written or expressed wishes, desires, values, and their meaning to the care plan. Discussions with providers, surrogate decision-makers, families, and caregivers are an essential tool in exploring the convergence of previous conversations with the patient with an understanding of who she is as a person and how that relates to treatment options. Timing, the individuals involved, and the content and context of such discussions are best planned and facilitated over the course of the patient's illness. Social workers are a natural fit to facilitate these conversations.

The rich interplay of an individual's own value system, health experiences, and culture exist within a sphere of societal norms, laws, and moral influences in the setting of a health care system. Being aware that all such influences are occurring simultaneously, although perhaps intermittently, increases understanding of the unique experience of each patient and family. The individual patient is experiencing the health setting on a multitude of levels, all intersecting at one time: being wealthy and feeling out of control, being poor with low medical literacy, being a man who feels vulnerable, being part of a marginalized ethnic or religious group, and/or speaking a different language. Realizing that patients have experiences at the intersection of everything that makes them unique individuals serves to help providers understand the intricate layers involved when patients are asked to make important health care decisions.

Grounded in the practice-guiding principle of honoring the person in his or her environment, social workers are trained to consider multiple facets of experience as they assist the patient, family, and providers in negotiating the best decision-making process along the illness trajectory. Social work brings a highly prized perspective to treatment decisions by raising moral and ethical questions and concerns. Creating opportunities for advance care planning, identifying agents and surrogate decision-makers, and providing support and guidance as they act in the patient's best interest are well within the realm of health social work practice. Social workers can lead valuable patient-centered discussions utilizing the existing patient support structure, family meetings, and consultative services. These discussions frame the individual patient and family within the institution's norms and policies and societal laws governing health care.

LEARNING EXERCISE

1. In the emergency department, a patient is brought in unresponsive, with no advance directive documentation other than a health care proxy appointing, a friend. The health care proxy arrives in significant distress, stating that she is uncomfortable with the role and has no knowledge of the patient's wishes or preferences. She does not know of any family or other friends to contact. What is the next best step? Who could be most helpful?
2. Select a colleague or fellow student to research position papers on physician aid in dying. Prepare a presentation that discusses the ethical, religious, public policy, and medical principles that influence the thinking of those who do or do not support the practice.

ACKNOWLEDGMENT

I would like to thank Beth Applebaum, Wayne State Law librarian, for her excellent research in support of this chapter.

ONLINE RESOURCES

The American Bar Association.
    Has compiled selected characteristics of state health care Power of Attorney laws:

www.americanbar.org/content/dam/aba/administrative/law_aging/
state-health-care-power-of-attorney-statutes.authcheckdam.p
Site for laws that identify who can be the substituted surrogate
decision-maker:
www.americanbar.org/content/dam/aba/administrative/law_aging/
2018-triggering-chart.authcheckdam.pdf
Center for Practical Bioethics. www.practicalbioethics.org/
The Center for Practical Bioethics is a nonprofit, free-standing,
and independent organization nationally recognized for its
proactive work in practical bioethics, calling attention to ethical
issues, developing programs, policies and publications to address
them. The Center assists patients and their families, health care
professionals, policymakers and corporate leaders with difficult
issues in health care and research, putting "practical bioethics"
into action.
The Conversation Project. www.theconversationproject.org/
The Conversation Project is dedicated to helping people talk about their
wishes for end-of-life care.
The Conversation Project: www.theconversationproject.org/wp-content/
uploads/2017/03/ConversationProject-ProxyKit-English.pdf
How to Choose a Health Care Proxy and How to Be a Health Care Proxy
The Hastings Center. www.thehastingscenter.org/
The Hastings Center is the world's first bioethics research institute,
a nonpartisan, nonprofit organization of research scholars from
multiple disciplines, including philosophy, law, political science, and
education. Staff includes members with expertise in communications,
publishing, and finance, and a worldwide network of elected Fellows,
an active board, and an advisory council. The Center produces books,
articles, and other publications on ethical questions in medicine,
science, and technology that help inform policy, practice, and public
understanding.
The Joint Commission.
www.jointcommission.org/assets/1/6/Lang%20Access%20and%20
Law%20Jan%202008%20(17).pdf
Has compiled laws that affect language access for patients when making
decisions in a health care setting.
National Council on Interpreting in Health Care (NCIHC). www.ncihc.org/
about
The NCIHC is a multidisciplinary organization whose mission is to
promote and enhance language access in health care in the United
States.

National Health Law Program. www.healthlaw.org/about
  Founded in 1969, the National Health Law Program (NHeLP) protects
  and advances the health rights of low-income and underserved
  individuals and families, and advocates, educates, and litigates at the
  federal and state levels.
National Healthcare Decisions Day (NHDD). www.nhdd.org/
  NHDD, an initiative of the Conversation Project, exists as a 50-state
  annual initiative to provide clear, concise, and consistent information
  on health care decision-making to both the public and providers/
  facilities through the widespread availability and dissemination of
  simple, free, and uniform tools (not just forms) to guide the process.
  NHDD entails 50 independent, but coordinated, state and local events
  supported by a national media and public education campaign.
National Hospice and Palliative Care Organization, www.caringinfo.org/i4a/
  pages/index.cfm?pageid=3286Caring Info
  Selecting Your Healthcare Agent:
Neuswanger Institute for Bioethics. www.hsd.luc.edu/bioethics/content/
  ethics-consultation-cases
  This website has access to skill-building materials for ethics case
  consultations, short videos, and a template for evaluating ethics
  consultations.
US Department of Veterans Affairs (VA), National Center for Ethics in
  Health Care. www.ethics.va.gov/integratedethics/
  This website has access to forms, templates, and pocket cards for the
  VA's system of using their CASES method of ethics consultation and
  articles and resources regarding ethics consultation.

REFERENCES

42 USC § 1395cc(f) and 1396a(w). *Agreements with providers of services: Enrollment processes*. Retrieved from www.ssa.gov/OP_Home/ssact/title19/1902.htm.
42 Code of Federal Regulations, Part 489, Subpart I. *Advance directives*. Retrieved from www.gpo.gov/fdsys/pkg/CFR-2016-title42-vol5/xml/CFR-2016-title42-vol5-part489.xml.
45 C.F.R. § 164.530(c). *Administrative requirements*. Retrieved from www.gpo.gov/fdsys/granule/CFR-2011-title45-vol1/CFR-2011-title45-vol1-sec164-530.
American Bar Association. (2017a). *Default surrogate consent statutes*. Retrieved from www.americanbar.org/content/dam/aba/administrative/law_aging/2014_default_surrogate_consent_statutes.authcheckdam.pdf.
American Bar Association. (2017b). *Living wills, health care proxies, and advance health care directives*. Retrieved from www.americanbar.org/groups/real_property_

trust_estate/resources/estate_planning/living_wills_health_care_proxies_advance_ health_care_directives.html.

Aulisio, M. P. (2016). Why did hospital ethics committees emerge in the US? *American Medical Association Journal of Ethics, 18*(5), 546–553.

Beachamp, T. L., & Childress, J. F. (1994). *Principles of biomedical ethics*, (4th ed.). New York: Oxford University Press.

Brinkman-Stoppelenburg, A., Rietjens, J. A. C., & Van Der Heide, A. (2014). The effects of advance care planning on end-of-life care: A systemic review. *Palliative Medicine, 28*(8), 1000–1025.

Buckley, J. W., & Abell, N. (2010) Life-sustaining treatment decisions: A social work response to meet needs of health care surrogates, *Journal of Social Work in End-of-Life & Palliative Care, 6*(1–2), 27–50.

Chamberlain, K. A. (2009). Looking for a good death: The elderly terminally ill's right to die by physician-assisted suicide. *Elder Law Journal, 17*, 61–93.

Cheon, J., Coyle, N., Wiegand, D. L., & Welsh, S. (2015). Ethical issues experienced by hospice and palliative nurses. *Journal of Hospice and Palliative Nursing, 17*(1), 7–13.

Cruzan v. Director, Missouri Dept. of Health, 110 S. (Ct. 2841, 1990).

Csikai, E. L., & Chaitin, E. (2006). *Ethics in end-of-life decisions in social work practice*. Chicago: Lyceum.

Deschepper, R., Distelmans, W., and Bilsen, J. (2014). Requests for euthanasia/ physician-assisted suicide on the basis of mental suffering: Vulnerable patients or vulnerable physicians? *Journal of the American Medical Association of Psychiatry, 71*(6), 617–618.

Emanuel, E. J., Onwuteaka-Philipsen, B. D., Urwin, J. W., & Cohen, J. (2016). Attitudes and practices of euthanasia and physician-assisted suicide in the United States, Canada, and Europe. *Journal of the American Medical Association, 316*(1), 79–90.

Fineberg, I. C. (2010). Social work perspectives on family communication and family conferences in palliative care. *Progress in Palliative Care, 18*(4), 213–220.

Ganzini, L., Volicer, L., Nelson, W. A., Fox, E., & Derse, A. R. (2004). Ten myths about decision-making capacity. *Journal of the American Medical Directors Association, 5*(4), 263–267.

Karsoho, H., Fishman, J. R., Wright, D. K., & MacDonald, M. E. (2016). Suffering and medicalization at the end of life: The case of physician assisted dying. *Social Science & Medicine, 170*, 188–196.

Ko, D. N., Perez-Cruz, P., & Blinderman, C. D. (2011). Ethical issues in palliative care. *Primary Care: Clinics in Office Practice, 38*(2), 183–193.

The Joint Commission. (2008). *Language access and the law*. Retrieved from www. jointcommission.org/assets/1/6/Lang%20Access%20and%20Law%20Jan%20 2008%20(17).pdf

Legal Information Institute. (n.d.). *Guardian*. Retrieved from www.law.cornell.edu/ wex/guardian.

Leiter, R.A. (2015). *National survey of state laws*. Retrieved from home.heinonline.org/ national-survey-of-state-laws/.

LexisNexis. (2014). Healthcare law—medical treatment: Advance health directives and surrogate decision-makers. *LexisNexis 50-State Surveys, Statutes & Regulations*. Retrieved from www.lexisnexis.com/50state/.

Lovell, A., & Yates, P. (2014). Advance care planning in palliative care: A systematic literature review of the contextual factors influencing its uptake 2008–2012. *Palliative Medicine, 28*(8), 1026–1035.

McCabe, M. S., & Coyle, N. (2014). Ethical and legal issues in palliative care. *Seminars in Oncology Nursing, 30*(4), 287–295.

Melhado, L. W. W., & Fowler Byers, J. (2011). Patients' and surrogates' decision-making characteristics: Withdrawing, withholding, and continuing life-sustaining treatments. *Journal of Hospice and Palliative Nursing, 13*(1), 16–28.

Meyer, C. (n.d.). *New designation for allowing a natural death ("A.N.D.") would eliminate confusion and suffering when patients are resuscitated against their wishes.* Retrieved from www.hospicepatients.org/and.html.

National Association of Social Workers. (2017). *NASW code of ethics.* Washington, DC: NASW Press. Available at www.socialworkers.org/About/Ethics/Code-of-Ethics/Code-of-Ethics-English.

National Hospice and Palliative Care Organization. (2016). *Download your state's advance directives.* Retrieved from www.caringinfo.org/i4a/pages/index.cfm?pageid=3289

National POLST Paradigm. (2017). *State programs.* Retrieved from polst.org/programs-in-your-state/.

Patient Self Determination Act, Omnibus Budget Reconciliation Act of 1990, Pub. L. No. 101-508, sec. 4206 and 4751, 105 Stat.1388, 1388-115, and 1388-204.

Perkins, H. S. (2007). Controlling death: The false promise of advance directives. *Annals of Internal Medicine, 147*(1), 51–57.

ProCon.org. (2017). *State-by-state guide to physician-assisted suicide.* Retrieved from euthanasia.procon.org/view.resource.php?resourceID=000132.

Pub. L. No. 104-191, 110 Stat. 1936. (1996). *Health insurance portability and accountability act of 1996.* Retrieved from www.gpo.gov/fdsys/pkg/PLAW-104publ191/pdf/PLAW-104publ191.pdf.

Quinlan, In re, 137 N.J. Super. 227, 348 A. 2d 801 (Ch. Div., 1975), re'd, 70 N.J. 10, 355 A. 2d 647, cert. denied sub nom. *Garger v. New Jersey,* 429 U.S. 922, 50 L. in part, *In re Conroy,* 98 N.J. 321, 486 A. 2d 1209 (1985).

Retkin, R., Brandfield, J., & Bacich, C. (2007). *Impact of legal interventions on cancer survivors.* New York: LegalHealth.

Schickedanz, A., Schillinger, D., Landefeld, C. S., Knight, S. J., Williams, B., & Sudore, R. L. (2009). A clinical framework for improving the advance care planning process: Start with patients' self-identified barriers. *Journal of the American Geriatrics Society, 57*(1), 31–39.

Schlairet, M. C., & Cohen, R. W. (2013). Allow-natural-death (AND) orders: Legal, ethical, and practical considerations. *HEC Forum, 25*(2), 161–171.

Silva, M. D., Genoff, M., Zaballa, A., Jewell, S., Stabler, S., Gany, F. M., & Diamond, L. C. (2016). Interpreting at the end of life: A systematic review of the impact of interpreters on the delivery of palliative care services to cancer patients with limited English proficiency. *Journal of Pain and Symptom Management, 51*(3), 569–580.

Silveira, M. J., Kim, S. Y. H., & Langa, K. M. (2010). Advance directives and outcomes of surrogate decision making before death. *New England Journal of Medicine, 362*(13), 1211–1218.

Skloot, R. (2010). *The immortal life of Henrietta Lacks.* New York: Crown.

Snow, A., Warner, J., & Zilberfein, F. (2008). The increase of treatment options at the end of life: Impact on the social work role in an inpatient hospital setting. *Social Work in Health Care, 47*(4), 376–391.

Sudore, R. L., Lum, H. D., You, J. J., Hanson, L. C., Meier, D. E., . . . Heyland, D. K. (2017). Defining advance care planning for adults: A consensus definition from a multidisciplinary Delphi panel. *Journal of Pain and Symptom Management, 53*(5), 821–832.

US National Library of Medicine. (2016). *Do-not-resuscitate order.* Retrieved from medlineplus.gov/ency/patientinstructions/000473.htm.

Van Scoy, L. J., Howrylak, J., Nguyen, A., Chen, M., & Sherman, M. (2014). Family structure, experience with end-of-life decision making, and who asked about advance directives impacts advance directive completion rates. *Journal of Palliative Medicine, 17*(10), 1099–1106.

Washington v. Glucksberg, 521 U.S. 702 (1997).

Zevon, M. A., Schwabish, S., Donnelly, J. P., & Rodabaugh, K. J. (2007). Medically related legal needs and quality of life in cancer care: A structural analysis. *Cancer, 109*(12), 2600–2606.

Special Issues in Children and Older Adults

TERRY ALTILIO, MEAGAN LYON LEIMENA,
BRIDGET SUMSER, ALLIE SHUKRAFT,
MARTHA SCHERMER, MERCEDES BERN-KLUG,
AND AMY L. LEMKE ■

A population that does not take care of the elderly and of the children and the young has no future because it abuses both its memory and its promise.

—POPE FRANCIS

INTRODUCTION

While children and adolescents may be distant in years from older adults, perhaps they are not so distant in the care, thoughtfulness, and expertise they need through the course of serious illness. There are interesting similarities to consider in the life of a person and the family they may be joining, with whom they are intimately entwined, or the family they may be leaving, no matter the age. The advent of disease, the news a child may be born with a life-threatening condition, the signs of emerging dementia, or the trauma of accident mark an unanticipated shift from the normal pattern of life and demand adaptation. As we may distance ourselves from the unimaginable experience of children who suffer and the affront that childhood disease and mortality is to the natural order, we may also distance ourselves from the suffering of older adults in a futile and unconscious effort to detach from the experience of aging and death. Given the enormity of the landscape, this chapter aims to provide a glimpse of these complex populations within which there is endless diversity yet common threads, weaving through and binding one human to another. It is enriched by the words and wisdom of social workers who inform the worlds of pediatrics and geriatrics as specialists who bring into plain sight, paths for intervention.

It is important to note that by discussing both populations, children and older adults together, we are not linking the two in a universal sense. Often, older adults are infantilized by professional and lay caregivers—described by well-intended providers as "cute" or "sweet." Increased dependency, a common theme in the trajectory of serious illness, often brings up ideas and feelings of being a child, and as such, we are mindful of the simile "treating like a child." There are obvious and significant differences between children and older adults. What we propose is that Erikson's developmental stages, often thought to layer over time in a linear fashion, may be interchangeable and relevant to life spans of all lengths. This highlights similarities in people living with serious illness at any point, be it day one or year 90.

Integrating Erikson's Developmental Stages

Erik Erikson conceptualized eight stages of development (Erikson, 1950). The first juxtaposes trust and mistrust, while the last contrasts integrity with despair. It is not hard to imagine that as children, adolescents, or older adults become ill, come to end of life, or more precipitously experience an event that derails them from a familiar path, trust and safety are as critical as at the beginning of life. Trust that care will be provided and comfort valued in the same way as medical treatments. Trust that just as sounds and touch reassure infants and children, perhaps as cognition fades or end of life approaches in elders, there may be times when comforting memories are evoked through voice and physical presence. Trust that time will be spent discovering values and beliefs to inform decision making and noticing whether autonomy is emerging as in children and adolescents or waning as in many elders. Trust that noticing will be reflected in respect for the life and values lived or make space for the challenges and joys in discovering preferences with a child or adolescent who is emerging. Trust there will be systems in place and clinician awareness to protect the most vulnerable from arbitrary judgments about the worth of a life – whether that life is a 22-week neonate or a 95-year-old living with dementia.

Integrity, Despair, and Dignity

It is possible that clinicians who are conscious of Erikson's concept of integrity will be present to the reflections of older adults and their families, not only of successes, sources of meaning, and satisfaction, but of regrets and wonderings. This reflects a real life reviewed, rather than a sanitized version that does not allow for authenticity. Is there a link to integrity versus despair when clinicians speak of the dignity we aspire to create, no matter the stage of illness or setting of care? Is there an opportunity to obviate despair in older adults by the way we meet their intimate needs when self-care is no longer possible? Perhaps dignity in the neonatal intensive care unit (NICU) is captured by the tenderness and respect paid to infants and parents, by efforts made to enhance bonding of parent and child, even in the cacophonous environment of light, tubes, and high technology.

Perhaps hope—adapted, lost, regained, or reframed—as a universal focus of care and intervention supports integrity. Joining families of children and adolescents in defining hope challenges our capacity to be present with the fluidity of life as it becomes clear that hopes evolve and that the hopes of parents, for example, might often be quite distinct from those of the child or adolescent. Hope moves beyond the length of life or life itself to legacy, defined not only in the most concrete sense of possessions or money, but also by the hearts and minds that have been touched over a lifetime—lives that include the generations and clinicians whose work and personal lives have been touched by caring for another, no matter the age or the outcome.

Meaning-Making

On the micro level, weaving palliative care tenets into services provided to persons and their families focuses on attributed meanings—discovering the meaning of events, treatments, behaviors, and the words or descriptors used by clinical providers, which create connections or distance. Whether children or older adults, a poignant theme is the contrast in meaning attached by families or friends to the responses of patients. The ability of an infant to wrap a tiny hand around the finger of a parent, explained by clinicians as "reflex," may be as profound for a particular family member as the holding of a hand by a person with end-stage dementia. The suggestion of opioid medication to manage pain or shortness of breath, while for the clinician an effort to comfort, may mean to families a threat to consciousness and connection that is prioritized above all else. It is these points of dissonance where the art of silence, recognition, and negotiation combines with expertise to create a shared consensus within which the integrity of individual meanings is not threatened, and care can proceed that privileges the well-being and wholeness of the person, regardless of age.

Dependence: A Comfort or a Threat to Identity

The natural dependence in infants and children contrasts with the meaning of forced dependence in adolescence when illness or accident may frustrate an expected drive toward autonomy and initiative. Understanding the importance of this developmental task in the setting of an evolving sense of self leads adolescents, parents, and clinicians to creative problem-solving, adaptation, discovery of a "new normal," and possibly a shared and unique grief and resilience as each recognizes not only what has been lost, but what remains as possible. For older adults, dependence may be expected and accepted, or may represent the suffering Eric Cassell describes as the threat to the integrity of the "whole person" (Cassell, 1991). It is instructive to link Erikson's tasks of early childhood, where autonomy is equated with personal control and expressed preferences, to clinical interventions, no matter the age. This restores a sense of control and uncovers preferences contributing to the understanding of the whole person. Physical dependence does not obviate the ability to direct one's care or the need to respect preferences, which may be explicitly expressed through words, writings, behaviors, and memories, or sometimes interpreted through the feelings, observations, and perhaps the projections of another. In the care of older adults, there is meaningful work in exploring the life lived, and creating a care plan enriched by discovery of the unique person. In the care of the young, the landscape is also one of a life lived, no matter the time frame, as well as the hopes and wishes imagined both by the self or others—adapted, actualized, or grieved.

Communication and Decision-Making

The families of children with serious disease or traumatic accident are forced into a dependent relationship and communication with fragmented health care systems speaking a unique language and often populated by rotating providers practicing in hurried environments. This dependence is often ongoing. Efforts to bridge transitions and create professional relationships of continuity have the potential to embody a shared history, sustain and support as complications and challenges arise requiring ongoing psychosocialspiritual interventions, decision-making, and care coordination (Konrad, 2008). Fragmentation increases the challenges in decision-making, which can be time-consuming processes and, most importantly, become the nexus for emotions, biases, and meaning-making infusing the care of children, adolescents, and older adults. As systems continue to be fragmented, technology can enhance connection, honoring the value of distant family, friends, and providers. Their virtual presence can diminish feelings of abandonment, affirm history, and build legacy.

Enhancing communication is central to the shared process of therapeutic and ethical decision-making. Often older adults who are seriously ill or cognitively impaired and have learned English as a secondary language are better able to participate when conversations are offered in their primary language. Assessing the range of ability and desire of the person with illness to participate requires time and skill. Children can be engaged in conversation about their care when communication is tailored to the individual's age and development, family considerations, and preferences, including thoughtful reflection on the preservation of hope (Sisk, Bluebond-Langer, Wiener, Mack, & Wolfe, 2016). This same adaptation often allows older adults with compromised cognition to share thoughts and values about their care and end of life. Social work advocacy and participation in these discussions assumes exquisite sensitivity to the emotions and impact on family members and the family system, ensuring that values are acknowledged and respected, and when challenged, that there is attention to the impact on the family going forward. Parents of children with serious, chronic conditions appreciate recognition of their knowledge of their child, their unique role, and clear candid communication (Jones, Contro, & Koch, 2014; Konrad, 2008). A similar respect is accorded families of older adults, when they are asked for their history, observations and shared experience with the patient. This further informs a sense of personhood while enriching decision-making with a congruence informed by the life lived, current circumstances of illness, and care options that exist. No matter the days or years lived or the setting of care, social work's respect for personhood and process, coupled with the ability to sit with silence and suffering, complements the best medical information, provided with clarity and compassion.

Beyond the emotional and cognitive demands of communication and decision-making within the health care system, families are often immersed in networks of friends and extended family who, from caring or curiosity, initiate or maintain contact. Families experience the emotional challenges of decision-making and then may feel compelled to share these complex processes with others—a sharing that may be therapeutic and empowering, or may create additional turmoil and stress. Social workers across settings, who are alert to this dynamic as a focus of assessment, can assist families to make informed decisions about sharing information. This conscious intention empowers families to define their parameters of confidentiality, informing decisions about the use of social media, voice mail recording, text messaging, and email to send group updates. This use of technology can allow for mobilizing resources while protecting from the emotional and cognitive distress that, for some, accompanies the telling and retelling of medical and updates.

Connection and Isolation

Social connection and isolation are psychosocial determinants of health with relevance across the life span (Heiman & Artiga, 2015). Maintaining and engaging social connections provide a semblance of normalcy and improves outcomes. The support of a larger community, whether a place of worship, neighborhood, advocacy groups, or expressed through public policy that privileges the needs of all patients and families, increases resilience and support systems essential to well-being over time. New relationships, with others on a similar path, promoted through disease- or life-span-specific groups in person and online, may provide validation and comfort. Access and availability to support from the micro to macro vary from person to person, reflective of relational choices made over time and geographic and socioeconomic realities. Identifying local resources allows social workers to make appropriate links to community resources and/or explore creative means for enhancing connection and support. For example, a woman whose partner dies after 50 years of marriage may be grieving, lonely, and struggling with her own illness. What is available to support her to maximize connections and mitigate feelings of abandonment and isolation? This may be the person who delivers the mail and notices when mail is not picked up, or the volunteer who delivers Meals on Wheels. Neighbors may bring food or check in on their way home from work. Support could involve community health social workers or hospice clinicians using tele-health technology such as Face Time or Skype to integrate distant family and prior providers who have been important to the lives of patients. The creative mobilizing of resources in consultation with older adults or families of children honors the integrity of family systems and creates the opportunity to engage available community support.

Pain and Symptom Management

Inattention to the assessment and treatment of pain in children and older adults results in increased suffering in populations who are particularly vulnerable (Paice & Ferrell, 2011). Social workers across settings and specialty practices share the responsibility of advocacy and management of symptoms for those who depend on our compassion and expertise where disease, accident, or cognitive changes are threats to the autonomy needed for self-report and self-advocacy. In addition to the pain caused by disease or accident, it is compelling to consider the experience of infants and children and those older adults with cognitive impairment when medical care requires clinicians to inflict pain, as when inserting an intravenous line or drawing blood for diagnostic processes. Often the most vulnerable, whose experience of fear, anxiety, and confusion is not tempered by analytical information and understanding, do not comprehend why they are being hurt. The shared commitment to ethical principles of beneficence and non-maleficence mandates social workers join with colleagues to use appropriate assessment tools and techniques found to minimize predictable pain. Discrepancy in the assessment of pain, or reluctance of family or clinicians to treat pain, is an invitation to an assessment to enhance shared understanding and negotiation of the intersecting factors that have created a circumstance where caring family and clinicians have allowed treatable pain to go unabated (See Chapter 3; "Physical Aspects of Care").

Conclusion

Serious illness in both children and older adults can extend over time, requiring complex care management, reorganization of family systems, linkage to community resources, and support and empowerment for caregivers and family members who may struggle to sustain and support self and others. A patient-centered, family-focused perspective responds to the needs of siblings where there is childhood illness, as well as attention to the needs of family caregivers who may provide and negotiate care of an older adult over days or years. This mandate requires social workers to attend to family systems, to assess, intervene, and model collaboration, linking to other providers, respecting and building on the work of colleagues. The essential focus on bridging transitions minimizes the demand that patients and families carry the emotional and cognitive work of new beginnings. Making connections with clinicians across settings strengthens the possibility that trust established is sustained, the identity and integrity of the person are communicated, and isolation and perceived abandonment is replaced by the possibility of informed relationships. This is support in action, an extension of therapeutic, relational work, which merges what has been learned about a person and family in this episode of their illness experience, honoring current developmental needs, to inform where they are going.

CHILDREN

Hope is the thing with feathers
That perches in the soul,
And sings the tune without the words,
And never stops at all.

—EMILY DICKINSON

Introduction

Hope is a unifying principle in palliative care across the life span—hope for lon-
gevity, hope for cure, hope for reduced suffering, and hope for meaning. Serious
or chronic illness in children, whether unexpected or anticipated due to a genetic condition, defies the assumption that there is a natural order to the world
and challenges the equilibrium of family systems. Regardless of how children
and their families come to illness, caring for and supporting the navigation of
illness resembles that of adults who also must be empowered to negotiate increasingly complex and fragmented health care systems (Friebert, 2012). Yet
for children and adolescents, the context is also one of ongoing development
and decision-making within the setting of an elusive and often more uncertain
illness trajectory (Sourkes et al., 2005).

A diagnosis of serious illness or sudden change in health status alters the
experience of childhood and increases the level of social vulnerability. As such,
the guiding principles of palliative care apply to children as they do to adults.
In the context of family life, the focus is to support development, growth, and
function to the fullest extent possible, to mitigate pain and suffering, and to
provide care contributing to a legacy, no matter what the outcome, of meaning,
respect, and compassion (Jones et al., 2014). This includes management of
symptoms and treatment side effects and attending to psychosocialspiritual and
developmental issues interrupted and influenced by illness. From a life course
perspective, diagnosis of and adjustment to a serious illness can impede or alter
developmental tasks (Sourkes et al., 2005). Social functioning, including the
ability to attend school, maintain friendships, develop an emerging sense of
sexuality and romantic relationships, and begin to form an autonomous self
are key aspects of childhood and adolescence reshaped by illness or a traumatic physical event. Children, from infants to young adults, exist within the
specific ecology of their families, and the impact of illness will be inherently
experienced through their micro and meso systems. Physical, emotional, and
cognitive development, legal and functional autonomy, and anticipation of
their future are essential considerations in planning for and providing care for

children. As legal minors, children are already more vulnerable to the effects of social forces because they lack agency to control much of their environment or to make choices about their lives. A child and adolescent identity is evolving in the context of family and community, and illness is an intervening variable, uninvited and unpredictable.

For families, adaptations may include adjusting to a life with their child and family that is different from what they had imagined, responding to a child or adolescent's physical or cognitive changes or difference, interfacing with medical systems, technology, and equipment, and integrating an uncertain life expectancy. Diseases such as cancer have a different trajectory in children than adults, as it is more unpredictable. Technology and treatments now may extend life for many years, provoking a range of adaptations and complex emotions, which may be both positive and challenging for patient as well as family (Sourkes et al., 2005). Decision-making involves adults and the child in an age-appropriate manner and occurs in the context of an evolving illness and the concurrent development of the child (Fromer, 2004). These dynamic processes extend beyond the micro to the meso levels of family and social systems, such as school, religious organizations, employment, and activities that may be meaningful to a child and may ground their families. There are myriad implications for siblings, as family routines are disrupted and they are asked to make practical and emotional accommodations and experience a range of normative sibling reactions such as jealousy, sadness, anger, resentment, and fear (Gaab, Owens, & Macleod, 2014; Humphrey, 2015; Sharpe, 2002).

It is evident that social workers have an important role in providing family-centered care with the child at the epicenter. Iterative assessment of needs, both developmental and practical, may help children and families work toward a new equilibrium and stability during challenging and difficult times, when an unpredictable course of disease and prognostic uncertainty can be overwhelming and immobilizing (Fromer, 2004; Konrad, 2008; Sourkes et al., 2005). Identifying and overcoming barriers, such as lack of access to resources, medications, or transportation, contribute to a care plan that is realistic and feasible (Beaune et al., 2014).

Honoring hopes and wishes, elevating child and adolescent voices in care planning, and respecting a developmentally appropriate role for the child in decisions about care can support autonomy and enhance a sense of control during potentially frightening and confusing experiences (Sisk et al., 2016).

Who Are the Children?

While the thought of serious or chronic illness often brings cancer to mind, congenital malformations, genetic, neuromuscular, and cardiovascular conditions are some of the leading life-threatening conditions in the United States for children. Of children aged 0–19, the group with the highest mortality rate is infants—in 2013, 55% of pediatric deaths occurred during infancy, two-thirds in the neonatal period. Infant mortality rates are disproportionately highest for non-Hispanic blacks (NHPCO, 2014), signaling in part the impact of poverty and discrimination on access to health care (Hauck, Tanabe, & Moon, 2011). In addition to the range of conditions, the definition of "pediatric" is pliable. A pediatric palliative care lens may benefit children and families before birth and through early adulthood in some disease trajectories (Juth, 2016; Levine et al., 2017; Sourkes et al., 2005). Pediatric care includes a range of family and social systems impacted by genetic conditions, disease, accident, and trauma. Reflective of this range, insurance providers cover children beyond age 18, and entitlements and benefits may be unique to pediatric populations. On a macro level, this variation drives advocacy for responsive policies such as concurrent care, where children and their families may have simultaneous access to both curative and life-extending treatments and hospice services.

Ecological Theory and Intersectionality

Generally, infants and children come complete with families, whether a single parent or a large extended network of parents, siblings, grandparents, aunts, uncles, and cousins. All come with values and beliefs, inherited or acquired, about parenting and health. Often families define themselves by the connection they have to one another, their culture, and community. A child may be the identified patient; however, family-centered care is a core concept of pediatric programs. Jones, Contro, and Koch (2014) have posited that family-centered care not only is best for families and consistent with needs identified in the research, but also meets the ethical standards of being in the best interest of the child and minimizing feelings of abandonment by maintaining relationships with the entire family (Fromer, 2004; Jones et al., 2014).

Using a lens of intersectionality brings into relief the dynamic and evolving processes of child and family interacting with illness or a traumatic event such as accident or violent injury. Many social systems of both privilege and oppression, including race, class, gender, gender identity, culture, language, education, sexuality, ability, and age, are in flux during all stages of childhood and are both separate from and directly influenced by parental and familial experience. While race and class are directly defined by parental identity and family circumstance, each individual child is learning about her unique identity. For example, Mai, a 13-year-old first-generation Chinese-American girl attending a diverse, urban public school exists at a different social location from her parents. She may or may not share their language as primary, yet needs care and connection driven by love, cultural expectation, respect, and survival. The demands of illness and treatment received in systems where clinicians speak English and preference Western medicine may place Mai, either as patient or sister of a patient, at the center of converging contexts requiring clinical discernment and advocacy to mitigate additional distress for both Mai and her family.

The Role of Social Work

Pediatric palliative care has experienced tremendous growth, yet there are still many children and families who would benefit from earlier introduction of palliative care services (Friebert, 2012). Given the challenges in access, availability, and time, coupled with the impact of disability and financial constraints, it is incumbent upon social workers to provide services "where the patient and family are" across practice settings. Building fluid and organic extended teams with clinicians and systems engaged in care enhances the ability of medical, health, and community supports to accommodate family needs (Friebert, 2012). Ideally, this means early assessment and support for palliative care needs, including pain and symptom management, informed decision-making, and psychosocialspiritual care throughout the course of the child's life-threatening condition. The use of a person-in-environment approach (Hollis, 1974) and ecological model (Bronfenbrenner, 1979) places the child and family in the context of their lives for the medical teams. Assessment includes the patient's current condition, related social determinants of health, and all components of social location and identity, highlighting the complexity of individual experience. With interventions that range from mitigating practical and financial challenges and resource finding to psychological interventions to enhance coping and resilience and support adaptation over time, social workers impact the life of child, adolescent, and family in the present, as well as mental health and well-being over time. Through this process, it is essential to visit and revisit how and when a child or adolescent can be engaged in discussions and decisions about his or her care. Clinical considerations of age, cognitive and emotional abilities, and preferences within the setting of family systems and culture build a foundation for co-constructing decision-making processes over time. Social workers are positioned to work with and often lead the efforts to have all voices heard to make the best and most appropriate plan of care.

Care Principles for Working with Children

Social workers are often called upon to facilitate and mediate communication both within and beyond the family. Modeling and facilitating clear communication is a skill set essential to clarifying complex medical, social, and family issues. Inquiry about the emotional, spiritual, and social aspects of illness, current impacts, and future implications introduces the scope and meaning of patient-centered family-focused care. These conversations can be painful and involve shared vulnerability. Infrequent, indirect cues from child, adolescent, and family may open the door to discussing emotional concerns (Pollak et al., 2007). Social work listening and response seek to understand the intersecting variables that influence communication, including the exchange of words and the choice of silence and presence, witnessing life, love, suffering, pain, joy, and all things in between.

Parents of children with serious, chronic conditions appreciate both recognition as they share an understanding of their child and the unique expertise that their role as caregiver brings, and the opportunity to communicate candidly with the medical team (Clarke & Fletcher, 2003; Goddard, Lehr, & Lapadat, 2007; Jones et al., 2014; Konrad, 2008; Prezant & Marshak, 2006). As parents often have to learn complex medical information and provide care under extraordinary circumstances, mentorship seems to be a valued aspect of parental team relationships, whether with the medical team or with parents who have been in the same situation. Mothers value collaborative relationships built on respect, mutuality, and trust, and communication that conveys concern, compassion, and connection. Equally important is the expertise of health care providers and their ability to individualize and express caring for the child, beyond a diagnosis, and for the family, understanding the intersecting variables that influence decision-making and the child's health care (Konrad, 2008). Social work skills in communication and family systems often contribute to building this caring relationship and collaboration, enhancing connection and shared understanding.

Issues of communication remain at the forefront, impacting everything from treatment adherence (Pollak et al., 2007; Sobo, 2004) to how caregivers feel about themselves and their role within their families (Nicholas, Beaune, Barerra, Blumberg, & Belletrutti, 2016). When faced with conversations about end of life, families value clinicians who are trained to discuss end-of-life concepts, are open and gentle and able to hear difficult stories and sit with suffering (Rattner & Berzoff, 2016) (See Chapter 8; "Care of Patients and Families at the End of Life").

Jesse

> Our children would be beloved. We would give them the best lives pos-
> sible and then prepare to give them the best deaths possible. And we
> would pray that we survived.
>
> —Lord (2014)

Jesse is a three-year-old child with hypoxic ischemic encephalopathy, a brain injury caused by a lack of oxygen during delivery. Resuscitated immediately, she spent weeks in the neonatal intensive care unit (NICU). The combined work of the NICU and palliative care teams focused on introducing her parents, John and Anna, to their first child within a landscape of her uncertain future and complex feelings of grief and loss of the healthy baby they had imagined. Medical information was titrated to their shared and unique emotional responses. The teams explored hopes and values, introducing over time concepts of medical decision-making and care planning. The parents quickly grasped that this process would continue throughout Jesse's life, which would likely be short and complicated. Anna had worked with children with developmental and medical needs with a Catholic youth group, learning basic personal care, a Catholic perspective on the value of the human soul, and the importance of service. She had planned to stay home full-time and felt prepared to care for Jesse. John shared the hope to sustain Jesse's life, supporting her development and survival, holding a belief that time and her evolving condition would bring clarity to decision-making. Psychoeducation and anticipatory guidance, combined with medical information, provided a foundation as Anna and John struggled to agree that they would set no limits on treatments and interventions, including resuscitation. At the same time, they were clear that if she made no developmental gains, "down the road" they would revisit this direction, stating, "We will know when."

Ongoing exploration of John and Anna's hopes, fears, vision, and thoughts about their future leads to a family conference with specialists to provide a medical update prior to discharge. The social worker assists John and Anna to do the emotional and cognitive work of formulating questions that might mitigate or confirm their worries about Jesse's uncertain future. The early integration of a palliative care team presumes that Jesse will likely be hospitalized in the future and the team might provide continuity of care and relationship for the family, providing a historical touchstone for ongoing decisions within a care plan focused on intensive efforts to sustain life. This model of bridging care across settings and building continuity extended into community care as physicians, nurses, and social workers ensured that each transition was marked by comprehensive "hand-offs."

Jesse's care at home is intensive, and physically and emotionally exhausting. The extended family and social support they had imagined waned over time. As family and friends meet Jesse, Anna and John see mixed reactions about their decision to care for her at home. Anna's parents, well intended, are afraid of hurting Jesse, and the medical tasks of tube feedings and frequent oral suctioning are daunting. Jesse's inability to clear secretions means that a parent or caretaker has to watch over her constantly, contributing to physical exhaustion. Family members do not offer respite or financial assistance, and Anna and John don't ask. Social work interventions focus on exploring the feelings and fears influencing their willingness to ask for help while encouraging the integration of self-care skills, both learned and preexisting.

Jesse's frequent visits with her developmental pediatrician and primary social worker are focused on coordinating early intervention therapies such as occupational, speech, and physical therapy. This social worker is the consistent source of psychosocialspiritual support, providing counseling, psychoeducation, and anticipatory guidance. They work together to maximize Jesse's care system and share the struggle to "know when" decisions regarding Jesse's care plan may be revisited. Essential to the shared goal of supporting Jesse's development is assisting to coordinate multiple appointments, communication across specialty providers, and helping family meet Jesse's changing needs, including access to adaptive and medical equipment.

John and Anna worry that they "push" Jesse with her schedule of therapies as they witness the intense efforts of the specialists. As the year passes, it is clear that Jesse's developmental gains are not what Anna and John had hoped to see. There are recurrent hospitalizations due to aspiration pneumonias and, most recently, social work assisted John and Anna as they came to the difficult decision to forgo a tracheostomy that was contrary to their goals for Jesse. They concur with a plan for rehospitalizations and trial intubations for what might be reversible conditions. During a "hand-off" communication between the hospital and primary community social worker, it becomes clear that a family conference replicating the comprehensive process that guided Jesse's care soon after her birth would be beneficial.

Jesse's needs continue to escalate; her parents sleep in shifts and rarely spend time together. They long to feel connected as a family yet rarely experience this—a source of great sadness. John and Anna perceive that Jesse is suffering, as are they. They feel they care for her physical body, but she does not seem to respond emotionally to her parents or environment. John and Anna need reassurance that they have done what is possible to support their daughter. They speculate to the social worker that perhaps the time of "we will know when" has come.

Bringing together the professionals who care for Jesse over time provides the most intimate environment for John and Anna to revisit their hopes and worries, and in response, the team offers a treatment recommendation. Those clinicians who are at a distance participate via conference call. John and Anna share feelings about caring for Jesse in the past and present, as they receive information regarding prognosis and the anticipated trajectory of her life. John and Anna accept a consensus recommendation to forgo future hospitalizations and antibiotics, caring for Jesse at home with hospice support as she comes to the end of her life.

Conclusion

The diverse and challenging paths that children and families walk when living with serious and chronic illnesses provide frequent opportunities for meaningful intervention. Through joining with children and their families in decision-making and care planning in the face of uncertainty, distress, and evolving needs, the social work purview and constellation of skills can be a source of continuity within a changing landscape. Social workers can provide context and compassion as families live with serious illness and strive to do their best for their children.

LEARNING EXERCISE

1. You are working at a specialty pediatric practice caring for a nine-year-old boy with chronic, complex medical issues from a genetic condition. He has frequent and extended visits where he and his family meet with you and medical providers. His parents report that his younger sister, age seven and unaffected by the genetic condition, has been attention seeking and acting out at home recently, behavior that her parents believe is rooted in jealousy. She is having difficulty at school and you have been contacted by the school social worker to discuss the situation. Write a developmentally sensitive assessment and plan of care for the family at home. How can you collaborate with the school social worker to contribute to a complementary plan for the patient's younger sister at school?

OLDER ADULTS

Older adulthood is a stage of life, not a permanent status. Every older adult was once a child. Like a set of Russian dolls, she carries within the lessons, fears, hopes, and dreams of childhood, youth, young adulthood, and middle age. It is this collection of experiences, accrued over decades, that can make working with older adults an interesting, challenging, satisfying, and sometimes poignant experience. The passage of time and the accumulation of experiences serve to accentuate individuality. There is tremendous physical, mental, spiritual, financial, cultural, and social heterogeneity within the group referred to as "older adults."

Older adults have had decades of their lives intertwined with others and have likely occupied many different roles, including child, sibling, friend, spouse, parent, employee, volunteer, and grandparent. Expectations accompanying these roles can come into conflict as illness progresses. People who have grown accustomed to being in control of their bodies, mind, decisions, and schedules for decades have new lessons to learn about accepting the limitations imposed and accommodations insisted on by illness. There are also opportunities for learning about asking for and accepting help. Although we are interdependent throughout the life course, ideals about independence and autonomy are often prized in Western culture. While it is sequential and reasonable to understand children as dependent on family members, the same is not always true for adults. Depending on one's culture, family history, and self-identity it can be extremely stressful *for the entire family system* to make the adjustments necessary for an older adult to receive and accept care. As care needs increase, boundaries can shift. As people require more assistance, they may find themselves feeling vulnerable, in a variety of areas, including the loss of privacy. Many older adults resist having caregivers (both paid and unpaid) in their home and underfoot because it diminishes their spatial privacy. Physical care needs that were once privately addressed may require the assistance of family members or paid caregivers, leading the older adult to feel exposed. There may also be the loss of financial privacy. Allowing someone else into one's financial affairs can add additional strain and can, unfortunately, at times lead to exploitation. These delicate situations require sensitivity, skill, tact, and finesse in order to preserve the dignity of the person receiving care.

Being in a caregiving relationship can be enriching, contributing to personal and interpersonal growth. Providing care to a loved one can be an opportunity to grow closer emotionally, reciprocate for care received earlier in life, and underscore the mutual give and take of being part of a family or network of friends. Accepting the assistance of others can be a welcomed experience of sharing time. It can provide relief from pressures or responsibilities that are taxing or tiring. It may lead to the healing of historic, relational dynamics that were challenging. Caring and being cared for may change the balance in a relationship, creating an opportunity for growth and opening doors for new understanding. The communication skills of social workers are essential tools in responding to what unfolds.

Alice

Alice is an 80-year-old, divorced, white woman with a diagnosis of recurrent breast cancer, including metastases to her pelvis and spine. In order to mitigate bone pain caused by the metastases, she has agreed to radiation treatments. Following these treatments, and in consultation with her oncologist, a decision will be made about pursuing further chemotherapy in the hopes of extending her life by a few months. Alice has four adult daughters whom she raised as a single parent. She lives in her home in a small town in a rural county, with her youngest daughter Suzanne. Another daughter, Annette, lives a few miles away but seldom visits. The other two daughters live out of state and communicate frequently by phone with their mother. In an initial social work assessment, Alice shares that historically Annette and Suzanne have had a strained relationship. Annette feels anger and frustration about the level of Suzanne's dependence on their mother. Suzanne is not employed outside the home and has struggled with depression. Her social worker learns that Suzanne's well-being is Alice's foremost concern. Not only does Suzanne reside in Alice's house, her only source of income is as a paid caregiver to Alice under the state's in-home assistance waiver. Suzanne is being paid to meet Alice's personal care needs. Alice and Suzanne have a close but at times contentious relationship, reflecting the intensity of living together and mutual dependence.

Alice is considering disease-modifying therapies, in part, to "buy" as much time as possible out of concern for how Suzanne will manage emotionally and financially after her mother's death. Alice expresses a desire for Suzanne to function more independently and for a more harmonious relationship among her daughters. Alice's other daughters believe she is being exploited and manipulated by their sister Suzanne. Having raised her children alone, with great pride in her independence and capacity as a parent, Alice wants to fulfill what she considers her responsibilities as a mother. She reports feeling uneasy and unsettled by their current circumstances and speaks about "finding peace" for her family.

Adaptations in Caregiving

The experience of older adulthood is often intergenerational. For many, like Alice, the desire to contribute to the well-being of others (generativity) remains strong. Social workers can help older adults create new ways to fulfill their desire for generatively while also adjusting to their own changing care needs. Older adults who are caregivers and then become ill may remain deeply committed to continuing to provide care—emotional, financial, and physical. In practice, it is not unusual to see older adults struggle to maintain the role as caregiver while learning to adapt to increased need themselves. Social workers can help support this process of adaptation by identifying aspects of the caregiving role that remain while exploring resources for securing additional support within their family and caregiving structures. This may include deputizing others to fulfill roles.

This twofold process capitalizes on elemental skills of social workers. Asking appropriate strengths-based questions aimed at demystifying family systems can help the social worker facilitate adjustment to changes on the part of the older adult and the support system. Social workers can use tools like genograms to map out key relationships (family and friends) in an older adult's life and to learn how major health changes and other potential crises have been responded to, as well as what roles have been assumed by members of the system to manage past events. These discussions can help identify emotional and practical resources within the older adult's circle of support, and prepare the older adult to anticipate family dynamics that may accompany the changing circumstances. When one person's need for care increases, it can affect the entire system. Ideally, members of the system will share the responsibilities of this stage of the family's life cycle, which requires open and frequent communication. In some cases, sharing is not likely or possible or even desired; it depends on the circumstances. It is important to remember that members of the family/close friend systems are each on their own emotional journey. Facilitating members' ability to articulate their needs and explore possible venues for resolution are key skills utilized by the family-systems-minded social worker. In all domains of practice, the roles of counselor and mediator are important to the individuals and families served.

Positionality

When working with older adults, we see up close the effects of cumulative advantage and cumulative disadvantage. We are witness to the influences of years of interacting forces, including social norms and public policies, employment histories, family dynamics, chance, and individual agency. We see the impact of the intersection of the various social identities held by the older adult, some of which may be privileged, and other identities marginalized. This is where our core conceptual frameworks help social workers understand the social context of an older adult's life and develop appropriate interventions. Through the lens of systems theory, the ecological theory, and the strengths perspective, we strive to understand and work with the whole person, especially as the illness progresses. This social context reflects both the present and the past. While a social worker will not be able to untangle a lifetime of family dynamics, we can help people identify what is most important to them and then work to develop a care plan honoring those values, preferences, and hopes.

In this narrative, engaging Alice in a conversation about the difficulties related to raising four children as a divorced woman during a time when doing so was uncommon and stigmatized may be both a path to life review and a reflection on family history. While validating the strengths of being a single parent, Alice can be invited to think about how to build on those same strengths to thrive in the situation she now faces. Individuals experiencing emotional distress can often forget the situations they have managed and overcome. Through their therapeutic exchange, Alice's social worker was able to facilitate Alice's reflection on her past and lessons learned. Utilizing cognitive reframing skills in a strengths-based perspective, the social worker is able to "remind" Alice of her fortitude under adversity and develop a possible strategy for mitigating her emotional struggle. Social work, informed by the principles of palliative care, can use these theories and frameworks as tuning forks for further assessment and intervention planning that are both deliberate and delicate. Helping people understand, integrate, and adjust to the changes and challenges of serious illness calls upon many core social work skills, including active listening, crisis management, identifying priorities, boundary setting, advocacy, group processing, accessing resources, and communication skills. These and other social work skills are useful in the context of palliative care, in part because despite the different paths people take to arrive at older adulthood, most have had to wrestle mightily with two issues: loss and hope.

Loss and Hope

Anyone who has lived seven or eight decades is well acquainted with loss, significant and small, prickly and profound, including loss of possessions, people, and familiar places, and loss of functional ability, stamina, and sometimes competence. Some older adults have learned how to dance with loss and not get their toes stepped on too hard. Others feel buried by loss and are barely hanging on. Most are somewhere in between when they come in contact with a social worker in a health care setting. Part of Erikson's psychosocial developmental challenge of "integrity versus despair" is related to the types of losses people have encountered and how they have been and are processing, integrating, and adapting (Erikson,

1950). In some cases, there may be complicating feelings of shame or guilt. Failing to process and resolve these feelings could lead to despair. For other individuals, losses have become an expected or accepted part of life. Through their personal strengths and coping strategies, they have been able to respond with grace and thus experience a sense of integrity. A social worker's ease in entering the world view of those in despair as well as facilitating recognition of this sense of integrity is an essential aspect of the therapeutic work with older adults.

Helping individuals acknowledge the losses exacerbated by illness is an important part of building a trusting relationship. Validating and normalizing these experiences is a central intervention. Through therapeutic rapport, people may feel comfortable sharing how they have dealt with previous losses, while discussing fears and hopes for the future. Social workers can provide emotional and informational support to facilitate reframing some hopes, setting aside others, and identifying and articulating new hopes, given the current reality and anticipated future.

Social workers may observe the effects of unresolved loss and grief complications when working with individuals and families around their hopes and goals for care. There may be disagreement, spoken or silent, among family members about what is in the best interest of the patient. As in the decision facing Alice, the patient may weigh medical interventions that carry the possibility of additional time risking the burden of the side effects of those interventions against the wish to savor the remaining time with family and friends untethered from medical treatments. In Alice's case, she may wonder which approach would be more likely to support her in continuing to care for her family. Which path may help her in encouraging independence in Suzanne? For Alice, helping Suzanne is a key aspect of a meaningful and peaceful end-of-life experience.

When we ask our patients about their hopes, we need to listen deeply. Sometimes patients mention hopes that are far reaching and challenging for clinicians to respond to in light of the clinical perception of illness trajectory. That initial hope may distract from others more immediate and potentially meaningful. It is important for clinicians to acknowledge the hope while exploring immediate wishes and desires that can be supported and engaged. Using clinical skills, we can invite a broader conversation that extends hope beyond illness circumstance, grounded in the immediate future, looking for opportunities for creative problem-solving and resource mobilization.

Alice initially identified a hope for a plan to support Suzanne's independence. Alice's role as a mother extended beyond the assurance that her own and Suzanne's basic needs would be met. Further discussion revealed that she was wrestling with deeper hopes. Alice wanted Suzanne to be independent, but she also wanted Suzanne and her other daughters to be reconciled. Alice longed for her final days to be marked with family cohesion and healing, not tension and distress. She wanted her children to learn how to be supportive of each other, especially after her death. Alice benefited from a skilled clinician who validated her initial hopes and who was able and willing to listen for and tease out the buried, emotional-based aspirations for herself and for her family.

The ability to work with patients and their families to establish meaningful goals toward quality of life, on their terms, requires empathic listening, observation of nonverbal communication, and the ability to work effectively as a member of an interdisciplinary team. Establishing goals and focus of care is a process, and thoughtful intervention, centered on personhood, will require ongoing attention and adjustments. Initial goals may entail working with patients and intimate partners to be able to discuss unspoken fears. At times these fears are based on past experiences—previous spouses gone too soon, children lost, careers that have ended—and require skillful listening and communication to elicit and process. Tangible goals, such as living long enough and with enough functional ability to attend a family event, easily come to mind. However, it is important for clinicians to address other meaningful and subtler goals, such as building physical strength in order to return home to rejoin a spouse of 60 years, management of potentially embarrassing symptoms such as incontinence in order to be more at ease when friends visit, or having the opportunity and support to reconcile with a loved one.

Alice (Continued)

After processing information from her oncologist and exploring priorities and goals with the social worker, Alice decides against chemotherapy. She continues to worry about the future for Suzanne and to feel guilt, knowing that she may be leaving her without many options. She is also feeling the weight of her children's strained relationships with each other and how it has meant less time together as a family. She longs for the physical presence of her daughters and reflects on meaningful times they shared together in the past. She is concerned about the amount of pain she will endure as the cancer progresses. The social worker suggests the possibility of moving to a local long-term care facility and enrolling in hospice services, where pain and symptom management will be a priority. Psychoeducation focuses on techniques for pain management, such as relaxation and breathing exercises she could try on her own, an approach that feels empowering and congruent with Alice's independent spirit. Placement at a long-term care facility is discussed as a potential benefit for her daughters, as they grieve the changes occurring with their mother and anticipate her coming to the end of her life. Moving to the long-term care facility would provide Suzanne with a period of time to "practice" living without her mother with supportive guidance from the hospice social worker. It would also facilitate visits by her other daughters by removing the tension that evolved when visits occur in Alice's home. The hospice social worker would be available to support conversations, processing feelings and thoughts about family relationships and patterns over the years. Through skilled communication, the social worker could facilitate recognition of Alice's hopes as mother—for a better, cohesive future for all of her daughters. Developing a plan to assist Suzanne involves not only preparing for Alice's death, but also having access to supportive services to stabilize her psychosocial status.

Alice decides to move to the facility and is able to spend her remaining weeks there with careful pain and symptom management and the satisfaction that her primary concerns have been heard. The hospice social worker helps bring the family together, creating a neutral space to acknowledge different experiences and Alice's wishes as she comes to the end of her life. By observing, clarifying, and brokering, the social worker was able to address a number of basic needs for Alice as well as for Suzanne. Alice come to the end of her life feeling affirmed as a mother, a role that was often difficult yet deeply meaningful to her. She shares the feeling that she grew as a person as she learned to navigate motherhood, and raising her daughters was a major accomplishment of her life. Although what will occur in Suzanne's future remains unknown, Alice ended her days with a sense of emotional resolution by having been heard and understood. She does not know what will transpire over time between her adult daughters, but feels that meaningful steps have taken place, a source of comfort and peace.

Conclusion

Engaging with older adults invites exploration of the history brought to an illness experience, which can be honored and explored in an effort to identify the strengths, resources, and vulnerabilities that may influence the navigation of illness. Listening with intention and curiosity can both affirm aspects of personhood and discover avenues for interventions that respond to worries and fears, which may be mitigated, if not fully resolved. Social workers across settings can provide interventions to enhance the experience of older adults and their families as they negotiate changing roles and relationships and establish connection to health care systems and maintain a sense of self and purpose.

LEARNING EXERCISE

1. You are working with a patient similar to Alice. She has both Medicare and Medicaid. What placement options would be available to her to support her desire for placement and high-quality symptom management? Consider how you would present these options to

her. If there is nothing available, what creative alternatives could be assembled?

2. A couple, married 60 years, are living together in an apartment in an assisted living facility. The wife has been living with dementia for the past five years and it has recently been determined, for both of their safety, that she cannot remain in their apartment, and she is to be moved to an adjoining skilled nursing facility. The uncertainty and changes associated with their impending separation are causing them both distress. As the receiving social worker in the skilled nursing facility, how could you prepare for her arrival in a way that best meets their needs as a couple? What modifications to routine or environment could you explore?

EPILOGUE

Jesse and Alice are years apart in age. Their families are at different developmental stages yet face challenges of loss and adaptation, profound decisions and a forced dependency on health care providers and systems which may be more or less responsive. The need for information, the therapeutic value of time and relationships which support integrity and honor hope, inform a landscape within which Jesse and Alice and their families create legacy and attempt to sustain and perhaps enrich relationships. Hopes are adapted and reframed—a process that is often at the core of social work intervention no matter the setting or diagnosis or outcome.

RESOURCES: CHILDREN

When working with families of children with serious illness, reach out to palliative care programs at the nearest children's hospital as they may guide, share resources, and save you and your families time and energy.

Aaron's Tracheostomy Page: Family run, this nonprofit page is intended to bring information about tracheostomies to pediatric families, as well as connect families hoping to network with others who are considering or whose children have tracheostomies. www.tracheostomy.com

The American Cancer Society: This website has articles about helping children when a family member has cancer, guiding family members or social workers. www.cancer.org/treatment/children-and-cancer/when-a-family-member-has-cancer.html

Courageous Parents' Network: This website contains videos about decision-making, quality of life, and coping with having a child with a serious illness, as well as resources, blog posts, and parent-matching resources to connect parents to others dealing with similar issues. www.courageousparentsnetwork.org

The Dougy Center: A National Center for Grieving Children and Families, based in Portland, Oregon, the center offers both local and national resources for grieving children, teens, and young adults, as well as families. Information can be printed for families, including helpful book lists and developmental information about grief and responding to national tragedies. www.dougy.org/

The MISS Foundation: A nonprofit, volunteer-based organization providing CARE (counseling, advocacy, research, and education) services to families experiencing the death of a child. They provide free support packets and match families with a HOPE mentor, support groups in some communities, and online, a network of trained counselors around the country searchable on their site. Families self-refer. www.missfoundation.org/

National Hospice and Palliative Care Organization (NHPCO): This website has a section dedicated to pediatrics with printable brochures for parents in English and Spanish, and an e-journal with informative articles from professionals, parents, and patients. www.nhpco.org/pediatric

The Tears Foundation: A resource for those who have limited funding for funerals, very common for families who lose a child. Families may self-refer. While unable to help in every situation, the foundation often connects social workers with other agencies. www.thetearsfoundation.org

Voicing My Choices and My Wishes: Advance care planning workbook geared specifically toward adolescents and young adults (Voicing My Choices) and children (My Wishes). The website has an FAQ section, but otherwise the site is for purchasing the workbooks. www.agingwithdignity.org/five-wishes/pediatric

RESOURCES: OLDER ADULTS

American Association of Retired Persons (AARP): A nonprofit, nonpartisan group focused on productive and healthy aging, with information and resources for older adults, their communities, and caregivers, specific to caregiving, health, insurance coverage, finances and prevention of financial abuse, and healthy living as an older adult. www.aarp.org

American Geriatrics Society: Nonprofit society for health care professionals dedicated to improving health, independence, and quality of life of older people. www.americangeriatrics.org

Association for Gerontology Education in Social Work: Provides leadership in gerontological social work education, research, and policy. www.agesw.org

Caregiver Action Network: Nonprofit family caregiver organization providing free resources to family caregivers, education, and peer support; and resources for cancer and rare disease caregivers. www.caregiveraction.org

CaringKind's Palliative Care for Advanced Dementia: Training and Implementation: Addresses the need for improving the quality of life and care for residents with advanced dementia living in nursing homes, through a program that generates special adaptations to make palliative care more effective for persons with advanced dementia and their families. www.caringkindnyc.org/palliativecare/

Centers for Disease Control and Prevention (CDC) Healthy Aging: Information and resources to help health professionals engage with initiatives around healthy aging, including the Healthy Brain Initiative, focused on cognitive impairment including Alzheimer's disease. www.cdc.gov/aging

Council on Social Work Education Gero-ed Center: Prepares social work faculty and students to meet the demographic realities of our aging society; online resource for social work faculty, students, and practitioners committed to enhancing gerontological competence. Course available on palliative care with older adults. www.cswe.org/Centers-Initiatives/CSWE-Gero-Ed-Center.aspx

Geriatric Social Work Initiative: Foundation for geriatric social work leadership, research, and practice innovation. www.gswi.org

National Alliance for Caregiving: Nonprofit coalition of organizations focused on family caregiving, promoting research, conducting policy analysis, developing programs, and supporting public awareness about issues in family caregiving. www.caregiving.org

National Center on Elder Abuse: National resource center to provide education and information to prevent elder abuse; provides technical assistance and training to states and organizations. www.ncea.acl.gov

National Council on Aging (NCOA): Partners with business, government, and nonprofits to provide community services and resources to promote healthy aging. Programs focus on falls prevention, chronic disease management, economic security, and nutrition. www.ncoa.org

National Coalition on Mental Health and Aging: Member organization working to improve availability and quality of mental health preventive and treatment services for older adults and their families. www.ncmha.org

REFERENCES

Beaune, L., Leavens, A., Muskat, B., Ford-Jones, L., Rapoport, A., Zlotnik Shaul, R., . . . Chapman, L. A. (2014). Poverty and pediatric palliative care: What can we do?. *Journal of Social Work in End-of-Life & Palliative Care, 10*(2), 170–185.

Bronfenbrenner, U. (1979). *The ecology of human development: Experiments by nature and design.* Cambridge, MA: Harvard University Press.

Cassell, E. J. (1991). Recognizing suffering. *Hastings Center Report, 21*(3), 24–31.

Clarke, J. N., & Fletcher, P. (2003). Communication issues faced by parents who have a child diagnosed with cancer. *Journal of Pediatric Oncology Nursing, 20*(4), 175–191. doi:10.1177/1043454203254040.

Dickinson, E. (2017, January 12). Hope is the thing with feathers (254). Retrieved March 15, 2017, from www.poets.org/poetsorg/poem/hope-thing-feathers-254.

Erikson, E. (1950). *Childhood and society.* New York: W. W. Norton.

Friebert, S. (2012). Best practice in pediatric palliative care: Giving voice to the voiceless. *Progress in Palliative Care, 20*(6), 327–330. doi:10.1179/0969926012z.00000000049.

Fromer, M. J. (2004). Palliative care for children. *Oncology Times, 26*(18), 25. doi:10.1097/01.cot.0000293218.06456.2f.

Fromer, M. J. (2004). Pediatric palliative care. *Oncology Times, 26*(17), 26–29. doi:10.1097/01.cot.0000292277.96386.e2.

Gaab, E. M., Owens, G. R., & Macleod, R. D. (2014). Siblings caring for and about pediatric palliative care patients. *Journal of Palliative Medicine, 17*(1), 62–67. doi:10.1089/jpm.2013.0117.

Goddard, J. A., Lehr, R., & Lapadat, J. C. (2007). Parents of children with disabilities: Telling a different story. *Canadian Journal of Counselling and Psychotherapy/Revue Canadienne de Counseling et de Psychothérapie, 34*(4), 273–289.

Hauck, F. R., Tanabe, K. O., & Moon, R. Y. (2011, August). Racial and ethnic disparities in infant mortality. *Seminars in Perinatology, 35*(4), 209–220.

Heiman, H. J., & Artigas, S. (2015). *Beyond health care: The role of social determinants in promoting health and health equity. The Kaiser Commission on Medicaid and the uninsured.* Retrieved from www.kff.org/disparities-policy.

Hollis, F. (1974). *Casework: A psychosocial approach.* New York: Random House.

Humphrey, L. M., Hill, D. L., Carroll, K. W., Rourke, M., Kang, T. I., & Feudtner, C. (2015). Psychological well-being and family environment of siblings of children with life- threatening illness. *Journal of Palliative Medicine, 18*(11), 981–984. doi:10.1089/jpm.2015.0150.

Jones, B. L., Contro, N., & Koch, K. D. (2014). The duty of the physician to care for the family in pediatric palliative care: Context, communication, and caring. *Pediatrics, 133*(Supplement), S8–S15. doi:10.1542/peds.2013-3608c

Juth, V. (2016). The social ecology of adolescents' cancer experience: A narrative review and future directions. *Adolescent Research Review, 1*(3), 235–244. doi:10.1007/s40894-016-0023-2.

Konrad, S. C. (2008). Mothers' perspectives on qualities of care in their relationships with health care professionals: The influence of relational and communicative competencies. *Journal of Social Work in End-of-Life & Palliative Care, 4*(1), 38–56. doi:10.1080/15524250802072161.

Levine, D. R., Mandrell, B. N., Sykes, A., Pritchard, M., Gibson, D., Symons, H. J., . . . Baker, J. N. (2017). Patients' and parents' needs, attitudes, and perceptions about early palliative care integration in pediatric oncology. *JAMA Oncology, 3*(9), 1214–1220. doi:10.1001/jamaoncol.2017.0368.

Lord, B. (2014). Courageous Parents Network. Retrieved from www. courageousparentsnetwork.org/about/our-story/.

Maddalena, V., O'Shea, F., & Murphy, M. (2012). Palliative and end of life care in Newfoundland's Deaf community. *Journal of Palliative Care, 28*(20), 105–112.

National Hospice and Palliative Care Organization (NHPCO). (2014). NHPCO Facts and Figures: Pediatric Palliative and Hospice Care in America. www.nhpco.org/sites/default/files/public/quality/Pediatric_Facts-Figures.pdf.

Nicholas, D. B., Beaune, L., Barrera, M., Blumberg, J., & Belletrutti, M. (2016). Examining the experiences of fathers of children with a life-limiting illness. *Journal of Social Work in End-of-Life & Palliative Care, 12*(1–2), 126–144. doi:10.1080/15524256.2016.1156601.

Paice, J., & Ferrell, B. (2011). The management of cancer pain. *CA: A Cancer Journal for Clinicians, 6*(1), 157–182.

Pollak, K. I., Arnold, R. M., Jeffreys, A. S., Alexander, S. C., Olsen, M. K., Abernethy, A. P., . . . Tulsky, J. A. (2007). Oncologist communication about emotion during visits with patients with advanced cancer. *Journal of Clinical Oncology, 25*(36), 5748–5752. doi:10.1200/jco.2007.12.4180.

Prezant, F. P., & Marshak, L. (2006). Helpful actions seen through the eyes of parents of children with disabilities. *Disability & Society, 21*(1), 31–45. doi:10.1080/09687590500373767.

Rattner, M., & Berzoff, J. (2016). Rethinking suffering: Allowing for suffering that is intrinsic at end of life. *Journal of Social Work in End-of-Life & Palliative Care, 12*(3), 240–258. doi:10.1080/15524256.2016.1200520.

Sharpe, D., & Rossiter, L. (2002). Siblings of children with a chronic illness: A meta-analysis. *Journal of Pediatric Psychology, 27*(8), 699–710.

Sisk, B. A., Bluebond-Langner, M., Wiener, L., Mack, J., & Wolfe, J. (2016). Prognostic disclosures to children: A historical perspective. *Pediatrics, 138*(3), e20161278. doi:10.1542/peds.2016-1278.

Sobo, E. J. (2004). Good communication in pediatric cancer care: A culturally-informed research agenda. *Journal of Pediatric Oncology Nursing, 21*(3), 150–154. doi:10.1177/1043454204264408.

Sourkes, B., Frankel, L., Brown, M., Contro, N., Benitz, W., Case, C., . . . Sunde, C. (2005). Food, toys, and love: Pediatric palliative care. *Current Problems in Pediatric and Adolescent Health Care, 35*(9), 350–386. doi:10.1016/j.cppeds.2005.09.002.

Epilogue

TERRY ALTILIO ■

I don't know how I got here.

—MICHAEL CAINE, *Youth (2015, film)*

Over two decades ago the Project on Death in America, funded by George Soros, launched the careers of clinicians across the country and across disciplines—many of whom would develop and lead the evolution of palliative care in the United States. Over time, social work would construct the foundation necessary to elevate its voice among interdisciplinary colleagues within the field. There is now a professional organization—Social Work Hospice and Palliative Care Network, credentialing, a journal, training opportunities, and an *Oxford Textbook of Palliative Social Work*. Palliative social work is a specialty.

In the time that has passed, palliative care has built an evidence base, and the demand for services continues to grow. There is an awareness that the values and principles of palliative care, rather than being the province of specialists, define good health care and ought to be accessible to all those living with serious illness. Hence the emerging focus on infusing palliative care into the practice of primary clinicians, toward the goal of providing person-centered, family-focused care and moving it from bedside to community.

Privileged to be a part of this evolution, I find myself now to be one of a generation of clinicians who have contributed to the birth of a specialty with an increased awareness that the core skills and values ought to be acknowledged as central to the practice of the thousands of health social workers who touch the lives of countless patients and families. The many hours of conversation between the editors of this book and the many iterations of the chapters have led to certain insights and changes in direction. For example, we came to truly realize, in heart and mind, that the boundaries between health social work and palliative social work are quite fluid, rather than rigid. As such, perhaps the task is to merge a knowledge base and skill set with collaboration and cooperation to ensure that the needs of patients and families are met and to know when specialists are needed for consultation.

Having lived through the evolution of a specialty, it has been a poignant experience to recognize, perhaps, that the important need to establish the specialty has blurred the landscape. Through the process of editing this book, the terrain has become a bit clearer—when health social workers are trained and free to work "at the top of their license," they are well able to meet the needs of patients and families living with serious illness. It is evident that as a profession we can model an approach that builds on each other's work and creates organic teams to respond to the unique needs of a specific patient and their family. At the same time, if we are to maximize the potential in our roles, no matter the setting, we need to further infuse our education with the requisite knowledge and skill and assert an expectation that institutions support health social workers as they work to "the top of their licenses."

Youth is a wonderful Italian movie about two men, older adults and best friends, who reflect on their lives while holidaying in the Swiss Alps. It is a story about many things, including age and youth, the past and the future. Michael Caine, in a tender moment of wondering about his history and his life, says, "I don't know how I got here." The process of editing this book has created moments of ongoing reflection about "how I got here" and how we, as a profession "got here." More important, with my co-editors Bridget Sumser and Meagan Lyon Leimena, it has forced reflection on where the second generation of palliative social workers will take us. Perhaps there will be less "wondering" because we are now able to work from a solid foundation. Perhaps we can build on the lessons and accomplishments of the past to move us forward.

PATIENT NARRATIVES

Chapter 1. The Convergence of Social Work Practice: Integrating Health Social Work and Specialized Palliative Care

Rafael, 23-year-old man, Puerto Rican, family (mother Flora and younger siblings) type I diabetes mellitus with multiple comorbidities. Clinical focus: Advocacy for appropriate symptom control and management, exploring parent-child dynamics around dependency and autonomy, partnering with community organizations, supporting autonomy and self-management, psychosocial functioning during medical crisis, assessing family system functioning, advance care planning pg 24.

Chapter 2. Structure and Processes of Care

Malcolm, 42-year-old man, African-American, family (including mother, partner and children), advanced heart failure and evaluation for heart device placement in hospital. Clinical focus: Building a therapeutic alliance to promote his agency and role within the plan of care, addressing psychosocial factors related to his evaluation for heart device, bioethics review, assessing health care team-patient dynamics, assessment of effects of social determinants of health pg 25.

Lisa, 30-year-old woman, Chinese-American, limited social connections and 8-year-old son who lives with her parents, HIV and end-stage renal disease admitted to the intensive care unit with a serious heart infection. Clinical focus: Assessing and contextualizing active substance use and mental health issues in relation to pain and management strategies with health care team, discovering values related to legacy, providing for son, exploring reconnection with family, discharge planning informed by patient values and preferences pg 41.

Chapter 3. Physical Aspects of Care

Mary, 50-year-old woman, Italian-American, family (spouse who is chronically ill, adult children, grandchildren) and pastor, lung cancer. Clinical focus: Navigating power dynamics with providers, clergy and patient about pain and medication, exploration of faith, pain and suffering, reframing losses and adaptation to illness, exploring psychosocial meaning of changes to employment, finances, housing, self-concept and impact on legacy through illness trajectory pg 60.

Chapter 4. Psychological Aspects of Care

Douglas, 64-year-old man, African-American, family (spouse Donna, adult children, grandchildren) and church, Congestive Heart Failure, admitted to cardiac unit. Clinical focus: Supporting patient and spouse in processing complex feelings about impact of behaviors on illness, grief and loss counseling integrating changes due to illness, assessing psychological functioning, discovering and promoting resilience within patient and family systems, family communication and adaptation pg 81.

Chapter 5. Social Aspects of Care

Mrs. Farahan, 89-year-old woman, Persian, family (three adult daughters), advanced cancer, care at home. Clinical focus: Assessing family systems functioning and dynamics in the setting of illness, using culturally humble approach to appreciate health belief systems about sharing of medical information, discussing prognosis and mutual pretense, respectfully exploring alternate possibilities around health beliefs and preferences, facilitating sharing of memories, activities and emotions to inform legacy pg 104.

Pam, a 35-year-old, lesbian, family (partner Susan, Susan's daughter Samantha, parents with strong religious values opposing what they believe is her "lifestyle"), pancreatic cancer, outpatient oncology practice. Clinical focus: Assessing functioning during a family systems crisis, assessment and referral for counseling services, psychoeducation about listening and developmentally appropriate reactions to illness, loss and dying among children, joining with individual family members to honor unique suffering within a family system, exploring meaning of guilt, shame, fear, allegiances within family, role of faith in illness experience pg 106.

Chapter 6. Spiritual, Religious, and Existential Dimensions of Care

Julia, 54-year-old woman, Latina, Spanish-speaking, Jehovah's Witness, colorectal cancer, Emergency Department. Clinical focus: Exploring root of decision to refuse blood transfusion, assessing comprehension of treatment options and consequences of refusal, perception and openness to learning about cultural, religious and spiritual influences on decision making, attentiveness to biases and values in health care systems marginalizing patients pg 128.

John Scott, 68-year-old man, white, self-identifies as gay, family (former spouse Marion, adult children Luke and Paula, grandchildren) penile and anal cancers. Clinical focus: life review, role playing to practice emotional conversations, referral to clergy, supporting exploration of attributed meanings to illness, shame, guilt, punishment and other spiritual themes pg 136.

Chapter 7. Cultural Aspects of Care

Araceli, 60-year-old woman, Puerto Rican, mother of Alejandro, 40-year-old man, divorced, colorectal cancer, living at home with mother and nursing services providing care, community mental health clinic. Clinical focus: Rapport and relationship building supporting therapeutic alliance, being culturally humble, curious and inquisitive to learn about health belief systems and cultural values shaping illness and health care experiences, rapport and relationship building supporting therapeutic alliance, validation of personal health belief systems for mother and son, including attributed meanings associated with illness such as disease as punishment from an authority, exploring opportunities for common ground between the two to enhance relationship and emotional support, facilitating communication about how medical information is shared pg 159.

Chapter 8. Care of Patients and Families at the End of Life

Timothy, 40-year-old, transgender man, critical care nurse with metastatic lung cancer. Clinical focus: Exploring history of pain being delegitimized (endometriosis) and locus of control re: his body, joining to understand influence of personal history and professional training and medication use, collaboration and planning with patient and team around safe prescribing and medication use pg 157.

Elise, 36-year-old woman whose mother is rapidly declining from liver cancer, shares history of traumatic loss of 10 day of baby. Clinical focus: Building therapeutic rapport to help identify past losses, current and ongoing needs for psychological support, anticipatory guidance around prognosis and expectations for end of life, referrals and coordination for bereavement support in the community pg 178.

Mrs. Eugenia Harris, 92-year-old woman, African-American, family (adult children Pamela and Lucien and granddaughter Daisy), dementia, transitions between skilled nursing facilities and hospitals. Clinical focus: Anticipatory guidance and psychoeducation about disease progression and dying process, advocacy for symptom management, building continuity and trust during transitions, joining with family to explore previous losses and understand impact on current decision making, assessing developmentally appropriate integration of children, bereavement support pg 183.

Chapter 9. Legal and Ethical Aspects of Care

Lynette, 44-year-old woman, African-American, family (young daughters Lana and Lenora and brother Thomas), friend Phyllis, church community, ovarian cancer. Clinical focus: Advance care planning including surrogate decision makers and guardianship for her children, exploration of values and preferences based on historical experiences of illness and decision making, psychoeducation and advocacy around symptom management, assisting patient and family elucidate and share goals and preferences for treatment in care conferences pg 210.

Chapter 10. Special Issues in Children and Older Adults

Children:
Mai, 13-year-old girl, Chinese-American, parents and siblings. Clinical focus: Awareness and appreciation of social location, intergenerational influences on family and identity pg 235.

Jesse, 3-year-old girl, parents John and Anna, hypoxic ischemic encephalopathy from childbirth injury, cared for at home by parents. Clinical focus: Anticipatory guidance and psychoeducation to support medical decision making, building continuity across settings over time and coordinating care, teaching self-care skills pg 238.

Older Adults:

Alice, 80-year-old woman, white, family (four adult daughters including Suzanne who lives with her mother), metastatic breast cancer. Clinical focus: Assessing family systems to uncover dynamics affected by illness, strengths based approaches to encourage resilience in patients and families, psychoeducation about relaxation and pain management techniques, exploration of hospice benefit for pain management and familial support pg 242.

GENERAL RESOURCES

This appendix of general resources is another tool for the integration of palliative care knowledge and principles into social work practice. It is meant to be a beginning for further exploration. Using the ecological framework, there are micro, meso and macro level resources here to inform clinical practice, education, writing, research and advocacy, as well as personal inquiry. This is not an exhaustive list and is intended as the start of a map of the universe of organizations, publications, research and activity by interested groups who might be useful to you, and encourage your creativity and thoughtfulness, in your professional journey.

TECHNICAL REPORTS AND ISSUE BRIEFS

- Training Opportunities
- Domestic Resources and Organizations
- International Resources and Organizations
- Hospice Eligibility and Benefits Information
- Multimedia

Institute of Medicine Reports

Dying in America: Improving quality and honoring individual preferences near the end of life (2015), nap.edu/18748

A consensus report from the Institute of Medicine (IOM); a committee of experts find improving the quality and availability of medical and social services for patients and their families could not only enhance quality of life through the end of life, but also contribute to a more sustainable care system.

Health literacy and palliative care workshop summary (2016), nap.edu/21839

A summary of a workshop to explore the relationship between palliative care and health literacy and the importance of health-literate communication in palliative care.

How far have we come in reducing health disparities? Progress since 2002, Workshop summary (2012), nap.edu/13383

A report of the 2010 Roundtable on the Promotion of Health Equity and the Elimination of Health Disparities, a public workshop focused on progress to address health disparities. Three major objectives were to assess progress made, to consider the scope and effectiveness of efforts to address the social determinants of health disparities, and to determine what still needs to be elucidated about efforts to address social determinants and reduce disparities.

Implications of health literacy for public health (2013), nap.edu/18756

A workshop summary to address the concerns raised in Health Literacy: A Prescription to End Confusion. Describes health literacy initiatives being undertaken by public health organizations and the implications of health literacy on community, health and safety, disease prevention, disaster management, and health communication.

Integrating the patient and caregiver voice into serious illness (2017), nap.edu/24802

A report of a roundtable that convened stakeholders from government, academia, industry, professional organizations, nonprofit advocacy organizations, and philanthropies to examine issues related to integrating the voice of patient and family caregivers into delivery of care.

Retooling for an aging America: Building the health care workforce (2008), nap.edu/12089

A report assessing the needs of the health care system for an aging population with a focus on training for professionals and informal caregivers and new models of health care delivery and payment.

The Irish Hospice Foundation

Loss and grief in dementia guidance document, hospicefoundation.ie/wp-content/uploads/2016/07/Final-Guidance-Document-3-Loss-Grief.pdf

This document provides reflections and guidance on supporting persons with dementia, as well as families, caregivers, and professionals working with persons with dementia in their experiences of grief and loss.

Agency for Health Care Research and Quality

Assessment tools for palliative care, technical brief, effectivehealthcare.ahrq.gov/sites/default/files/pdf/palliative-care-tools_technical-brief-2017.pdf

This document provides an overview of palliative care assessment tools designed to be completed by or with patients or caregivers; it indicates which tools have been applied to clinical care, as quality indicators, or in evaluations of interventions, and identifies needs for future palliative care assessment tool development and evaluation.

Social Work Policy Institute

Hospice social work: Linking policy, practice, and research (2010), www.socialworkpolicy.org/news-events/hospice-social-work-linking-policy-practice-and-research.html

The report explores the connections between quality hospice social work services, the mission of hospice, federal requirements, professional standards, and the current state of hospice research by social workers.

TIMELINE OF SEMINAL PUBLICATIONS, DECISIONS, AND EVENTS

Publications, Decisions & Events	Author(s)/ Organization	Year	Website
Standards for Social Work Practice in Palliative and End of Life established	NASW	2004	www.socialworkers. org/ practice/standards/ Palliative.asp
Journal of Social Work in End of Life and Palliative Care launched	Csikai, E. (Ed.)	2005	www.tandfonline.com/ toc/wswe20/current
Social Work Competencies in Palliative and End-of-Life Care published	Gwyther, L., Altilio, T., Blacker, S., et al.	2005	www.ncbi.nlm.nih.gov/ pubmed/17387058
Social Work Hospice and Palliative Care Network launched	SWHPN	2007	www.swhpn.org/
NASW Certification Advanced Certified Hospice and Palliative Social Worker established	(ACHP-SW)	2008	www.socialworkers.org/ credentials/list.asp
Creating Social Work Competencies for Practice in Hospice Palliative Care published (Canada)	Bosma, H., Johnston, M., Cadell, S., et al.	2009	www.chpca.net/media/ 7868/Social_Work_ Competencies_July_ 2009

NASW Certifications Certified Hospice and Palliative Care Social Worker established	(CHP-SW)	2009	www.socialworkers.org/credentials/list.asp
National Center for Gerontological Education; Council on Social Work Education; Palliative Care with Older Adults	Christ, G., & Blacker, S. J.	2009	www.cswe.org/CentersInitiatives/CurriculumResources/MAC/Reviews/Health/22739/22700.aspx
Hospice social work linking policy, practice, and research.	Social Work Policy Institute	2010	www.socialworkpolicy.org/news-events/hospice-social-work-linking-policy-practice-and-research.html.
Publication of the *Oxford Textbook of Palliative Social Work*	Altilio, T., & Otis-Green, S.	2011	global.oup.com/academic/product/oxford- textbook-of-palliative-social-work textbook-of-palliative-social-work
Core Competencies for Palliative Social Work in Europe: An EAPC White Paper; Parts 1 and 2 published	Hughes, S., Firth, P., & Oliviere, D.	2014, 2015	www.eapcnet.eu/Themes/Education/Socialwork.aspx

SOURCE: Altilio, T, McKinnon, A., Rivas, N. (2017), Palliative Care: Evolution and Scope of Practice. DOI: 10.1093/obo/9780195389678-0253 *Encyclopedia of Social Work.*

TRAINING OPPORTUNITIES

California State University Institute for Palliative Care (overview course, skills, and post-Master's certificate; Internet courses), csupalliativecare.org/search/?q=palliative+social+work

New York University, Silver School of Social Work, Zelda Foster Program (Master's level), socialwork.nyu.edu/academics/zelda-foster-studies.html

National Association of Social Workers Foundation, Social Work HEALS: Social Work Health Care Education and Leadership Scholars, (training program supporting social work students studying and committed to health social work www.naswfoundation.org/social_work_heals.asp New York University,

Palliative and End of Life Care (post-Master's certificate), socialwork.nyu.edu/alumni/continuing-education/post-masters/palliative-care.html

Smith College School of Social Work (post-Master's certificate), www.smith.edu/ssw/acad_cont_graduate_elc.php

Stanford School of Medicine, Palliative Care Training Portal

(training exercises and videos for clinicians to learn about palliative care principles) palliative.stanford.edu/transition-to-death/the-illlness-progresses

DOMESTIC RESOURCES AND ORGANIZATIONS

Agency for Healthcare Research and Quality (AHRQ), www.ahrq.gov/tools/index.html

American Academy of Hospice and Palliative Medicine, www.aahpm.org/

Americans for Better Care of the Dying, www.abcd-caring.org/

Association of Oncology Social Work, www.aosw.org/

Association of Pediatric Oncology Social Workers, www.aposw.org

Caring Conversations, www.practicalbioethics.org/files/caring-conversations/Caring-Conversations.pdf

Center for the Advancement of Palliative Care (CAPC), www.capc.org

Five Wishes, www.agingwithdignity.org/five-wishes/about-five-wishes

National Association of Social Workers (NASW), www.socialworkers.org

The National Palliative Care Research Center (NPCRC), www.npcrc.org

National Hospice and Palliative Care Organization (NHPCO), www.nhpco.org/nchpp-sections/social-worker

National POLST Paradigm, POLST.org

Palliative Care Network of Wisconsin (PCNOW), www.mypcnow.org/fast-facts

INTERNATIONAL RESOURCES AND ORGANIZATIONS

The Association of Palliative Care Social Workers, www.apcsw.org.uk/the-people/

The Canadian Hospice and Palliative Care Association, www.chpca.net/about-us.aspx

The European Association for Palliative Care, www.eapcnet.eu

European Association for Palliative Care Task Force on Social Work in Palliative Care, www.eapcnet.eu/Themes/Education/Socialwork.aspx

The International Association of Hospice and Palliative Care, hospicecare.com

Palliative Care Australia, palliativecare.org.au

HOSPICE ELIGIBILITY AND BENEFITS INFORMATION

Medicare Hospice Benefits and Eligibility Criteria, www.medicare.gov/Pubs/pdf/02154-Medicare-Hospice-Benefits.PDF

Medicaid Hospice Benefits and Eligibility Criteria, www.medicaid.gov/medicaid/benefits/hospice/index.html

MULTIMEDIA

Brené Brown, *The Power of Vulnerability*, www.ted.com

Brené Brown, Ph.D., LMSW, is a research professor at the University of Houston Graduate College of Social Work. She has spent the past decade studying vulnerability, courage, worthiness, and shame.

Amy Herman *Visual Intelligence*, www.ted.com

Amy Herman developed and conducts all sessions of *The Art of Perception* using the analysis of works of art to improve perception and communication. While working as head of Education at the Frick Collection, she instituted the program for medical students to improve their observation skills. She presents to social workers, medical professionals, and institutions such as the New York City Police Department and the FBI. www.youtube.com/watch?v=4v_tn4nyjwE

National Public Radio, *23 Weeks 6 Days: Radiolab*

A radio interview of Kelley Benham and her husband Tom French, whose daughter was born at 23 weeks and 6 days, covers a range of questions about the lines between life and death, reflex and will, and the balance between doing no harm—and doing everything possible to help. www.radiolab.org/story/288733-23-weeks-6-days/

ADDITIONAL READING

Berlinger, N., & Crowley, M. (2008). *Birth to death and bench to clinic: The Hastings Center bioethics briefing book for journalists, policymakers, and campaigns*. New York: The Hastings Center.

Bern-Klug, M. (Ed.) (2010). *Transforming palliative care in nursing homes: The social work role*. New York: Columbia University Press.

Byock, I. (2004). *The four things that matter most: A book about living*. New York: Atria Books.

Chow, R., Chow, S., & Chow, E. (2015). Social work in end-of-life care: A review of the most highly cited papers. *Journal of Pain Management, 8*(4), 331.

Crawley, L. M., Marshall, P. A., Lo, B., & Koenig, B. A. (2002). Strategies for culturally effective end-of-life care. *Annals of Internal Medicine, 136*(9), 673–679.

Ellis, G., Whitehead, M. A., Robinson, D., O'Neill, D., & Langhorne, P. (2011). Comprehensive geriatric assessment for older adults admitted to hospital: meta-analysis of randomised controlled trials. *BMJ, 343*, d6553.

Gawande, A. (2014). *Being mortal: medicine and what matters in the end*. New York: Metropolitan Books.

Kagawa-Singer, M., & Blackhall, L. J. (2001). Negotiating cross-cultural issues at the end of life: you got to go where he lives. *JAMA, 286*(23), 2993–3001.

Kalanithi, P. (2016). *When breath becomes air*. New York: Random House.

Sontag, S. (2001). *Illness as metaphor and AIDS and its metaphors*. New York: Macmillan.

Aaron's Tracheostomy Page, 248
AARP, 249
Active dying, 179–81
    definition of, 179
Active listening, 101
Activities of daily living (ADL), resources
        and guidelines for, 119
Acute illness, disease trajectory in, 167
Addiction, 46, 53
    fears and misconceptions about, 53
    learning exercises, 65–66
    narrative examples, 211
ADL. *See* Activities of daily living (ADL)
Adolescent(s) and young adults
    advance care planning for, 249
    and care planning, 236
    dependence and, 229
    grief in, resources on, 116
    serious illness in, 233–40
    social forces affecting, 233–34
Advance care planning, 23, 24, 169,
        199–201
    for adolescents and young adults, 249
    for children, 249
    components of, 199
    documentation in, 200 (*see also* Ad-
        vance planning documents)
    health care setting and, 199–200
    for homeless population, 44–45
    learning exercise, 220
    narrative example, 210–14, 217–18, 258

patient preferences in, 200
    resources on, 207
    steps in, 200
Advance directive(s), 32, 200–1, 202
    culture and, 158–59
    federal regulation on, 207
    homeless persons and, 44–45
    travel through systems of care, 201
Advance planning documents, 200–1, 202
Advocacy, 6
    in care of person with serious
        illness, 26
    cultural sensitivity and, 105,198, 199
    in end-of-life care, 171
    for pediatric care, 234–35
    as social work role, 41, 72
    in spiritual care, 135
    in symptom management, 54
    for underserved populations, 72
Agency for Health Care Research and
        Quality, 263
    *Assessment tools for palliative care, tech-
        nical brief,* 260–61
Aging population. *See also* Older adults
    health care system and, 260
Allow natural death (AND) order, 202
ALS. *See* Amyotrophic lateral sclerosis
Alzheimer's disease, 182–83
    facts and figures for, 188
American Academy of Hospice and Pallia-
        tive Medicine, 263

American Bar Association, online resources from, 220–21
American Cancer Society, resource for helping children when family member has cancer, 248
American Geriatrics Society, 249
Americans for Better Care of the Dying, 263
Amyotrophic lateral sclerosis, prevalence and impact of pain in, and linkage to intervention, 57
Anger
   as coping process, 39
   in family member/spouse, 84–85
   as protective strategy, 39
Anhedonia, 78, 79
Anticipatory guidance, 63–65, 72, 76–77, 85–86, 107, 108, 135, 167, 169, 178, 199, 206
Anxiety, 53, 76
   and delirium, differentiation of, 75–76
   interventions for, 76–77
   medications for, abuse/misuse concerns about, 53
   with pain, 59
Argot(s), 12–13
Artificial hydration and nutrition, 140, 150, 183, 211, 216
Aries, Phillippe, on medicalization of death, 165–66
Assessment, 32, 193–96. *See also* Social assessment
   comprehensive, 32
   of decision-making capacity, 192–93, 194
   domains of, 173–75
   ecological framework and, 38, 60–63, 64
   in end-of-life care, 173–75, 177
   focus of, 173
   initial, 32
   interdisciplinary, 97
      person-centered, 99
   as intervention, 173
   pace of, 173
   in pediatric palliative care, 236
   process of, 173
   resources for, 66

social work, 32
spiritual, 131–32
   documentation of, 138–39
   tools for, 100–1
   resource on, 260–61
Association for Gerontology Education in Social Work, 250
Association of Oncology Social Work, 263
Association of Palliative Care Social Workers, 263
Association of Pediatric Oncology Social Workers, 263
Assumption(s)
   avoiding, 83
   erroneous, 103–4
      about religion or spirituality, 132, 142
   language reflecting, 46–48
Attunement
   clinical, 141–44
   definition of, 142
Autonomy
   ethical principle of, 196, 197
   patient access to medical information and, 40–41
Avoidance, 74–75
   adaptive vs. maladaptive, 75

Behavioral descriptors, effects on care, 45–48
Behavioral interventions, 72
   for anxiety, 76–77
Belief systems. *See also* Religion; Spirituality
   conflicts among, 160
   social worker's, 144–45
Beneficence, ethical principle of, 196, 197
Benham, Kelley, 264
Bereavement, 71, 177–78
   children's, resources on, 115
   complicating factors, 178
   high-risk, 178
Bereavement care, 72
Bereavement Risk Index (BRI), 100–1
   modified, 115
Bereavement services, hospice and, 172
Bias(es), 156–57

clinicians', and advance care planning, 199–200
reflective practice as antidote to, 156–57
therapeutic, language and, 45–46
Binary thinking
about health and illness, 21–22
moving away from, 27–28
Bioethics
consult, value to clinicians and patients, 40
narrative example, 37
multicultural perspective and, 40
online resources on, 221, 222
research, online resources on, 221
Blood transfusion(s), religion and, 128–29
Brown, Brené, *The Power of Vulnerability,* 264
Burial, arrangements for, 182
Byock, Ira, on human dimension of dying, 165

Caine, Michael, 253, 254
Canadian Hospice and Palliative Care Association, 263
Cancer
assessment and interventions in ecological framework for, 59–63
narrative example, 59–63, 256
disease trajectory in, 167
end-of-life care with, *narrative example,* 210–14, 217–18, 258
in older adult, *narrative example,* 242, 244, 245–47
pain management in
learning exercise for, 65–66
narrative example, 35, 256
prevalence and impact of pain in, and linkage to intervention, 57
Care conference(s), 99, 110–12, 135. *See also* Family meetings
debriefing after, 112
functions of, 214
pre-meeting, 111, 213, 218
process for, 111–12
provider preparation for, 111–12, 214
SPIKES protocol for, 111, 115

Care delivery, patient and caregiver voices in, 260
Caregiver Action Network, 250
Caregivers, patients as, role change and, 107–8
Caregiving
adaptations, older adults and, 242–43
resources and guidelines for, 119
Care planning, 32. *See also* Advance care planning; Care conference(s)
in hospice care, 172
interdisciplinary, 97
for seriously ill child or adolescent, 234, 236
social, 112
spiritual and religious concerns and, 130
Caring Conversations, 263
CaringInfo, 115
CaringKind's Palliative Care for Advanced Dementia, 250
Case management, 21
CASES method, 222
Cassell, Eric, 229
Center for Practical Bioethics, 221
Center for the Advancement of Palliative Care, 263
Centering, of self, 27
Centers for Disease Control and Prevention (CDC), Healthy Aging, 250
Center to Advance Palliative Care (CAPC), definition of palliative care, 1–2, 18
Certification, 18–19, 23, 261, 262
CHF. *See* Congestive heart failure
Child(ren). *See also* Pediatric care
adult, as interpreters for parents, 210
advance care planning for, 249
care of, Pope Francis on, 226
and care planning, 234, 236
care principles for, 237
death of, resources for family with, 116, 249
dependence of, 229
grief in, resources on, 115, 116

Child(ren) (*cont.*)
  health/wellness of, social determinants
    and, 7–8
  helping
    when family member has cancer,
      188, 248
    when family member is dying, *narra-*
      tive example, 185–86
  loss experienced by, resources on, 115
  palliative care for, need (identified de-
    mand) for, 2
  serious illness in, 233–40
    causes of, 234–35
    concurrent care for, 234–35
    issues with, 226–32
    learning exercise, 240
    narrative examples, 258
    resources related to, 248
  social forces affecting, 233–34
  talking to, about death, 188
Children's Grief Education Association, 115
Chodron, Pema, on compassion, 71
Chronic obstructive pulmonary disease
  disease trajectory in, 167
  prevalence and impact of pain in, and
    linkage to intervention, 57
City of Hope Pain and Palliative Care Resource Center, 66
Clinical social work, discharge planning
  and, 21
Cognitive-behavioral therapy, 72
  for anxiety, 76–77
Cognitive therapy, in support of family
  member of dying person, 171, 181
Columbia University Loss, Trauma, and
  Emotion Lab, 92
Communication, 229–30. *See also*
  Conversations
  clinician–patient, standards for, 23
  coercive, 45–46
  culturally attuned, 158–59
  about death and dying, 169
  with dying patient, 180
  in families, 72

  high- and low-context, 10–11
  issues with, 192
  legal and ethical aspects of, 206–10
  macro-level intervention and, 26
  in pediatric care, 237
  therapy first approach in, 46–48
Community, as resource for care, 3–4, 231
Community linkage, in spiritual care,
  135, 140
Compassion, 71
Competency(ies). *See also* Social work
  competency(ies)
  in palliative care, 18–19, 261
    relevance of, 4–5
  for palliative social work in Europe, 262
Concurrent care, 234–35
Confidentiality, ethical principle of, 197
Congestive heart failure
  and depression, ecological framework
    for, 86, 89
  prevalence and impact of pain in, and
    linkage to intervention, 57
Connection
  skills that enhance, 141–42
  spirituality and, 127
Consent, statutes on, 221
Continuity, in daily life, resources and
  guidelines for, 113–14, 117
Continuity of care, 85–86, 87
  in care of person with serious ill-
    ness, 26
Conversation Project, The, 221
Conversations
  culturally attuned, 158–59
  about decision-making, 201–5
  about disease trajectory, spiritual and
    religious concerns and, 199
  about end-of-life care, 169, 221
    resources on, 207
  about prognosis, spiritual and religious
    concerns, 130, 173, 199
  about religious or spiritual matters, with
    patients and family, 142–44
COPD. *See* Chronic obstructive pulmonary disease

Coping process
    action-focused, 39–40
    emotion-focused, 39–40
    family/caregiver, with dying rela-
        tive, 180–81
    locus of control and, 39–40
    patients', vs. institutional values, 150
    PVEST framework for, 39
    spirituality and, 127
Council on Social Work Education, 262
    Gero-ed Center, 250
Counseling
    spiritual themes in, 131, 134–35
    therapeutic aims of, 134–35
Countertransference, 80–81
Courageous Parents' Network, 116
Creating Social Work Competencies for
        Practice in Hospice Palliative
        Care, 261
Credential(s), in hospice and palliative
        care, 18–19
Cremation, arrangements for, 182
Cruzan, Nancy, 207
Cultural anthropology, 156
Cultural competence, 148–49, 150–54,
        161–62
    narrative example, 159–61, 257
Cultural domain, of palliative care, 5,
        33, 149–50
    narrative example, 159–61, 257
Cultural humility, 152, 155–57
Cultural sensitivity
    advocacy and, 105
    and bioethics, 40, 192,198, 199
    with grief and loss, 77
    and pain and symptom management, 56
    in social work practice, 48, 148–49
        narrative examples, 35, 159–61, 255
Culture(s)
    and advance care planning, 199
    and assessment and intervention, 103
    definition of, 148, 150–51
    and end-of-life care, 175
    exploration of, with patient and fam-
        ily, 158–59

groups/components/identities in, 150–51
    and health care, 149
    high- and low-context, 10–11
    learning exercises related to, 163
    palliative care and, 26
    patient preferences grounded in, explo-
        ration of, 158–59
    patients', vs. institutional values, 150
    and post-death arrangements, 181–82
    and serious illness, 148–49
    spiritual or religious considerations and,
        127, 140–41
    subgroup diversity in, 152
Curiosity, language that encourages, 46–48

Death(s). See also Good death
    autobiographical vs. biological, 167
    of child, resources for family
        experiencing, 116, 249
    communicating with patient/family
        about, 169
    desire for, 54, 80
    developmental perspective on, 165–66
    dissimulation of, 165–66
    of family member, and coping pro-
        cess, 39
    final arrangements after, 181–82
    hastened, requests for, 215
    at home, 170–71
        feasibility of, assessment, 175
    meaning of, for patient and family,
        166–67
    medicalization of, 165–66
    medication-related, 53
    pediatric
        age distribution of, 234–35
        causes of, 234–35
    preparation for, assessment of, 174–75
    prior experience of, and bereave-
        ment, 178
    setting for, 166–67, 170–71
    social meanings of, 165–66
    speaking of, cultural considerations
        and, 104, 140–41
    sudden, 167

Decision-making, 229–30. *See also* Medical decision-making; Surrogate decision-making
  changing contexts and, 193–96
  competing values and principles in, 196
  conversations about, 201–5
  family's sharing of, with interested others, 230–31
  health care
    components of, 199
    online resources for, 221, 222
    social work role in, 199
  information about, 201–5
  informed, 108–9
  patients', vs. institutional values, 150
  in pediatric care, 234, 238, 239
Decision-making capacity, assessment for, 192–93, 194
Delirium, 75–76
  definition of, 75–76
  hyperactive, 75–76
  hypoactive, 75–76
  interventions for, 76
  symptoms of, 75–76
  terminal, 179–80
Dementia, 182–83
  disease trajectory in, 167, 182, 183
  prevalence and impact of pain in, and linkage to intervention, 57
  resource on, 260
  as terminal illness, 183
Demoralization, 62, 78
  assessment of, 62–63
  and depression, differentiation of, 78
  interventions for, 78
Denial, 74–75
  adaptive vs. maladaptive, 75
  and avoidance, 74–75
Dependence, 229
  Children and, 226
  older adults and, 229, 241
  related to illness progression, 31, 148
  narrative examples, 148, 165
Depression, 62, 79–80
  and agitation, 76
  and anxiety, 76

assessment and interventions in, 62–63, 79
  narrative example, 81–86, 256
  caregiver, with Alzheimer's disease, 182–83
  and delirium, differentiation of, 75–76
  and demoralization, differentiation of, 78
  and desire for death, 80
  diagnosis of, 79
  DSM-5 diagnostic criteria for, 79
  ecological framework for, 86, 89
  interdisciplinary approach to, 80
  as life-threatening disorder, 79–80
  masked, 83
  mistreatment of, 83
  pain and, 82, 83–84
  physical symptoms of, 56, 79, 83–84
  prevalence of, in patients at end of life, 79
  screening for, 79
  serious illness and, 79
  severe, 79–80
  and suicide, 80
  treatment of, 80
Despair, integrity vs., 228, 244–45
Destiny, interrelatedness of, 97
Development
  and coping processes, 39
  Erikson's theory of, 165–66, 227–28
Diagnosis, disclosure of, cultural considerations, 103–4
Dickinson, Emily, poem on hope, 233
Dignity, 97, 196, 228
Dignity Therapy, 87
Disability
  effects of, 55
  reframing of, 63
  symbolic meaning of, 55
Discharge planning, 21
  Social work interventions for, 87, 170
Disclosure of diagnosis, cultural considerations, 103–4
Disease trajectory(ies), 167, 168
  in children, 234
  conversations about, spiritual and religious concerns and, 199

Diversity, 149
  of cultural subgroups, 152
  organizational commitment to, 156–57
  in staff and programs, 156–57
Diversity wheel, 151
DNAR. *See* Do not attempt resuscitation
  (DNAR) order
DNR. *See* Do not resuscitate (DNR) order
Documentation. *See also* Legal documents;
  Medical documents
  in advance care planning, 200. *See also*
  Advance planning documents
  language used in, importance of, 11–12
  learning exercise for, 48, 92
  narrative, of interdisciplinary care,
  86–92
  of spiritual assessment and interven-
  tion, 138–39
Domain(s), of palliative care, 5, 32–35
  components of, 32–35
Do not attempt resuscitation (DNAR) or-
  der, 200–1, 202
Do not resuscitate (DNR) order, 200–1, 202
Dougy Center, 116
DPOA. *See* Durable medical power of
  attorney
Drug abuse, fears and misconceptions
  about, 53
  assessment, 44, 46
Drug misuse, fears and misconceptions
  about, 53
Duke-UNC Functional Social Support
  Questionnaire, 115
Duke-UNC Social Support Scale, 100–1
Durable financial and legal power of
  attorney, 202
Durable medical power of attorney,
  200–1, 202
Dying. *See also* Active dying; Physician aid
  in dying (PAD); End of life care
  ecological framework for, 102, 166
  family/caregiver coping with, 180–81
  as high-context experience, 11
  human dimension of, 165
  physical changes in, education of family
  about, 179–80

speaking of, cultural considerations
  and, 104, 140–41
Dyspnea (shortness of breath), 53, 54–55
  and anxiety, 76
  cultural aspects of, 56
  distress caused by, 62
  medications for, abuse/misuse concerns
  about, 53

Ecological framework, 38, 60–63, 64,
  82–86
  assessment and, 38, 60–63, 64
  for cancer care, 59–63
  and cultural humility, 156
  for depression and congestive heart failure, 86, 89
  for dying, 166
  for interventions, 60–63, 64
  for legal and ethical issues, 192–93
  and medications for pain, 61–62
  for mental health and well-being, 72
  for pain assessment, 60–63, 64
  for pain management, 60–63, 64
  for pediatric care, 235–36
  person-in-environment approach
  and, 97
  psychoeducation in, 63–65
  social work practice within, *narrative
  examples,* 35, 256
  for social assessment, 97
  for spiritual care, 124
Ecological Systems Theory, 6–7, 38. *See
  also* Macro level; Meso level; Micro
  level; Phenomenological variant of
  ecological systems theory
Education. *See also* Psychoeducation
  of patient and family, social work's role
  in, 22
  professional, 23
  public, about care for persons with
  serious illness, 24
Ego psychology, in support of family
  member of dying person,
  171, 181
Elderly. *See also* Older adults
  care of, Pope Francis on, 226

Emotional distress, 72. *See also* Psycholog-
    ical distress
Emotional support, 112
Empathy, social worker's, 145–46
Empowerment, of patients, 154–55
End-of-life care, 22
    advocacy in, 171
    assessment in, 173–75
    conversations about, 169, 221
        resources on, 207
    cultural considerations in, 175
    as domain of palliative care, 5, 33
    domains important in, 166–67
    empowerment of patient in, 154–55
    homeless persons and, 44–45
    intersectional experience in, 175
    IOM recommendations for, 22–24
    learning exercise related to, 187–88
    legal and ethical issues in, *narrative
        example,* 210–14, 217–18
    narrative examples, 71, 183–86, 257–58
    online resources for, 188
    patient preferences for, 32, 205–6
    planning for, 169
    psychoeducation on, 41, 171
    psychological and spiritual tasks
        in, 176–77
    seriously ill child and, 237, 240
    social work competencies in, 261
    social work role in, 183–87
    spiritual and religious considerations
        in, 140–41
    standards of practice for, 98
End-stage renal disease
    assessment and interventions in, *narra-
        tive example,* 41–44, 255–56
    prevalence and impact of pain in, and
        linkage to intervention, 57
Entitlements, 113
Environment, and coping processes, 39
Equity
    in health, 8–9
    in illness experience, 8–9
Erikson, Erik, developmental theory of,
    165–66, 227–28, 244–45
ESRD. *See* End-stage renal disease

Ethical challenges, 196
Ethical distress, 196
Ethical principles
    conflicts among, in treatment
        decisions, 196
    of Western medicine, 196, 197
Ethics
    and communication, 192
    as domain of palliative care, 5, 33, 192–93
    and pain treatment, 52–53
Ethics committees, 215–16
Ethics consultations, online resource
    on, 222
European Association for Palliative
    Care, 263
    Task Force on Social Work in Palliative
        Care, 264
Euthanasia, 214–15
Evil eye, 160
Explanatory model(s), 152, 153
    eliciting, 152–54

Family
    assessment and interventions for, re-
        sources and guidelines for, 118
    bereavement of, 39
    communication in, 72
    grief reactions in, 39
    information-sharing by, 230–31
    interfaith, 132
    of older adults, social work's respect
        for, 230
    role changes in, 61–62
    of seriously ill child, 234
    shared experience of illness, 61–62
Family Caregiver Alliance National Center
    on Caregiving, 188
Family-centered care, in pediatric care,
    234, 235
Family meetings, 72, 85–86, 135, 218. *See
    also* Care conference(s)
    in pediatric care, 238, 239
Family-oriented care, 23, 25–26
    narrative examples, 35, 255
Family system. *See also* Patient-family
    system

assessment of, 174
of older adults
    and adaptations in caregiving, 242–43
    care needs and, 241
    narrative example, 242, 244, 245–47
    pain and symptom management and, 55
    seriously ill child in, social work
        with, 237
Fast Facts and Concepts—Palliative Care
    Network of Wisconsin (PCNOW),
    66, 92–93
Fatalism, 62
Feeding, for dying patient, 180
FICA (spiritual assessment tool), 133
Fidelity, ethical principle of, 197
Finances, 113
    and final arrangements, 182
    resources and guidelines for, 116
Financial documents, resources and
    guidelines for, 116
Five directions, 27
Five Wishes, 263
Feeding, for dying patient, 180
Francis (Pope), on care of elderly and chil-
    dren, 226
Frankl, Viktor, on meaning, 122
French, Tom, 264

Generativity, 242–43
Geriatric Social Work initiative, 250
Goal(s), older adults', in palliative care, 246
Good death
    definition of, 166–67
    reconceptualizing, 166–67
Grief, 61, 71, 77
    assessment of, 77
    children's, resources on, 115
    complicated, 178
        risk factors for, 178
    cultural aspects of, 77
    dementia and, resource on, 260
    intuitive vs. instrumental, 71
    normal, 77
    online resource about, 188
    outlets for, 77–78
    resources on, 116

symptoms of, 77
Guardian, court appointment of, 202
Guardianship, hospital petition for, 205–6

Hallenbeck, James, 10–11
Hallucinations, in dying patient, 180 (See
    also Deleriumterminal)
Hastings Center, 221
Healing Center (Seattle, WA), 188
Healing language, 46–48
Health, social determinants of, 7–8
Health care, as social work's place, 1
Health care agent, 200–1, 202
    selection of
        narrative example, 210–14, 217–
            18, 258
    resource on, 222
Health care proxy(ies), 202
    being, online resource on, 221
    choosing, online resource on, 221
Health care system, human-centered, 14
Health disparities, resource on, 260
Health literacy, 108–9, 157–58, 206–10,
    259, 260
Health social workers
    and palliative care, 18, 253–54
        narrative example, 24–26, 255
    role in medical care and treatment pla-
        nning, 31
    at the top of their license, 254
Heart failure. *See also* Congestive heart
    failure
    assessment and interventions in, *nar-
        rative examples,* 35–41, 81–86,
        255, 256
    disease trajectory in, 167
Herman, Amy, *Visual Intelligence,* 264
HIPAA, 207
HIV/AIDS, assessment and
    interventions in, *narrative
        example,* 41–44, 255–56
Home
    continuity in, importance of, 113–14
    death at, preferences for, 170–71
    leaving, 113–14
    loss of, 63

Home Health Pain Management Work-
    sheet, 66
Homeless population
    advance care planning for, 44–45
    concerns of, 44–45
    end-of-life preparations in, 44–45
    interventions for, 44–45
Hope, 228, 233
    Dickinson's poem about, 233
    older adults and, 244–46
HOPE (spiritual assessment tool), 133
Hospice
    continuing care in, 85–86, 87
    eligibility and benefits information, 172
        resources on, 264
    federal regulation on, 188
    national credential in, 18–19
    for seriously ill child, 240
    social work partnering with, 72
Hospice care, 172
    and bereavement services, 172
    care plan in, 172
    at home, 172
    interventions provided in, 172
    narrative examples, 183–86, 257–58
    psychoeducation on, 37–38, 41
    in skilled nursing facility, 172
Hospice social work, 262
    resource on, 261
Hospital(s), palliative care teams in,
    19, 20–21
Hospital admission(s), need (identified de-
    mand) for palliative care among, 2
Hospital palliative care, need (identified
    demand) for, 2
Housing
    changes in, 63, 113–14
    resources and guidelines for, 116

IADL. See Instrumental activities of daily
    living (IADL)
IASP. See International Association for the
    Study of Pain
ICU Delirium and Cognitive Impairment
    Study Group, 93

Identity, 104–5
    assessment and interventions for, re-
        sources and guidelines for, 117
    delegitimizing of, 42, 175, 257
    fluidity and, 9
    illness-related assaults on, 61, 62, 124
    interconnected nature of, 155
    intersectional, 104–5
        spirituality and religion in, 127–29
    social location and, 9
Identity conflict, 105–6
Illness. See also Serious illness
    disease trajectory in, 167 (see also
        Disease trajectory(ies))
    as high-context experience, 11
    nature of, resources and guidelines
        for, 117
    social determinants and, 7–8
In Plain Sight, C0/Front Matter
Informed consent, 103, 156, 192, 195, 197
Institute of Medicine (IOM)
    Dying in America, 259
    Health literacy and palliative care work-
        shop summary (2016), 259
    on hospice and palliative care, 2
    Implications of health literacy for public
        health, 260
    Integrating the patient and caregiver
        voice into serious illness, 260
    recommendations for care of people liv-
        ing with serious illness, 22–24
    report on health disparities, 260
    Retooling for an aging America, 260
Instrumental activities of daily living
    (IADL), resources and guidelines
    for, 119
Insurance, 113
    and pediatric care, 234–35
    resources and guidelines for, 116
Integrity, 228
    Erikson's concept of, 228, 244–45
    as social work value, 196
Interdisciplinary team approach
    narrative documentation of, 86–92
    in palliative care, 18

International Association for the Study of
    Pain, definition of pain, 54
International Association of Hospice and
    Palliative Care, 264
Interpreter(s), 128, 157–58
    family member as, 109, 157–58,
        206–10
    medical, 109, 157–58
    online resources for, 221
    professional, 109, 157–58, 206–10
    provision of, mandate for, 157–58
    untrained, 157–58, 206–10
Interprofessional team, 17–18
Intersectionality, 9, 38, 44, 72–73,
        104–5, 154–55
    and older adults, 243–44
    and pediatric care, 235–36
    and physical symptoms, 56
Intervention(s)
    for cases with ethical and legal
        challenges, 197
    ecological framework for, 60–63, 64, 102
    extension beyond medical, 52
    for homeless population, 44–45
    macro-level, 26, 41, 44–45, 72
    meso-level, 25–26, 40–41, 44, 72
    micro-level, 24–25, 38, 43–44, 62, 72
    spiritual, documentation of, 138–39
    spiritually focused, 134–35
Intimacy, illness and, 40
Iranian communities, cultural
        considerations with, 103–4
Irish Hospice Foundation, *Loss and
        grief in dementia guidance
        document,* 260

Jargon
    effects on care, 45–46
    and paternalism, 40–41
Jehovah's Witness(es), 128–29
Joint Commission, 216
    online resources from, 221
*Journal of Social Work in End of Life and
        Palliative Care,* 261
Joy, 27

Judgment
    language reflecting, 45–46, 47
    language that avoids, 46, 47
Justice, ethical principle of, 197

King, Martin Luther, Jr., on interrelated-
        ness of life, 97
Kleinman, Arthur, 152 (See
        alsoexplanatory models)

Label(s)/labeling, of patients, effects on
        care, 45–46, 81, 83
Laing, R. D., 17
Language
    abstract, effects of, 45–46
    coercive, 45–46
    dynamics of, 12
    effects in care, 45–46, 172–73
    empowerment-based, 46–48
    feminist, 12
    harmful, 45–46, 83
    healing, 46–48
    medical, 108–9, 169
    in medical communication, 157–58
    modeling, as intervention, 11–12
    non-English, 109, 157–58
    patient-centered, 12–13, 46–48
    power of, 11
    religious or spiritual, exploring, with
        patients, 143–44
    respectful, 12–13
    shorthand, 12–13, 172–73
    spiritual/religious, 134, 135
    terror, 45–46
    that defers judgment, 46–48
    that fosters curiosity, 46–48
    that invites further exploration, 46–48
    that reports observation, 46–48
    therapy first, 12
    whole-person, 12–13
Language access. *See also* Interpreter(s)
    in health care, 109, 157–58, 206–10
    online resource for, 221
    for older adults, 230
Latino culture, 161

Learning exercise(s), 28
  for advance care planning, 220
  culture-related, 163
  for documentation, 48, 92
  for end-of-life care, 187–88
  for pain and symptom management, 65
  for pediatric care, 240
  for social aspects, 114–15
  for spiritual care, 146
  for work with older adults, 247
Legacy, 228
Legacy activities, 87,104, 169
Legal documents, 113
  resources and guidelines for, 116
Legal domain, of palliative care, 5, 192–93
Licensure, 23
Life-Course Theory, 165–66
Life expectancy, prediction of, difficulty/
      uncertainty of, 168
Life review, 39–40, 87, 137
Life-sustaining treatment. See also Phy-
      sician orders for life-sustaining
      treatment (POLST)
  Forgoing or withholding, 140, 192
  right to refuse, 206, 207
  spiritual or religious considerations
      and, 140
  withdrawal of, 206, 207
  narrative examples, 210
Liquid intake, for dying patient, 180
Listening. See also Active listening
  with spiritual attunement, 141–44
Living will, 200–1, 202, 205–6
Locus of control, and coping
      process, 39–40
Loss, 77(see alsoGrief)
  adaptive responses to, gender
      differences in, 77
  ambiguous, with dementia, 183, 184–85
  assessment of, 77
  children's, resources on, 115
  cultural aspects of, 77
  dementia and, resource on, 260
  experience of, and coping process, 39
  of home, 63

  of identity and self-esteem, 61
  illness-related, 61, 62
  older adults and, 244–46
  prior experience of, and bereave-
      ment, 178
  transitions as, 170
Low-income populations, resource for, 222

Macro level
  dying process at, 166
  in Ecological Systems Theory, 6–7
  interventions at, 26, 41, 44–45, 72
  legal and ethical issues at, 192–93
  and religious concerns, 129
Major depressive disorder. See also De-
      pression
  DSM-5 diagnostic criteria for, 79
Marshall, Kerry James, 1
MCC. See Medical crisis counseling
Meaning, Frankl on, 122
Meaning-making, 27, 73–74, 228–29
  patients', vs. institutional values, 150
  therapeutic process and, 63
Medicaid, 116
  Hospice Benefits and Eligibility
      Criteria, 264
Medical crisis counseling, 43–44
Medical decision-making, spirituality and,
      129–30, 135
Medical documents, 113
  resources and guidelines for, 116
Medical equipment, in home, significance
      of, 113–14
Medical model
  and religious concerns, 129
  and strengths approach, differences
      between, 73
Medicare, 116
  Hospice Benefits and Eligibility
      Criteria, 264
Medication(s)
  abuse/misuse concerns about, 53
  attributed meaning of, 53
  availability, socioeconomic factors
      and, 7–8

discontinuation of, 179
fears and preconceptions about, 53
management of, intersectional experi-
    ence of, 175–76
for pain, ecological framework
    and, 61–62
as tool to support aspects of self, 62
Mental health
    definition of, 72
    ecological vision of, 72
Mental status, changes, with active dy-
    ing, 179–80
Meso level
    dying process at, 166
    in Ecological Systems Theory, 6–7
    interventions at, 25–26, 40–41, 44, 72
    legal and ethical issues at, 192–93
    and religious concerns, 129
Micro level
    dying process at, 166
    in Ecological Systems Theory, 6–7
    interventions at, 24–25, 38, 43–44, 62, 72
    legal and ethical issues at, 192–93
    and religious concerns, 129
    of symptom assessment, 61
MISS Foundation, 116
MND. See Motor neuron disease
Mortuary, arrangements with, 182
Motor neuron disease, prevalence and
    impact of pain in, and linkage to
    intervention, 57
Mourning, cultural aspects of, 77 (see
    alsoGrief)
MS. See Multiple sclerosis
Muller, Wayne, 122
Multiple sclerosis, prevalence and impact
    of pain in, and linkage to interven-
    tion, 57
My Wishes, 249

Narrative therapy, 43–44
    in support of family member of dying
        person, 171, 181
NASW. See National Association of Social
    Workers (NASW)

National Alliance for Caregiving, 250
National Association of Social Workers
    (NASW), 263
    Certification, 261, 262
    standards of practice, 18–19, 98, 115,
        148–49, 261
National Center for Gerontological Edu-
    cation, 262
National Center on Elder Abuse, 250
National Coalition on Mental Health and
    Aging, 250
National Consensus Project (NCP)
    clinical practice guidelines, 115
    Clinical Practice Guidelines for Quality
        Palliative Care, 98
    Eight Domains of Palliative Care, 5
    social aspects of palliative care, 98, 99
National Council on Aging, 250
National Council on Interpreting in
    Health Care, 221
National Healthcare Decisions Day, 222
National Health Law Program, 222
National Hospice and Palliative Care Or-
    ganization (NHPCO), 18–19, 115,
        188, 222, 263
    pediatric resources, 117
National Palliative Care Registry™, on
    palliative care in hospitals, 2
National Palliative Care Research Cen-
    ter, 263
National POLST Paradigm, 263
National Public Radio, 23 Weeks 6
    Days, 264
National Quality Forum
    preferred practices for hospice, 115
    preferred practices specific to social
        aspects of palliative care, 98, 99
NCP. See National Consensus Pro-
    ject (NCP)
Neuswanger Institute for Bioethics, 222
New normal, with serious illness, 123
NHPCO. See National Hospice and Pallia-
    tive Care Organization (NHPCO)
Non-maleficence, ethical principle of,
    196, 197

Observation, in spiritual/religious assess-
        ment, 131–32, 177
Older adults
    in caregiver role, 242, 244, 245–46
    care needs of, social work and, 241
    dependence and, 229, 241
    financial privacy of, 241
    generativity and, 242–43
    goals of care, 246
    heterogeneity of, 240–41
    and hope, 244–46
    infantilization of, 227
    and intersectionality, 243–44
    and loss, 244–46
    and positionality, 243–44
    privacy of, caregivers and, 241
    resources for, 249–50
    serious illness in, 226–27
        narrative example, 242, 244,
            245–47, 259
    social context of, 243–44
    social work with, 240–41
        learning exercises for, 247
    strengths-based approach with, 243–44
Opioid(s). See also Medication(s)
    access to, disparities in, 56
Oppression. See also Intersectionality
    systems of, 9, 10, 154–55
Outcome data, use in advocacy efforts, 72
Oxford Textbook of Palliative Social
        Work, 262

PAD. See Physician aid in dying (PAD)
Pain. See also Total pain
    and anxiety, 76
    congenital insensitivity to, 53–54
    cultural aspects of, 56
    definition of, 54, 59
    and depression, 82, 83–84
    emotional component of, 54, 59
    experience of, 52
    functions of, 53–54, 59
    interdisciplinary approach for, 52
    prevalence and impact of, 53–54
        linkage to intervention, 56–59
    procedural, 54–55, 231–32

studies of, 53–54
subjective nature of, 54
symbolic significance of, 54–55
undertreatment of, 52–53
Pain assessment, 54
    ecological framework for, 60–63, 64
    in nonverbal adults, 180
        tools for, 67
    in vulnerable patients, 231–32
Pain management, 231–32
    disparities in, 56
    ecological framework for, 60–63, 64
    ethical considerations in, 52–53
    intersectional experience of, 175–76
    learning exercises for, 65
    medications for, abuse/misuse concerns
        about, 53
    multidimensional considerations in, 54
    narrative examples, 256
    preemptive, 54–55
    psychosocial aspects of, 55
    resources for, 66
    in vulnerable patients, 231–32
Pain Management—US Department of
        Veterans Affairs, 66
Pain Scales in Multiple Languages, 66
Palliative care
    barriers to, 2
    components of, congruence with social
        work, 4
    definition of, 1–2, 18
    evolution of, 253
    goal of, 1–2, 97
    as high-context culture, 10–11
    misconceptions about, 149–50
    national credential in, 18–19
    need (identified demand) for
        in children, 2
        global, 2
        at hospital admission, 2
    relevance of, 21–22
    in social work, 18–19
    as specialty in social work, 18–19
    as standard of care, IOM on, 2
    standards of practice for, 98
    training in, IOM on, 2

Palliative Care Australia, 264
Palliative care consult teams, 215–16
Palliative Care Network of Wisconsin
(PCNOW), 263
Fast Facts and Concepts, 66, 92–93
Palliative medicine, definition of, 1–2
Palliative social work, and health social
work, collaboration of, 21
Panic attack, 76
Parents, of seriously ill children
collaborative relationships with, 237
communication and, 230, 237
mentorship of, 237
social work with, 230, 237
Parkinson's disease, prevalence and impact
of pain in, and linkage to intervention, 57
Paternalism, 40–41
Patient advocate designation, 200–1, 202
Patient-centered care, 48
narrative examples, 35, 255
Patient descriptors
effects on care, 45–46
to invite curiosity and defer judgment, 46–48
Patient-family system. See also Family system
conflict in, 105–6
social aspects, narrative example,
104, 256
social assessment of, 103
social context of, 101
Patient Self-Determination Act (1990),
200–1, 207, 216
Payment systems, and care for persons
with serious illness, 23
Pediatric care, 234–35
assessment in, 236
communication in, 237
ecological framework for, 235–36
family-centered care in, 234, 235
learning exercise, 240
narrative example, 235–36, 238–40, 258
person-in-environment approach
for, 236
role of social work in, 236

Peer support, 41
Personalismo (personalism), 161
Person-centered care, 19, 23, 25–26
spiritually sensitive, 124
Personhood
illness and, 56, 60–62
social work's respect for, 230
threat to, 55
Phenomenological variant of ecological
systems theory, 39
Physical domain, of palliative care, 5,
33, 52
Physical symptoms. See also Pain
of depression, 83
interdisciplinary assessment and management of, 52
intersectionality and, 56
Physician aid in dying (PAD), 214–15
state laws on, 207, 214–15
Physician orders for life-sustaining treatment (POLST), 200–1, 202
Policy(ies), and care for persons with serious illness, 23
POLST. See Physician orders for life-
sustaining treatment (POLST)
Positionality, 104–5
and older adults, 243–44
Poverty
and health, 7–8
and illness outcomes, 7–8
Power. See also Intersectionality
in health care system, 21, 22
patient access to medical information
and, 40–41
social location and, 9
systems of, 9, 10
Power of attorney, 200–1, 202
state laws on, 220–21
Prayer, 135
Primary palliative care, 17–18, 253–54
Principles, of palliative care, congruence
with social work, 4
Privacy
financial, of older adults, 241
older adults' care needs and, 241
Privacy rule(s), HIPAA, 207

Privilege. *See also* Intersectionality
  in health care system, 21
Process of care, as domain of palliative
     care, 5, 33
Prognosis
  conversations about, spiritual and reli-
       gious concerns and, 130, 173, 199
  difficulty of, 168
  patient/family desire for, assessment
       of, 169
Project on Death in America, 253
Protected health information (PHI),
     HIPAA and, 207
Psychiatric domain, of palliative care, 5
Psychoeducation, 108–9
  about depression after heart attack,
       83–84, 86
  about dying process, 179–80
  in ecological framework, 63–65
  in end-of-life care, 171
  on end-of-life care, 41
  about financial and legal planning, 113
  on hospice care, 37–38, 41
  about illness and emotional/social
       functioning, 31
  in pain and symptom management,
       61–62
Psychological distress, 71
  in serious illness, common forms of, 75
  severe, risk for, 74
Psychological domain
  in palliative care, 62–63, 71
  of palliative care, 5, 33
Psychological themes, in end-of-life
     care, 176–77
Psychosocial Pain Assessment Form—City
     of Hope, Duarte, CA, 67
PVEST. *See* Phenomenological variant of
     ecological systems theory

Quality of life, 18, 72
Quinlan, Karen Ann, 207

Racism, 37, 38
Reflective statements, 82–83
Reframing, of serious illness, 63

Relationships
  illness and, 39
  importance of, as social work value, 196
  strengths-based asset mapping of, 107–8
Religion, 125. *See also* Spiritual care
  and advance care planning, 199
  and culture, 127
  and end-of-life care, 140–41
  and experience of health care, 128–29
  and illness, *narrative example,*
       136–38, 257
  and intersectional identity, 127–29
  learning exercises related to, 146
  and pain and symptom manage-
       ment, 61–62
  patient participation in, 127
  and post-death arrangements, 181–82
  screening and assessment tools,
       132, 133
  social worker's, 144–45
  and spirituality, differentiation of, 124–25
  visual clues about, 131–32, 177
Resilience, 73–74
  behavioral manifestations of, 73–74
  definition of, 73
  spirituality and, 127
Respeto (respect), 161
Risk management services, 215–16

Safety, resources and guidelines for, 117
Self-awareness, social worker's, 144–45
Self-care, social worker's, 26–27, 145
Self-determination, 97
Self-esteem, illness-related assaults on, 61
Sense of coherence, 74
Serious illness. *See also* Child(ren), serious
     illness in
  in adolescents and young adults, 233–40
  continuity of care in, 26
  culture and, 148–49
  depression and, 79
  new normal with, 123
  in older adults, 226–27
       narrative example, 242, 244,
       245–47, 259
  peer support in, 41

people living with
  case example, 24–26
  improved care for, 22–24
  psychological distress in, common
      forms of, 75
  psychological factors in, 73
  reframing of, 63
  and spirituality, 123–24
Sesame Street in Communities, 115
Settings, for palliative care, 3–4
Sexual expression, illness and, 40
Sexual identity/orientation
  and conflict, 105–6
  and experience of health care, 128
  spiritual concerns and, narrative
      example, 136–38, 257
Shortness of breath. See Dyspnea
    (shortness of breath)
Siblings, of seriously ill child, 234
  social work with, learning exercise, 240
Social aspects
  learning exercise for, 114–15
  narrative example, 104, 256
  of palliative care, 98, 99, 102
  resources for, 115–19
Social assessment, 101–3
  tool for, 100
Social care plan, 99
Social connection, 231
Social Determinants of Health, 7–8
Social domain, of palliative care, 5, 33,
      98, 99
Social isolation, 231
  illness-related, 61, 62
Social justice, 6, 9, 155, 196
  patient access to medical information
      and, 40–41
  treatment of pain and, 52–53
Social Security, 116
Social support, 112
Social system(s), assessment and
      interventions for, resources and
      guidelines for, 118
Social work
  core values of, 18–19
  ethical principles of, 18–19

as high-context culture, 10–11
  palliative care in, 18–19
  place of, in health care, 1
  and social aspects of care, 98
  and spirituality, 124–25, 126–27
Social Work Assessment Tool (SWAT),
      100, 101
Social work competency(ies)
  in end-of-life care, 261
  in palliative care, 3, 261
Social worker(s)
  as context interpreters, 175
  demographics of, 149
  in hospitals, conflicting demands
      on, 20–21
  as participant-observers, 162
  role in medical care and treatment pla-
      nning, 31
  self-awareness of, 144–45
  self-care by, 26–27, 145
  spiritual and religious considerations
      for, 144–45
Social Work Hospice and Palliative Care
      Network, 253, 261
Social Work Policy Institute, Hospice social
      work, 261, 262
Socioeconomic status, and health/well-
      ness/illness, 7–8
Soros, George, 253
Specialist practice, 17–18, 253–54
  convergence with health social work,
      narrative example, 24–26, 255
  development of, historical patterns
      in, 20
  palliative care as, 18–19
  palliative care principles and, 4–5
SPIKES protocol, 111, 115
SPIRIT (spiritual assessment tool), 133
Spiritual care, 122–23
  advocacy in, 135
  clinical attunement in, 141–44
  collaboration across health care teams
      and providers in, 141
  community linkage in, 135, 140
  documentation of, 138–39
  ecological framework for, 102, 124

Spiritual care (*cont.*)
  at end of life, 140–41
  intervention in, 134–35
  resources in, 135
Spiritual domain
  in pain and symptom management,
    61–62
  of palliative care, 5, 33
Spirituality, 122–23, 125. *See also*
    Spiritual care
  and advance care planning, 199
  and complicated family dynamics 71
  and culture, 127
  domains of, 125–26
  and end-of-life care, 176–77
  as evolving, 123
  and illness, *narrative example,* 71, 97,
    136–38, 257
  and intersectional identity, 127–29
  learning exercises related to, 146
  and medical decision-making, 129–30
  and religion, differentiation of, 124–25
  and screening and assessment, 131–32
  screening and assessment tools,
    132, 133
  serious illness and, 123–24
  and social work, 124–25, 126–27
  social worker's, 144–45
  as unique to person, 123
  visual clues about, 131–32
Status, assessment and interventions for,
    resources and guidelines for, 117
Stoicism, 62, 77
Strengths, 27
  spirituality and, 127
Strengths-based approach, 170, 171
  narrative examples, 35, 255
  with older adults, 243–44
  in support of family member of dying
    person, 171, 181
Strengths-based asset mapping, 107–8
Strengths perspective, of social work, 73
Stress
  caregiver
    with Alzheimer's disease, 182–83
    with early-onset dementia, 182–83

and cognitive functioning, 169
Structure of care, as domain of palliative
    care, 5
Substance use, narrative therapy
    and, 43–44
Substitute decision maker(s), state laws
    on, 221
Suffering, 55
  psychological, 71
Summarizing, 82–83
Support
  emotional and social, 112
  resources for, 107–8
Surrogate decision-making, 205–6
  narrative example, 210–14, 217–18, 258
  state laws on, 213, 214, 221
SWAT. *See* Social Work Assessment
    Tool (SWAT)
Symptom(s). *See also* Physical symptoms
  complex meanings of, 54–55
  multidimensional aspects of, 52, 54
  prevalence and impact of, linkage to
    intervention, 56–59
  and suffering, 54
  symbolic significance of, 54–55
Symptom management, 72, 231–32
  language barriers and, 206–10
  multidimensional considerations
    in, 54
  resources for, 66
Systems change, advocacy for, social work
    and, 41

Team(s)
  collaborations among, 13
    narrative examples, 35, 255
  concept of, 13
  formal, 98
  informal, 98
  input from, in assessment, 32
  interdisciplinary, 98
    in assessment and management of
      pain and physical symptoms, 52
  negotiations among, 13
  of creation, 14, 31, 43
  palliative care, in hospitals, 19, 20–21

reciprocal learning across, *narrative example,* 37

Tears Foundation, The, 249

Terror language, 45–46

Theoretical frameworks, 6

Therapeutic bias, language and, 45–46

Therapy first approach, 46–48

language and, 12

Timing

of interventions and clinical decisions, 60–61

of medical interventions, 112

Total pain, 55, 97

Training, 23

IOM on, 2

resources for, 262

Transference, 80

Transgender status, intersectional experience of, 175–76

Transition(s), 170–71

in pediatric care, 238

social work role in, *narrative examples,* 31, 183–86, 257–58

Trauma, social worker's, in caring for dying patients, 145

Trauma-informed care, 72

Trauma stewardship, 27

Treatment options

ethical challenges with, 196

resources and guidelines for, 117

Trust, 227

Truth-telling, 196, 199

Underserved populations

advocacy for, 72

resource for, 222

US Department of Veterans Affairs

ethics resources from, 222

pain management resource from, 66

VA. *See* US Department of Veterans Affairs

Value(s)

conflicts among, in treatment decisions, 196

cultural alignment of, 154–55

in Latino culture, 161

of palliative care, 150

congruence with social work, 4

patient's, 150

exploration of, 201–5

of providers and health care systems, 150

in social work, 150

Veracity, ethical principle of, 197

Veterans Administration, health benefits, 116

Voicing My Choices, 249

Wellness, social determinants of, 7–8

WHO. *See* World Health Organization (WHO)

Whole person, threat to integrity of, 229

Words

abbreviated, 12–13

power of, 11

World Health Organization (WHO)

definition of palliative care, 1–2, 18

Promoting Mental Health, 93

Worth of the person, 97, 196

Young adults. *See* Adolescent(s) and young adults

Youth (movie), 253, 254